PRAISE FOR THE ENTERPRISE UNIFIED PROCESS

"The Enterprise Unified Process *is required reading for all team members in an IT organization. Its holistic focus on delivery and production support is second to none and it is an outstanding read for those wanting to achieve an effective Enterprise Architecture."*
—David Hecksel, Senior Java Architect, Sun Microsystems

"EUP *captures the set of enterprise activities and post-deployment issues that we have needed since RUP was defined."*
—Doug Hill, VP Center of Software Development Innovation, Number Six Software

"If RUP is the process vehicle you are driving, think of the EUP as your SUV. Only you will get better mileage, and your whole organization will travel more safely than in that klunker you've been nursing along. If your organization is pursuing iterative software development, the EUP is the Road Atlas that completes the map started by the RUP."*
—Gary K. Evans, Senior Consultant, Agile Software Practices, Evanetics, Inc.

"EUP *does for IT what RUP did for the project team. Thank You!"*
—Geri Winters

"Today's enterprise demands agile processes in order to achieve lower TCO, better software quality, and reduction in risk. The ability to achieve these goals requires the savage pursuit of balance between people, processes, and tools. This book takes a pragmatic approach and provides guidance on practices used within IT and serves as a wonderful blueprint for achieving success on large-scale enterprise projects."*
—James McGovern, Enterprise Architect, The Hartford

"The Enterprise Unified Process *is the book for you. With its myriad tips (including anti-patterns) you will be able to adapt the Unified Process to all of your work. The tips alone are worth the cost of the book."*
—Johanna Rothman, Rothman Consulting Group, Inc., Author of Hiring the Best Knowledge Workers, Techies, and Nerds

"The Enterprise Unified Process *significantly expands the scope of the RUP, adding support for such disciplines as operations, portfolio management, and enterprise architecture—areas of concern that are rarely mentioned in books on software process. Instead of focusing on the development of a single project, this book provides a roadmap for the entire IT process. This book should be required reading for anyone interested in providing leadership to an IT organization."*
—Mark Nichols, Corporate Vice President, Fortune 100 Company

"The Enterprise Unified Process *is a good read for anyone involved in developing information systems in an organization. In other words, if your group is responsible for more than one application, you need this to succeed!"*
—Michael Boggs, RUP Mentor

THE ENTERPRISE UNIFIED PROCESS: EXTENDING THE RATIONAL UNIFIED PROCESS

THE ENTERPRISE UNIFIED PROCESS: EXTENDING THE RATIONAL UNIFIED PROCESS

SCOTT W. AMBLER,
JOHN NALBONE, MICHAEL J. VIZDOS

PRENTICE
HALL
PTR Prentice Hall Professional Technical Reference

Upper Saddle River, NJ • Boston • Indianapolis • San Francisco • New York • Toronto
• Montreal • London • Munich • Paris • Madrid • Capetown • Sydney • Tokyo •
Singapore • Mexico City

The publisher offers excellent discounts on this book when ordered in quantity for bulk purchases or special sales, which may include electronic versions and/or custom covers and content particular to your business, training goals, marketing focus, and branding interests. For more information, please contact:

U.S. Corporate and Government Sales
(800) 382-3419
corpsales@pearsontechgroup.com

For sales ouside of the U.S., please contact:

International Sales
international@pearsoned.com

Visit on the Web: www.phptr.com

Library of Congress Catalog Number: 2004114355

ISBN 0-13-191451-0
Text printed in the United States on recycled paper at R.R. Donnelley in Crawfordsville, Indiana.
First printing, February 2005

Scott:
For Bev. Thank you for bringing love into my life.

Michael:
For Lo, Dominic, and Kenton. Thank you. For everything.

John:
For Mom. We miss you.

Contents

About the Authors

Scott Ambler is a senior consultant with Ronin International, Inc. specializing in software process improvement, adoption, and mentoring. He has contributed to the RUP and has been working with organizations since 1999 to adopt and extend the RUP. He is the thought leader behind the Enterprise Unified Process (EUP), Agile Model Driven Development (AMDD), the Agile Data (AD) method, and the process patterns of the Object-Oriented Software Process (OOSP). He has worked in the information technology (IT) industry since the late 1980s in a wide range of roles within a variety of industries, including financial, retail, military, and health. He has either authored or co-authored numerous books, including *The Object Primer, The Practical Guide to Enterprise Architecture, Agile Database Techniques*, and the four-book Unified Process series. He is a senior editor with *Software Development* (www.sdmagazine.com) and an international speaker in the IT field.

John Nalbone is a senior consultant with Ronin International, Inc. He has worked in the information technology (IT) industry since the late 1980s in a variety of roles. Although he started his career as a coder, his experience covers a wide range, including being an analyst, designer, architect, developer, project manager, and process engineer. He has worked on a variety of projects over the years, including debugging operating systems, developing expert systems, and enterprise architecture efforts, with a number of different clients, including startups, government agencies, and Fortune 500 companies. His current focus is on helping companies with their process improvement efforts; in particular helping them to adopt both the RUP and/or the EUP.

Michael Vizdos is President of Ronin International, Inc. Michael has more than 15 years of experience in the IT industry and has worked in all aspects of the system lifecycle. He came to Ronin with a variety of experience, including six years at Electronic Data Systems and two start-up companies. His specialty is building successful Professional Services teams, and he is also a Certified Scrum Master (www.michaelvizdos.com). Michael speaks and writes about various process IT-related topics.

Ronin International, Inc. is based in Evergreen Colorado, just outside of Denver. The team at Ronin is known and respected as a market leader for planning, improving, and implementing various software practices throughout the world. Ronin consultants are in the "knowledge transfer" business. Their goal is to transfer knowledge from their experts to your team members. They work with clients to develop working software, create or improve new software process improvement efforts, and facilitate long-term strategic planning sessions for your IT organization.

Foreword

My first development job in the 1970s was as an APL programmer in a large insurance company. We had to build, operate, maintain, and retire large systems used by hundreds and sometimes thousands of people. Some things have changed radically since then: the IBM mainframe had around 8MB of memory, cost more than the GDP of some nations, and occupied the entire floor of an office building! But some things remain the same, and I recognize in this useful guide lessons learned long ago, and lessons I should have learned but didn't. Although its subject is officially the Enterprise Unified Process, don't let that mislead you into thinking it has nothing to offer unless you are a RUP organization. Quite the opposite, it's a valuable learning aid for everyone involved in enterprise IT.

Scott, Michael, and John have superbly organized, summarized, and synthesized many of the key skills in running an IT organization and the IT lifecycle with plenty of tips and pointers to excellent literature for more learning. And perhaps most importantly, they express these skills in the spirit of agility and iterative, evolutionary development that we now know is so critical for success. I've known Scott to be a passionate and thoughtful, yet utterly pragmatic advocate of modern development practices for years, and I have always benefited from his advice. I'm sure you will too.

—Craig Larman, Chief Scientist, Valtech
Rome, Italy, December 2004

Preface

It was a dark and stormy night, and suddenly a shot rang out. The information technology (IT) department had failed to deliver once again, and that was the last straw for the business stakeholders—it was time to outsource the entire department.

Sound familiar? This is happening to IT departments all over the world because they don't provide sufficient value to their business stakeholders. Stakeholders have grown tired of projects being delivered late and over budget, if they're delivered at all. They're tired of paying for the same functionality over and over again, insufficient system support, systems that don't work together, and the ever-increasing bill for IT-related services. Many IT departments are at a crossroads—either they need to change the way they work, or they need to be prepared to be replaced by other organizations that are more effective at delivering working software.

Since 1999, Ronin International, Inc. has been helping organizations adopt the Unified Process to enable them to become better at software development. At first, most clients needed help to adopt the Rational Unified Process (RUP), but later they realized that they needed help extending the RUP to address issues that go beyond software development. We at Ronin International started seeing significant commonality between customers, motivating us to develop the Enterprise Unified Process (EUP), which extends the RUP to become a full IT lifecycle. The RUP is a great starting point for many IT departments, and the EUP takes it to the next level.

One of the first things that you'll notice about this book is that we present a slightly different approach to the Unified Process. We don't work for IBM Rational, and as a result, we're in a position to objectively describe what actually works in practice. Don't worry, within the scope of the RUP, we don't deviate all that much because frankly IBM Rational has done a pretty good job within their chosen area. The value in this book is the extensions to the RUP—two new phases and eight new disciplines—making the RUP truly ready for real-world IT departments. Just take a quick look at the table of contents to see what we mean.

The bottom line is that this book looks at process from the viewpoint of an entire IT department, not just a single project or system, discussing the difficult issues that IT professionals face every day. The book features a wide range of figures that illustrate what you need to do. The text describes the issues you'll face and strategies for overcoming them, but it doesn't waste your time with minute details. In every organization where we've worked, we discovered that they had good people who knew what they were doing, but what was missing was a unifying vision for getting them to work together effectively. This book won't turn you into an expert portfolio manager, enterprise architect, or whatever, but it will explain the fundamental issues and strategies that these roles address within your IT organization.

Features of This Book

This book has several features that will make it a valuable resource for you:

- It is practical: This book provides practical advice in an easy-to-read manner.

- It covers the critical issues: This book focuses on the fundamental issues that you will face on a daily basis and describes options for addressing the issues. It does not, however, waste your time covering extraneous details, which are typically unique to your organization anyway.

- It is consistent with the RUP: The chapters describing the new phases and disciplines include many workflow diagrams that follow the same approach within the RUP product. Existing RUP practitioners will instantly recognize and understand them.

- It includes case studies: We share our experiences, most good (although some bad), gained by introducing the RUP and EUP into organizations since 1999.

- It includes Reader Return on Investment (ROI) boxes: Each chapter begins with a summary of the critical points made within the chapter, providing a quick overview of the chapter.

- It contains suggested resources: Each chapter ends with suggestions for where to look for more information.

Who Should Read This Book

This book is written for IT professionals who are experienced at the RUP who want to improve and extend their approach to IT. You're competent at your job, but you realize that your organization, and perhaps you as well, need to change your approach with IT if you're going to succeed in the coming years. This book will provide the insights you need to identify where you're going wrong and will provide strategies for addressing those challenges.

Acknowledgments

We would like to acknowledge the following people for helping us, often in the form of incisive feedback, throughout the development of this book: Michael Boggs, Susan Burk, Beverley Dawe, Gary K. Evans, John Harrison, Doug Hill, Mauricio Iannini, Ben Lawson, Pete McBreen, Paul Petralia, Gary Pollice, Bob Rhubart, Rebecca Savoie, Graeme Simsion, Michael Thurston, Michelle Vincenti, Kenneth Vizdos, Kenneth Ward, Lars Wendestam, and Brad White.

Part I

From the RUP to the EUP

Chapter 1

Introduction

Reader ROI

■ There is more to IT than system development—the RUP is a good start, but you need more.

■ The EUP extends the RUP to cover the entire system lifecycle, including both production and system retirement.

■ The EUP also extends the RUP to cover cross-system issues. It was introduced in 1999 and has evolved since then; it will continue to evolve over time.

Many information technology (IT) departments are struggling to fulfill their primary mission—to deliver, operate, and support systems that enable the organization to meet its business goals. Business stakeholders want new systems that meet their needs, delivered on time and on budget. They want to pay for functionality once and then reuse it whenever appropriate, and they want their systems to work together effectively. Business stakeholders also want their systems to be properly operated and supported. They can't afford to have systems become unavailable, nor can they afford to not receive help when it's required. From the point of view of business leaders, these expectations are very reasonable, yet many information technology departments seem unable to fulfill these demands. If this describes your situation, you either need to change the way you work or be prepared to be replaced by someone who can get the job done. Our recommendation is the former.

This book defines the Enterprise Unified Process (EUP), which was introduced by Scott Ambler in 1999 (Ambler 1999b) and later was enhanced by his team at Ronin International, Inc. (`www.ronin-intl.com`) to support a wider variety of clients. The EUP is an extension to the industry standard IBM Rational Unified Process (RUP) (IBM 2004), whose lifecycle diagrams are depicted in Figures 1-1 and 1-2. Both the EUP and RUP are instantiations of the Unified Process (UP) (Jacobson, Booch, and Rumbaugh 1999). The UP, also known as the Unified Method or the Unified Software Development Process (USDP), was originally a framework from which system processes were to be instantiated. A system process defines the roles people fulfill, the activities they perform, and the artifacts they create to develop, operate, and support one or more computer systems. Over the years the primary focus of IBM Rational has been evolving the RUP.

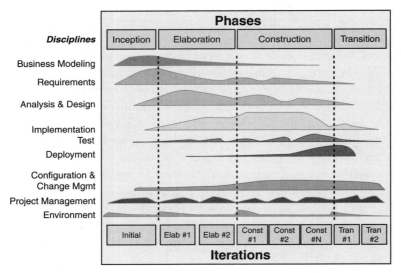

FIGURE 1-1   *The RUP v2003 system lifecycle.*
Reprint Courtesy of International Business Machines Corporation
Copyright 2005 © International Business Machines Corporation

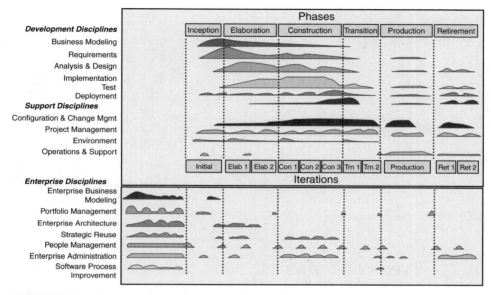

FIGURE 1-2   *The EUP v2004 IT lifecycle.*

Whereas the RUP defines a software development lifecycle, the EUP extends it to cover the entire information technology (IT) lifecycle. Figure 1-3 summarizes the complete lifecycle of a system, from the point at which it begins as someone's idea to when it is retired from service. An important part of that lifecycle is its initial development and release into production, as well as its continued evolution and maintenance over time. The EUP extends the RUP to include the operation and support of a system after it is in production and its eventual retirement. Furthermore, because all but the smallest organizations have more than one system, the EUP also handles cross-system enterprise issues such as portfolio management, enterprise architecture, and strategic reuse. Whereas the RUP defines a very good software development lifecycle, it is only a start—you need the EUP to address the entire IT lifecycle.

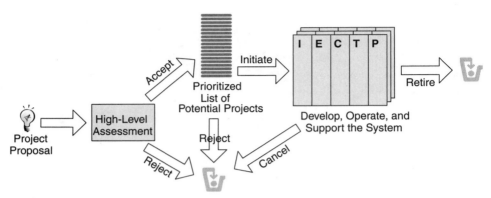

FIGURE 1-3   *The complete lifecycle of a system.*

TYPES OF PROCESS

A process lifecycle defines the scope of a process and the relationships between its activities. It is important to distinguish between four kinds of process lifecycles, each of which is a superset of the previous one, as depicted in Figure 1-4:

1. **System development lifecycle:** This lifecycle encompasses the activities required to develop a system and put it into production. The RUP and Extreme Programming (XP) (Beck 2000) are system development lifecycles.

2. **System lifecycle:** This lifecycle extends the system development lifecycle to include the activities required to operate and support a system after it is in production and to eventually retire that system when it is no longer needed. The scope of a system lifecycle includes the development of a project's first version; the development, operation, and support of all subsequent versions; and the retirement of the final version. The ISO 12207 standard (ISO 1998) defines a high-level system lifecycle.

3. **Information technology (IT) lifecycle:** This lifecycle encompasses the activities of an IT department, adding the enterprise management disciplines required to effectively manage your organization's portfolio of systems. This scope expansion makes IT lifecycles very different from traditional development and system lifecycles. In many ways, an

IT lifecycle really defines an environment in which system lifecycles are instantiated. The EUP is an IT lifecycle.

4. **Organization/business lifecycle:** This lifecycle encompasses the activities of your entire organization, including both IT and business aspects. Your IT lifecycle must fit into your overall organization lifecycle if it is to be effective.

Figure 1-4 depicts the different scope of each of the four types of lifecycles. It shows how each "level" of lifecycle encompasses the previous level. Although it is important to have an effective software development process to be truly effective at IT, you need to look at the entire picture. Where you choose to set the scope boundaries of a process can have a significant impact on it. For example, if your lifecycle doesn't address strategic reuse across systems, reuse efforts will probably receive little attention. Compare the RUP system development lifecycle of Figure 1-1 with the EUP IT lifecycle of Figure 1-2—the EUP covers the full range of issues faced by modern IT organizations, whereas the RUP covers only those issues faced by project teams. The organization/business lifecycle is beyond the scope of this book; your organization will need to address it as part of your enterprise business modeling efforts (see Chapter 7, "The Enterprise Business Modeling Discipline").

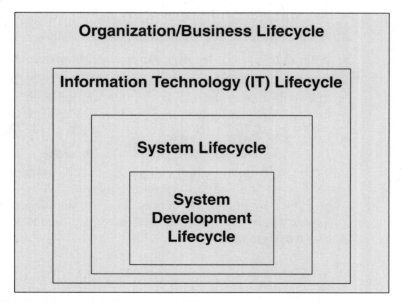

FIGURE 1-4 *The scope of the four types of lifecycles.*

HISTORY OF THE ENTERPRISE UNIFIED PROCESS

To understand the history of the EUP, we must also look at the history of both the UP and the RUP. The RUP is an endeavor of IBM's Rational division, formerly Rational Software Corporation. Rational is best known for its development toolset—including Requisite Pro, Rational Rose/XDE, and Rational ClearQuest—and as the same people who introduced what has become the industry standard modeling notation, the Unified Modeling Language (UML). The UML is now maintained by the Object Management Group (OMG) at www.uml.org. People often assume that the RUP, the IBM Rational toolset, and the UML are inextricably linked. However, you'll see in this book that you can follow an instantiation of the UP without using any of IBM Rational's tools or even the UML. Nonetheless, IBM Rational offers some very good tools that you should consider, and we believe that every IT professional should understand at least the fundamentals of the UML.

A good way to understand the EUP is to know its historical timeline. Here are some critical events in the evolution of the EUP:

- **1988:** Objectory v1.0 is defined by Ivar Jacobson's Objectory AB company. The Objectory process defines the core from which the RUP and the EUP later evolve.

- **1995:** Objectory v3.8 released. The first online version.

- **1995:** Rational Corporation purchases Objectory AB.

- **1996:** Rational Objectory Process (ROP) 4.0 is developed. Rational extends Objectory with internal Rational architecture concepts and introduces iterative concepts to it.

- **June 1998:** Rational Unified Process (RUP) 5.0 is released. This is the renamed ROP, extended with process material obtained from other tool companies purchased by Rational Corporation as well as material developed by the RUP group led by Phillipe Kruchten. This version describes how to apply UML diagrams in the development of object-based systems.

- **February 1999:** *The Unified Software Development Process* (Jacobson, Booch, and Rumbaugh 1999) is published. This book describes the Unified Process framework in detail.

- **June 1999:** RUP 5.5 is released. Major enhancements focus on real-time and web-based development.

- **October 1999:** An enhanced lifecycle for the RUP is first proposed, which extends the RUP with a production phase and a cross-system discipline called Infrastructure Management (Ambler 1999b).

- **February 2000:** RUP 2000 is released. Major enhancements include the addition of business engineering techniques (Jacobson, Ericsson, and Jacobson 1994) to the business modeling discipline and a more extensive approach to requirements.

- **2000–2002:** The Unified Process series of books (Ambler and Constantine 2000a-c, 2002) is published, repositioning the enhanced RUP lifecycle as the EUP. These books reprint a large collection of articles originally published in *Software Development* (www.sdmagazine.com) that describe topics not yet covered by the RUP. Some topics, such as improved testing and agility, have since been added to the RUP.

- **March 2002:** *Agile Modeling* (Ambler 2002) is published, showing how it is possible to take an agile approach to modeling on a RUP project.

- **August 2002:** IBM purchases PriceWaterhouseCooper (PWC), developers of the Summit methodology. Material from Summit is later adopted into the RUP.

- **December 2002:** IBM purchases Rational Corporation.

- **May 2003:** RUP 2003 is released. Some of the material from the Unified Process series, in particular an enhanced test discipline and some agile concepts, is now covered by the RUP.

- **Spring 2003:** The EUP site, www.enterpriseunified process.com, and the EUP mailing list (visit the site for details) go online. All EUP-related material published by Ronin International, Inc. is published here.

- **January 2004:** EUP v2004 is released. Enhancements include the addition of the retirement phase and the expansion of the enterprise management discipline (formerly the infrastructure management discipline) into seven detailed disciplines.

- **Spring 2005:** RUP v2005 is released. Major enhancements include the adoption of PWC's Summit project management practices and partial support for production-related activities.

WHY AN IT PROCESS?

It is crucial for an IT organization to follow one or more software processes. A system development process helps guide project teams in a consistent, affordable, and (relatively) predictable approach, which results in high-quality systems that meet the needs of stakeholders. However, you need to look beyond development. The operation and support of a system after it is in production is not only difficult—it is critical to your success. Why bother building the system if you can't run it? The retirement of a system that is no longer needed or that is to be replaced by another system is also difficult. Both production and retirement efforts require different skill sets and activities from the system development lifecycle; therefore, you need at least one system process if you want to cover the full lifecycle of a system.

It doesn't end here—most organizations deal with more than one system at a time, so they need a process that reflects this reality. Failing to address cross-system issues can lead to stovepipe applications, among other problems. A stovepipe application is one that stands on its own, does not interact with or build on other applications, and can be difficult to maintain and enhance. Although few people actively seek to build stovepipe applications, they inadvertently do so when they don't take enterprise issues into account and because the application is usually created to address a specific set of requirements. From a project perspective, it is a success: the team has fulfilled the requirements by implementing the functionality that was requested. From an enterprise perspective, however, it can be a nightmare due to a plethora of technologies used across your entire system portfolio, the inconsistent repetition of functionality between systems, and the lack of interoperability. In a nutshell, stovepipe applications are successful in the tactical sense but not in the strategic sense. The EUP addresses the entire IT lifecycle.

However, it is very possible (and unfortunately common) for project momentum to grind to a halt when inefficient or unrealistic enterprise processes are thrust upon individual project teams. Enterprise groups must recognize that they exist not only to protect the enterprise but also to actively enhance system development efforts. They must support development teams, not hinder them. In every chapter, this book presents strategies that have been proven in a wide variety of organizations.

This Book

This book is organized into four parts. The first part covers both the RUP and the EUP in detail. The second part describes how to extend the RUP to become a full system lifecycle. The third part describes how to extend the RUP to encompass the full IT lifecycle described by the EUP. The fourth part describes how to succeed with the EUP. The chapters within each part are as follows:

Part I: From the RUP to the EUP

- Chapter 1: Introduction
- Chapter 2: The Rational Unified Process (RUP)
- Chapter 3: Introduction to the Enterprise Unified Process (EUP)

Part II: Beyond Development

- Chapter 4: The Production Phase
- Chapter 5: The Retirement Phase
- Chapter 6: The Operations and Support Discipline

Part III: The Enterprise Management Disciplines

- Chapter 7: The Enterprise Business Modeling Discipline
- Chapter 8: The Portfolio Management Discipline
- Chapter 9: The Enterprise Architecture Discipline
- Chapter 10: The Strategic Reuse Discipline

- Chapter 11: The People Management Discipline
- Chapter 12: The Enterprise Administration Discipline
- Chapter 13: The Software Process Improvement Discipline

Part IV: Putting It All Together

- Chapter 14: Adopting the Enterprise Unified Process
- Chapter 15: Parting Thoughts

Appendices

- Appendix A: Roles
- Appendix B: Artifacts
- Appendix C: Glossary
- Appendix D: Acronyms and Abbreviations

SUMMARY

Effective software processes are critical to the success of your IT organization. The Unified Process (UP) is a framework from which a software process may be instantiated, and both the Rational Unified Process (RUP) and the Enterprise Unified Process (EUP) are UP instantiations. The scope of the RUP is that of system development; the EUP extends the RUP to become a full IT lifecycle that encompasses both the full system lifecycle as well as cross-system issues required for successful enterprise system management.

Chapter 2

The Rational Unified Process

> ## Reader ROI
>
> - The RUP is an industry-standard prescriptive system development process.
> - RUP phases represent the four major stages, or "seasons," that a project goes through over time.
> - RUP disciplines encompass the logical activities that take place throughout a development project.
> - RUP best practices capture development concepts proven to work in practice.

The IBM Rational Unified Process (RUP) is a prescriptive, well-defined system development process, often used to develop systems with object- and/or component-based technologies. It is based on sound software engineering principles such as taking an iterative, requirements-driven, architecture-centric approach to software development (Kruchten 2004). It provides several mechanisms, such as relatively short-term iterations with well-defined goals and go/no-go decision points at the end of each phase, to provide management visibility into the development process. IBM Rational has made, and continues to make, a significant investment in the RUP, including an HTML-based description of the RUP that your organization can tailor to meet its exact needs (IBM 2004).

Figure 2-1 depicts the RUP lifecycle, commonly referred to as the "hump chart" diagram. The horizontal "humps" for each discipline give a rough estimate of the relative effort for each discipline throughout the four phases. For example, a large portion of Business Modeling takes place in Inception, although it does continue through to early Transition. Work on Deployment usually doesn't start until Elaboration and doesn't really kick into high gear until the middle of Construction. The hump chart is a visual mechanism to provide a rough overview of the extent to which each discipline is executed in each phase. We like to characterize the RUP lifecycle as serial in the large and iterative in the small, delivering incremental releases over time through the application of proven best practices.

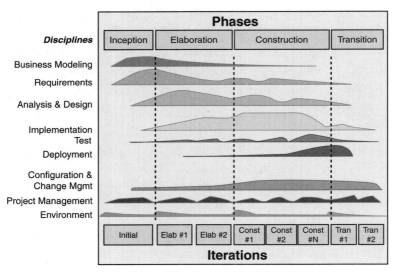

FIGURE 2-1   *The RUP v2003 lifecycle.*
Reprint Courtesy of International Business Machines Corporation
Copyright 2005 © International Business Machines Corporation

SERIAL IN THE LARGE

The RUP is structured in two dimensions: phases, which represent the four major stages that a development project goes through over time, and disciplines, which represent the logical activities that take place throughout the project. The serial aspect of the RUP (in many ways a management view) is captured in its phases, and the iterative nature (in many ways a technical view) of the RUP is captured in its disciplines. You see in Figure 2-1 that the four phases—Inception, Elaboration, Construction, and Transition—are listed across the top of the lifecycle.

Each phase ends with a well-defined milestone. At these points, the stakeholders assess the project, including what has been done and the plans for moving forward. A go/no-go decision is made about whether to proceed with the project. Each phase has a specific set of goals, which are addressed within the iterations of the phase, so that the phase milestone can be met. Figure 2-2 shows the primary activities and milestones of each phase; each phase is explored in detail in the following sections. Table 2-1 summarizes each phase and its corresponding milestones.

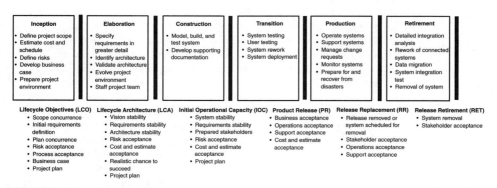

FIGURE 2-2 *The RUP phases and their milestones.*

TABLE 2-1   *The Four Phases of the RUP*

Phase	Description	Milestone
Inception	The primary goals are to achieve stakeholder consensus regarding the objectives for the project and to obtain funding. To do this you will develop a high-level requirements model, which will delimit the scope of the project. You will start to install the work environment and tailor the process for the team. You will also develop a high-level plan for how the project will proceed.	Lifecycle Objectives (LCO): Your stakeholders assess the state of the project and must agree that the scope of the project has been established, the initial requirements have been identified (albeit without much detail), your software development plan is realistic, the risks have been identified and are being managed appropriately, the business case for the project makes sense, and the development process has been tailored appropriately.
Elaboration	During Elaboration you specify requirements in greater detail and prove the architecture for the system. The requirements are detailed only enough to address architectural risks and to ensure that there is an understanding of the scope of each requirement for subsequent planning. The point of proving the architecture is to ensure that the team can actually develop a system that satisfies the requirements.	Lifecycle Architecture (LCA): Your stakeholders assess the state of the project and must agree that the project vision has stabilized and is realistic; the requirements for the project have been established (although they will still evolve); the architecture is stable and sufficient to satisfy the requirements; risks are continuing to be managed; the current expenditures are acceptable, and reasonable estimates have been made for future costs and schedules; there is a realistic chance for the project team to succeed; and detailed iteration plans for the next few Construction iterations, as well as a high-level project plan, are in place.

(continues)

TABLE 2-1 *The Four Phases of the RUP (Continued)*

Phase	Description	Milestone
Construction	The focus of the Construction phase is to develop the system to the point where it is ready for deployment. Emphasis shifts to prioritizing requirements and completing their specification, analyzing them, designing a solution to satisfy them, and coding and testing the software. If necessary, early versions of the system are released, either internally or externally, to obtain user feedback.	Initial Operating Capacity (IOC): Your stakeholders assess the state of the project and must agree that the software and supporting documentation are acceptable to deploy; the stakeholders (and the business) are ready for the system to be deployed; the risks are continuing to be managed effectively; the current expenditures are acceptable, and reasonable estimates have been made for future costs and schedules; and detailed iteration plans for the next few Transition iterations, as well as a high-level project plan, are in place.
Transition	The Transition phase focuses on delivering the system into production. There will be testing by both system testers and end users, and corresponding reworking and fine-tuning. Training of end users, support, and operations staff is done.	Product Release (PR) milestone: Your stakeholders assess the state of the project and must agree that the system is ready, including supporting documentation and training; the current expenditures are acceptable, and reasonable estimates have been made for future costs; the system can be operated after it is in production; and the system can be supported appropriately after it is in production.

Several critical observations can be made concerning the RUP phases:

- **Activities continue in each phase:** Traditionalists often mistakenly think that the Inception phase corresponds to the traditional requirements phase, that Elaboration corresponds to design, that Construction corresponds to coding, and that Transition corresponds to testing. Nothing could be further from the truth. Look at Figure 2-1 again—the nine disciplines (which are discussed in the following sections) cross into each phase. You'll be designing, coding, and testing in an iterative manner during all four phases.

■ **Artifacts evolve during each phase:** Your project artifacts— models, plans, source code, and documents—evolve throughout the life of your project. Your artifacts aren't finished until you release your system into production; in fact, you may find that you'll be doing requirements modeling the day before you release.

■ **The project is planned in a rolling wave:** With a rolling-wave approach (Githens 1998), detailed planning is done for things closer to you (like the relative height of the crest of a wave), and less-detailed work is performed for things further away (in the trough behind the wave). As your project progresses and tasks get closer, detailed planning for them is done.

■ **Risk management is crucial to your success:** IT professionals who say, "We know the risks; there's no need to document them" or "There are so few risks, it's not worth our time to record them" are asking for trouble. Though everyone might "know" of certain risks, they might not agree on their exact nature. If risks are few in number, little time will be required to record them. Identifying risks and response strategies is time well spent.

■ **Each phase ends with a go/no-go decision:** Your stakeholders must agree to move forward into the next phase. This may entail reworking your strategy for proceeding, or even canceling the project. A project may be canceled because it's unacceptable due to quality concerns or lack of appropriate documentation, because it is deemed too expensive to deploy and/or support, or because the strategic direction for the company has shifted. Although it is rare, a project may even be canceled at the end of Transition.

Typical RUP projects spend approximately 10% of their time in Inception, 25% in Elaboration, 55% in Construction, and 10% in Transition, although these figures vary from organization to organization and even from project to project. For example, a "green field" project in a new technical area may spend more time in Elaboration as the team addresses new architectural issues. A project that is heavily dependent on business processing may spend more time in Inception figuring out new business processes and how (or if) technology can support them. A project consisting of minor enhancements and fixes to an existing system may spend very little time in Inception and Elaboration. The bottom line is that every project is different, and the process that each project follows must be tailored to meet its needs.

ITERATIVE IN THE SMALL

RUP phases are divided into one or more iterations, although the term "increments" might be more appropriate. Each iteration has a fine-grained plan with a specific goal and addresses only a portion of the entire system (unlike the waterfall approach, which attempts to do it all at once). Iterations build on the work done by previous iterations and assemble the final system incrementally. Iterations are indicated along the bottom of Figure 2-1, with each phase being subdivided into one or more iterations. When an iteration ends, in particular during the Construction phase, a small subset of the system has been completed that could conceivably be deployed to users as a release, even if only as an alpha or beta version.

The iterative nature of the RUP is reflected in how you approach its disciplines, which are logical groupings of activities that take place over the lifetime of a project. During an iteration, the portion of the requirements selected for that iteration are analyzed, designed, coded, tested, and integrated with the products from earlier iterations. As new or changed requirements are identified throughout a project, they are prioritized and either incorporated into the current effort, put off for later efforts, or rejected.

The disciplines, summarized in Table 2-2, are collections of tasks that ultimately produce a set of artifacts.

TABLE 2-2 *The Nine Disciplines of the RUP*

Discipline	Goal
Business Modeling	To understand the business of the organization, usually confined to the scope of the business that is relevant to the system being developed.
Requirements	To elicit, document, and agree on the scope of what is and what is not to be built. This information is used by analysts, designers, and programmers to build the system, by testers to verify the system, and by the project manager to plan and manage the project.
Analysis & Design	To analyze the requirements for the system and to design a solution to be implemented, taking into consideration the requirements, constraints, and all applicable standards and guidelines.
Implementation	To transform the design into executable code and to perform a basic level of testing—in particular, unit testing.
Test	To perform an objective evaluation to ensure quality. This includes finding defects, validating that the system works as designed, and verifying that the requirements are met.
Deployment	To plan the delivery of the system and to execute the plan to make the system available to end users.
Configuration and Change Management	To manage access to the project artifacts. This includes tracking artifact versions over time, controlling the versions, and managing changes to them.
Project Management	To direct the activities that take place on the project. This includes managing risks, directing people (assigning tasks, tracking progress, and so on), and coordinating with people and systems outside the scope of the project to be sure that it is delivered on time and within budget.
Environment	To support the rest of the effort by ensuring that the proper process, guidance (standards and guidelines), and tools (hardware, software, etc.) are available for the team as needed.

An important concept when working within an iteration is that work does not proceed strictly serially, as it does in a waterfall approach. Yes, you still start with requirements, perform analysis, and then design and code, but you do not have to finalize one step before you can move to the next. With RUP, a typical approach is to address some subset of the requirements, do some analysis, go back and rework some of the requirements, move to design, rework some requirements and/or analysis, start coding, and then rework the design. In order for this to work, you need a team that works together on projects. Requirements people need to work with designers, who work with coders, who work with testers. Of course, this works best if the same people can perform requirements analysis, design, coding, and testing, but it's not strictly necessary. The important point is that work proceeds in a serial nature in the broader sense but that artifacts are revised as needed by latter phases instead of being finished and handed off to other team members.

Iterations are planned according to risks. Higher-priority risks are addressed in earlier iterations, while lower-priority risks are addressed later. This concept is at the heart of a risk-management approach to developing software.

Near-term iterations are planned in greater detail than longer-term iterations. The longer-term iterations may change in scope or goal depending on what happens in earlier iterations. Planning for iterations further down the line should be assumed to be of lower accuracy with a higher degree of variance based on current information, which may change and cause changes to iteration planning. That does not mean that planning for later iterations should be taken lightly. It just means that the best planning based on current data should be done but that things may change before the iteration is realized. It can, in fact, be misleading to stakeholders and others if you attempt to plan work that is far in the future with any specificity.

DELIVERING INCREMENTAL RELEASES OVER TIME

The first version of a system is usually just one of many; systems evolve over time. New functionality is added, user-requested enhancements are incorporated, new standards are adopted and supported, and so on. A pass through the four RUP phases creates a single version of a system called a production release.

During or after the Transition phase, a new project may be started to address any outstanding requirements. The new project may begin at the Inception phase again, although some teams may decide to start in the Elaboration phase or even the Construction phase if appropriate. As Figure 2-3 depicts, this process can continue indefinitely, as long as new requirements are identified that the stakeholders agree are worthy of a new version of the software.

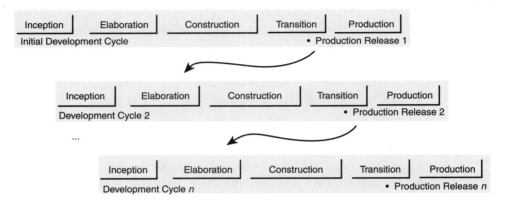

FIGURE 2-3   *The incremental release of a system into production.*

FOLLOWING PROVEN BEST PRACTICES

The RUP is based on six best practices—develop iteratively, manage requirements, use component architecture, model visually (UML), continuously verify quality, and manage change—gleaned from many years of experience on many projects. We have reworked two of the best practices to capture their core essence and added a few more practices to round them out. The best practices that we promote are as follows:

- **Develop iteratively:** Developing in iterations allows projects to address risks on a priority basis. It allows for a constant measuring of progress, as iterations have a fixed time window and a specific goal to be met. At the end of each iteration, stakeholders are provided a view of how the project is proceeding and can set realistic expectations for the remainder of the project based on the actual progress of working code.

- **Manage requirements:** A key to delivering a system that meets the stakeholders' needs is identifying and then managing the requirements for the system. This includes gathering, documenting, and maintaining requirements, incorporating changes in a systematic manner, and potentially even tracking and tracing the requirements to the design. Your requirements management process can be very well defined and prescriptive, often involving significant effort and expense but with the benefit of producing accurate and detailed documentation of your decisions. It also can be something as simple as the index-card–based planning game from Extreme Programming (XP) (Beck 2000). It can be somewhere in between these two extremes. The RUP can and should be tailored to meet a project's exact needs.

- **Proven architecture:** The RUP product uses the term "use component architecture," but the reality is that many architectures aren't component-based. For example, web services are another architectural option, as are procedural languages such as COBOL, and you can easily extend the RUP to work with these technologies. The true best practice is to identify and then prove through prototyping an architecture that is appropriate for the system you are building.

- **Modeling:** Although the RUP product uses the term "model visually" (IBM 2004), the reality is that some models such as use cases, business rule specifications, and Class Responsibility Collaborator (CRC) cards are nonvisual in nature. Although you might be tempted to think of writing a use case as simply writing documentation, what you're really doing is modeling how people will interact with your system. Modeling helps people envision and think through concepts and then share those ideas with others. Modeling can be done with high-powered, GUI-based software applications or can simply be sketches on whiteboards. A quick visit to the Agile Models Distilled home page (`www.ailemodeling.com/artifacts/`) quickly reveals that a wide range of models is available to you.

- **Continuously verify quality:** Testing happens throughout each iteration of a RUP project instead of as a single, large testing effort at the end. Ensuring quality goes beyond testing software to ensure it meets requirements. Reviews of requirements, design, and mockups with stakeholders are also part of continuous quality verification. Testing for and catching defects early is much more efficient than a comprehensive approach to testing at the end. An effective way to ensure quality is an implementation technique called test-driven development (TDD), which is based on the idea that developers should write a test before they write new business code to ensure that they always have a 100% regression unit test suite for their system (Beck 2003; Astels 2003).

- **Manage change:** Change is a given in software development. Change must be expected and handled appropriately for a project to run smoothly and to take advantage of changes that may give it a competitive advantage. A wide range of artifacts—documents, models, plans, tests, code, and so on—will potentially be affected by any changes; as agilists point out, you want to travel as light as possible to minimize the impact.

- **Collaborative development:** Systems are built by teams of people, and if these people don't work together effectively, the overall project risks failure. The agile software development community (`www.agilealliance.org`) has done significant work in identifying and promoting collaborative development techniques. Primary techniques include pair programming, where two people work together to develop code (Williams and Kessler 2003); modeling with others, which promotes the concept that several people are more effective modeling together than they are working separately; and active stakeholder participation, which promotes the concept that project stakeholders should provide information and make decisions in a timely manner and be involved with the development effort itself (Ambler 2002).

- **Look beyond development:** Not only do you need to build and deploy a system into production, but you also need to operate and support it after it's there. Good developers know this and understand that they need to work with operations and support professionals to ensure that their needs are met. Furthermore, good developers also realize that their system must fit into the overall organization, the implication being that they need to ensure that their system reflects common enterprise norms—their systems will take advantage of the existing architecture and infrastructure and will follow accepted enterprise guidance (standards and guidelines).

- **Deliver working software on a regular basis:** The primary measure of success for a software development project should be the delivery of working software that meets the needs of its users. Effective developers deliver working software on an incremental basis, delivering the highest-priority functionality remaining at each iteration.

- **Manage risk:** Effective project teams strive to identify and then manage the risks they face, either mitigating them or reducing their potential impact as appropriate. Chapter 8, "The Portfolio Management Discipline," describes risk management in greater detail.

WHY THE RUP?

The RUP has become a de facto industry standard for prescriptive software processes. The RUP works; it's here to stay, and the RUP product (IBM 2004) contains most of the information you require to define your own software process (and probably more information than you need). The RUP is based on best practices gleaned from many years of experience on many projects. It has been successfully applied by many organizations in many domains. A growing number of professionals are proficient with the RUP, making it easier to find people with RUP expertise. It doesn't make sense to develop your own process when such a wealth of proven material already exists.

The RUP as a system development process can be tailored to meet the specific needs of different organizations. Using the RUP as a base, organizations can pick and choose the portions they wish to use and add new items particular to their environment. It can be tailored to implement an iterative and incremental approach (the default), a waterfall approach (not recommended), an agile approach, and others as needed. Augmentations to the RUP product (called "plug-ins") are developed and shared by many organizations to speed the adoption of a particular aspect of software development or technology.

The RUP's iterative and incremental approach has several advantages over serial/waterfall strategies:

- **Regular feedback to stakeholders:** Stakeholders can see portions of the system sooner and receive assurances that they will receive what they want. If they don't like what they see, they can provide course corrections at a much earlier point than with the waterfall approach.

- **Improved risk management:** Working incrementally allows bigger risks to be addressed early. If there is a question about whether a requirement can be met or whether a technical challenge can be overcome, it can be addressed in an early iteration. If it cannot be implemented, or if it can be implemented but in a manner that does not meet the stakeholders' needs, the project can be refocused or canceled outright.

- **You implement the actual requirements:** Developing a system incrementally reflects the fact that change is inevitable. Expecting to define requirements once at the beginning of a project and to not have to change them is unrealistic, as is expecting to design an entire system before writing a line of code. By developing systems in smaller iterations, you can react to any changes and thereby build software that meets the actual needs of your stakeholders instead of their perceived needs, which were documented months or years earlier. Changes in requirements that impact later iterations do not impact the work being done on the current iteration. In addition, changes to requirements within the current iterations are easier to deal with because the scope of requirements for each iteration is smaller. Changes to previous iterations are simply scheduled as new requirements in future iterations.

- **You discover what works early:** The goal of the Elaboration phase is to ensure that your architecture works early in your project. Every architecture works on paper, but many don't work in practice. By developing a proof-of-concept (POC) prototype during Elaboration, you mitigate much of the technical risk on your project. By developing the system in iterations, you regularly ensure that your architecture and design continue to meet the changing needs of your stakeholders.

TIP	**Cancel Problematic Projects Early**

Cancel Problematic Projects Early
Canceling a project early is actually a good thing. Implementing an entire system before finding out that it does not meet the stakeholders' needs or is no longer relevant is an expensive way to find out that you've failed. The earlier you can discover that a system is not going to meet your needs, the better off you are.

THE RUP AS A PROCESS FRAMEWORK

The RUP is not only a system development process but also a system development process *framework*. That is, it is a structure from which a process can be created. It was never intended to be a silver bullet that organizations should apply "as is." IBM Rational clearly advocates that organizations customize the RUP to create a process that specifically meets their particular needs.

Although the main concepts remain the same, the specifics of the customization process vary somewhat. This allows organizations to tailor the process to meet their specific business priorities, personnel skill sets, and philosophical—or cultural—approach. For example, if an organization develops shrink-wrapped software, it would tailor the deployment aspects to reflect the manufacturing of software and documentation; an IT organization that only develops for internal use doesn't worry about that aspect. An organization may also, for example, decide to do more (or less) business modeling than is typical for a RUP implementation. The RUP also allows for the addition (or deletion) of phases and/or disciplines.

Each organization must decide how much of the process to implement and which roles, activities, and artifacts it will use. It is not unusual for organizations to have several tailorings of the RUP for use in the different types of projects it normally executes. This reflects the reality that process needs differ across projects as well as across organizations.

The Enterprise Unified Process (EUP) is an extension to the RUP that is best for organizations with multiple systems and multiple development teams. The EUP includes new disciplines and phases, which should be tailored into the standard RUP, making it more effective for these types of organizations. See Chapter 3, "Introduction to the Enterprise Unified Process," for an overview of the extensions to RUP that the EUP encompasses.

SUMMARY

The Rational Unified Process is a product offered by IBM Rational. It is a system development process geared toward object-oriented and component-based system development. It consists of four phases: Inception, Elaboration, Construction, and Transition, which execute sequentially. Work is grouped into logical activities called disciplines, which are performed iteratively throughout the four phases. The RUP is not only a system development process but also a system development process framework that can be tailored to meet organizations' individual needs.

Suggested Reading

Philippe Kruchten's *The Rational Unified Process: An Introduction*, Third Edition, published by Addison-Wesley, provides a detailed summary of RUP from the leader of the team that developed it.

Chapter 3

Introduction to the Enterprise Unified Process

Reader ROI

- The Enterprise Unified Process (EUP) extends the RUP with two new phases: Production and Retirement.

- The EUP adds the Operations and Support discipline to the RUP.

- The EUP adds seven enterprise management disciplines—enterprise business modeling, portfolio management, enterprise architecture, strategic reuse, people management, enterprise administration, and software process improvement—that address cross-system issues.

- Become successful with the RUP first, and then gradually adopt portions of the EUP in priority order based on your specific needs.

As you learned in the first two chapters, the scope of Rational Unified Process (RUP) is a single production release of a system—you will cycle through the RUP lifecycle for subsequent production releases. The RUP is a great start because it provides a foundation for your information technology (IT) organization system process. However, most IT organizations deal with more than simply the development of a single system. They must analyze their needs and identify systems to be built, they must operate and support systems they develop, they must retire systems when they are no longer required, and they must address cross-system concerns such as enterprise architecture, strategic reuse, and portfolio management.

It is possible to build on the foundation of the RUP to support these critical needs; that's what the Enterprise Unified Process is all about. In this chapter we discuss

- Transitioning from a development to a system lifecycle
- The information technology (IT) lifecycle
- The Zachman Framework (ZF) and the EUP
- Common threads throughout this book
- How the EUP works in practice

FROM A DEVELOPMENT TO A SYSTEM LIFECYCLE

The RUP lifecycle of Figure 3-1, described in detail in Chapter 2, "The Rational Unified Process (RUP)," clearly addresses the fundamentals of software development. However, a large portion of the cost and effort for systems, upwards of 75% (Gartner 2000), occurs after systems are deployed. This includes their operation and support in production, maintenance fixes, and their eventual retirement. Our experience is that these efforts are often quite complex and that the people performing them need defined processes just as much as software developers do. Therefore, any organization that wants to be successful at IT needs to look beyond the software DEVELOPMENT lifecycle to consider system lifecycle activities.

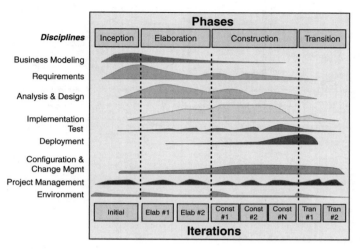

FIGURE 3-1 *The RUP v2003 lifecycle.*
Reprint Courtesy of International Business Machines Corporation
Copyright 2005 © International Business Machines Corporation

The EUP extends the RUP lifecycle to include an Operations and Support discipline, along with two new phases, Production and Retirement. By doing so, it reflects the lifecycle of an entire system, spanning the creation of the first release to its support and eventual retirement. Figure 3-2 depicts the system lifecycle aspects that the EUP adds to the RUP, and Figure 3-3 summarizes all of the EUP phases and their corresponding milestones.

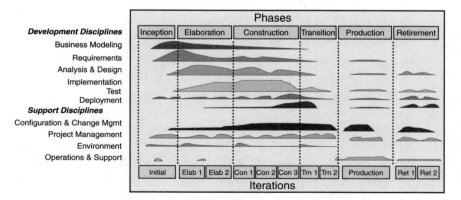

FIGURE 3-2 *Extending the RUP to reflect the system lifecycle.*

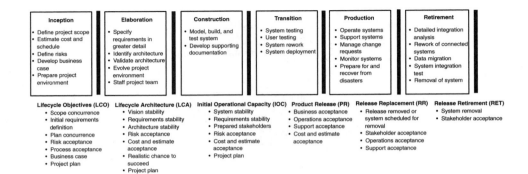

Inception	Elaboration	Construction	Transition	Production	Retirement
• Define project scope • Estimate cost and schedule • Define risks • Develop business case • Prepare project environment	• Specify requirements in greater detail • Identify architecture • Validate architecture • Evolve project environment • Staff project team	• Model, build, and test system • Develop supporting documentation	• System testing • User testing • System rework • System deployment	• Operate systems • Support systems • Manage change requests • Monitor systems • Prepare for and recover from disasters	• Detailed integration analysis • Rework of connected systems • Data migration • System integration test • Removal of system

Lifecycle Objectives (LCO)	Lifecycle Architecture (LCA)	Initial Operational Capacity (IOC)	Product Release (PR)	Release Replacement (RR)	Release Retirement (RET)
• Scope concurrence • Initial requirements definition • Plan concurrence • Risk acceptance • Process acceptance • Business case • Project plan	• Vision stability • Requirements stability • Architecture stability • Risk acceptance • Cost and estimate acceptance • Realistic chance to succeed • Project plan	• System stability • Requirements stability • Prepared stakeholders • Risk acceptance • Cost and estimate acceptance • Project plan	• Business acceptance • Operations acceptance • Support acceptance • Cost and estimate acceptance	• Release removed or system scheduled for removal • Stakeholder acceptance • Operations acceptance • Support acceptance	• System removal • Stakeholder acceptance

FIGURE 3-3   *The EUP phases and milestones.*

THE PRODUCTION PHASE

The Production phase, described in Chapter 4, encompasses the period of the system lifecycle where you operate and support a system until it is either replaced with a new version or retired and removed from use. The primary focus of this phase is on operations and support, although change management of reported defects and new requirements is also critical to ensure that changes are assigned to future development cycles. This phase applies to the lifetime of a single release of your software. To develop and deploy a new release of your software, you need to cycle through the four development phases, as described in Chapter 2.

THE RETIREMENT PHASE

The focus of the Retirement phase (Chapter 5) is the removal of a system from production. Software systems do not last forever. Eventually they become obsolete or are superseded by other systems and must be removed (often referred to as "sunsetting"). A system may be removed from production for two fundamental reasons: the system is not needed anymore, or it is being replaced. Sometimes a system is put in production to fulfill the legal requirements imposed by government legislation, but then the legislation is repealed, thus negating the need for the system. We also commonly see homegrown systems (such as ones for human resource functions) being replaced by commercial off-the-shelf (COTS) systems.

Sometimes a legacy system needs to be replaced by a COTS system for competitive reasons or to show an increase in your financial bottom line.

Many people will question the need for a retirement phase, either because it is rare to remove a system from production or because they treat the retirement of an existing system as a sub-project of the initial deployment of the system replacing it. Yes, it is rare to truly retire a system—as we learned during the Year 2000 (Y2K) crisis, many systems remain in production decades after they were originally implemented—but it still happens. It is quite common to treat system retirement as a sub-project of the replacement project, but this is just a management convenience; the fact remains that retirement is still part of the lifecycle of the original system. As you saw in Chapter 1, systems are conceived, developed, operated, and supported, new releases are developed, and eventually the system is retired. This is the entire lifecycle of a system; how you manage and pay for that lifecycle is up to you.

System retirement is usually complex and risky. An existing system could have thousands or even millions of users, many of whom you may not know or may not be able to contact. Other systems may rely on the system you intend to retire (perhaps they require data feeds or invoke functionality implemented by the system) and therefore will need to be refactored. Significant analysis of the existing systems and IT infrastructure may be required before a system may be safely retired. Because system retirement is a difficult and complex endeavor, it requires a specialized skill set and supporting processes.

THE OPERATIONS AND SUPPORT DISCIPLINE

The purpose of the Operations and Support discipline (Chapter 6) is exactly as the name implies: to operate and support your production systems. Operations activities include monitoring and tuning systems, upgrading hardware, and archiving data. Support activities include responding to user requests, escalating serious problems, and recording suggested fixes and improvements to existing systems. It also includes maintaining your infrastructure, such as the application of patches; maintaining the code base; and keeping your operating systems, databases, and all internal systems running in the production environment. This also includes planning for and recovering from disasters.

Operations and support are both complex endeavors that require defined processes. This new discipline spans several phases. During the Construction phase, and perhaps as early as the Elaboration phase, you need to develop operations and support plans, documents, and training manuals. During the Transition phase, you continue to develop these artifacts, reworking them based on the results of testing. Finally, during Transition, you need to train your operations and support staff to effectively work with your software. During Production, your organization must contend with the support activities to maintain the system within the environment. This also happens during the Retirement phase, when you enter the process of shutting down an existing system in production.

THE INFORMATION TECHNOLOGY (IT) LIFECYCLE

Successful IT departments look beyond the needs of a single system. As you learned in Chapter 1, the IT lifecycle extends the system lifecycle to address the cross-system issues that your IT organization must deal with on a daily basis. Figure 3-4 depicts the full lifecycle of the EUP, which extends the system lifecycle of Figure 3-2 to include disciplines that address the cross-system issues that are critical to your success.

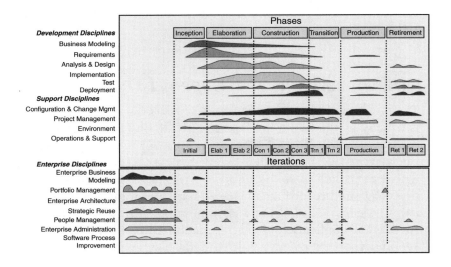

FIGURE 3-4   *The EUP lifecycle.*

The EUP includes seven new enterprise management disciplines that tackle the cross-system issues that organizations should address to be successful at IT.

- **Enterprise Business Modeling:** The goal of this discipline, described in Chapter 7, is to explore the business structure and processes of the enterprise. It provides a common understanding of the business activities, customers, and suppliers of the business. Enterprise business modeling helps identify problems and areas that are candidates for automation.

- **Portfolio Management:** Organizations often have suites of applications, called programs, that can be better managed as a whole than as individual applications. This discipline enables you to track and plan your organization's entire software portfolio as well as individual programs within your overall portfolio. Doing so allows you to schedule and implement new requirements in a more strategic fashion. This also helps avoid implementing the same functionality within different applications. This discipline is further described in Chapter 8.

- **Enterprise Architecture:** This discipline addresses the overall architecture issues associated with your organization. It consists of models that define it, prototypes and working models that demonstrate how it works, and frameworks that make it easier to use. The Enterprise Architecture discipline, described in Chapter 9, helps ensure consistency across systems and greatly facilitates application architecture efforts.

- **Strategic Reuse:** This discipline, described in Chapter 10, promotes development and reuse of assets across projects, the goal of which is to enable you to develop higher-quality applications more quickly by reusing assets instead of developing them anew each time. It also helps improve quality, as it allows you to use artifacts that have already been tested and proven to work.

- **People Management:** Managing software development efforts includes far more than the technical tasks of creating and evolving project plans and schedules. People exist within your organization, and you need to manage your staff and mediate the interactions between them and other people. This discipline, covered in Chapter 11, describes the process of organizing, monitoring, coaching, and motivating people in a manner to ensure they work together well and successfully contribute to projects within the organization.

- **Enterprise Administration:** This discipline includes setting up and administering tools, processes, and facilities that are key infrastructure components of your IT organization. This discipline is covered in Chapter 12.

- **Software Process Improvement:** This discipline, described in Chapter 13, addresses the need to manage, improve, and support the multiple processes in use across your organization. Remember, one process does not fit all.

All of the new enterprise management disciplines come at a cost. Any attempts at implementing them should be applied judiciously and with minimal interruption to your current business functions. These new disciplines can provide significant savings in the long run by streamlining how your IT department operates—if you choose to implement them in a non-bureaucratic manner.

It is important to understand that although some overlap exists between the enterprise management discipline activities and existing RUP activities, the scope is different. For example, the Enterprise Architecture discipline includes many of the same activities as the RUP Analysis and Design discipline. Your enterprise architecture is concerned with the architecture that spans multiple systems, whereas the architecture that is done during the Analysis and Design discipline of a project is for a single system only. Similarly, Enterprise Business Modeling (EBM) and Business Modeling (BM) disciplines are similar as far as the activities are concerned. The difference is that EBM takes a broad and shallow look at the entire business, whereas BM typically looks at the business as it relates to only a single system. BM will most likely go into more detail in a specific area, as it may be required to do so in order for a particular system to be developed.

THE ZACHMAN FRAMEWORK AND THE EUP

A fundamental question that people frequently ask about enterprise modeling and modeling in general is how various approaches such as enterprise business modeling, enterprise architectural modeling, and design modeling for a single project all relate to one another. The Zachman Framework (ZIFA 2002), created in the 1980s by John Zachman, describes an approach to addressing this very question. The Zachman Framework (ZF), depicted in Figure 3-5, describes a collection of perspectives pertinent to enterprise modeling. The rows of the framework represent the views of different types of stakeholders, and the columns represent different aspects or views of your architecture. Traditionally, within a column, the models are evolved/translated to reflect the views of the stakeholders for each row and within a single row should be consistent with one another.

	What (Data)	How (Function)	Where (Locations)	Who (People)	When (Time)	Why (Motivation)
Scope {contextual} **Planner**	List of things important to the business	List of processes that the business performs	List of locations in which the business operates	List of organizations important to the business	List of events/ cycles important to the business	List of business goals/strategies
Enterprise Model {conceptual} **Business Owner**	e.g. Semantic Model	e.g. Business Process Model	e.g. Business Logistics System	e.g. Workflow Model	e.g. Master Schedule	e.g. Business Plan
System Model {logical} **Designer**	e.g. Logical Data Model	e.g. Application Architecture	e.g. Distributed System Architecture	e.g. Human Interface Architecture	e.g. Process Structure	e.g. Business Rule Model
Technology Model {physical} **Implementer**	e.g. Physical Data Model	e.g. System Design	e.g. Technology Architecture	e.g. Presentation Architecture	e.g. Control Structure	e.g. Rule Design
Detailed Representation {out-of-context} **Subcontractor**	e.g. Data Definition	e.g. Program	e.g. Network Architecture	e.g. Security Architecture	e.g. Timing Definition	e.g. Rule Definition
Functioning System	e.g. Data	e.g. Function	e.g. Network	e.g. Organization	e.g. Schedule	e.g. Strategy

FIGURE 3-5 *The Zachman Framework.*

The Zachman Framework has several strengths. First, it has been well accepted within the data community, which considers it the de facto standard for enterprise architecture (Hay 2003). Second, and more importantly, it defines the perspective that your enterprise models should encompass, the implication being that you can apply its guidance within a process such as the EUP. Third, it explicitly communicates that enterprise modeling has several stakeholders, not just enterprise architects and developers, whom you should involve in your modeling efforts.

However, the Zachman Framework suffers from several weaknesses. First, it can lead to a documentation-heavy approach (although this does not have to be the case). There are 36 cells in Figure 3-5, each of which could be supported by one or more models. Second, it can lead to a process-heavy approach to development—you can see the opportunity to define a collection of rigorous processes to support the framework (which is not our recommendation). Third, it isn't well accepted within the development community, and few developers seem to have even heard about it—it's very rare to see a programming or software design book that even mentions the framework. Fourth, it seems to promote a top-down approach to development. When people first read about it, they tend to think that it implies an approach where you start with the models in row 1, then work on row 2 models, and so on. This doesn't have to be the case, though; you can in fact start in any cell and then iterate from there. Fifth, it appears to be biased toward traditional, data-centric techniques (thus explaining its popularity within the data community).

Our experience is that it is possible to apply the Zachman Framework successfully within the EUP if you focus on its strengths and address its weaknesses. Figure 3-6 shows how we have extended the Zachman Framework so that it aligns with the EUP.

	What (Structure)	How (Function)	Where (Locations)	Who (People)	When (Time)	Why (Motivation)	Cost/Benefit (Finances)
Enterprise Business Modeling	Most significant business concepts (Enterprise glossary)	Enterprise business processes (Data flow diagram)	International view of locations (Location map)	Organizational strategy (Organization chart)	Business events	Enterprise vision/ mission	Corporate financials
Portfolio Management	List of systems and inter-relationships	Map business processes to systems	Map project teams to locations	Project team assignments	IT planning	IT vision	IT department's budget and actuals
Enterprise Architecture	Domain architecture (UML component diagram)	Workflow architecture	Network architecture (UML deployment diagram)	Actual and potential interactions	Technical architecture		Enterprise architecture team's budget and actuals
Strategic Reuse Management	Domain components	Functions (Web services, CICS transactions)		User interface components			Reuse group's budget and actuals
People Management	Positions and relationships between positions	Roles played in each location and relationships between roles	Offices and relationships between them	Human resource philosophies and strategies	Annual reviews, project milestones	Career management strategies	Human resource department budget and actuals
Enterprise Administration	Information assets (Corporate data sources)	Guidance (Standards and guidelines)	Physical assets				Enterprise administration budget and actuals
Software Process Improvement		Software process definition		Software engineering process group (SEPG) mandate		IT department improvement goals	Process group's budget and actuals
Business Modeling	Most significant business concepts (Project glossary)	Project mission, strategies processes (Data flow diagram)	Project view of locations (Location map)	Affected positions (Organization chart)	Business events	System vision/ mission	Business modeling budget and actuals
Requirements	Domain model (CRC Cards, UML Class Model)	Usage of the system (Use cases)			Timing requirements (Business rules)	Business rules	Requirements modeling budget and actuals
Analysis and Design	Structural design (UML Class Diagram, Physical Data Model)	Implementation design of functions/ operations	Map of processes to location	User interface design	Scheduled events		A&D budget and actuals
Implementation	Source code	Source code	Hardware, network, middleware	Implementation of user interface	Implementation of system triggers	Implementation of business rules	Implementation budget and actuals
Test	Test suite	Tests			Testing framework	Quality goals	Testing budget and actuals
Deployment	Installation packages	Installation scripts					Deployment budget and actuals
Configuration and Change Management	Configuration builds					C&CM plan	C&CM budget and actuals
Project Management	Project task list (Gantt chart)	Project schedule (Gantt chart)		Staffing plan	Project schedule (Gantt chart)	Project charter	Project management budget and actuals
Environment	List of required tools and guidance						Environment budget and actuals
Operations & Support	Deployed classes, components, tables, ...	Deployed functions/ operations	Deployed hardware, middleware, and software	Deployed user interface (including documentation)	Deployed systems	Deployed software	Operation and support budget and actuals

FIGURE 3-6 *Extending the Zachman Framework for EUP.*

As you can see, we have made significant changes to the Zachman Framework:

- **Discipline-based rows:** We've replaced the six rows with the 17 disciplines of the EUP, providing a more finely detailed collection of views. The enterprise management columns are listed first and then the project-level disciplines to remain consistent with its top-down approach. The primary benefit of showing the disciplines as rows is that it clarifies how to apply the questions represented by the framework columns to each aspect of the EUP. Unfortunately this approach could exacerbate many of the weaknesses of the Zachman Framework.

- **The cost column:** At the Data Management Association (DAMA) 2004 conference, Graeme Simsion mused on a panel that the columns of the framework reflect single-word English interrogatives and that if John Zachman had spoken another language, it may have looked different. For example, French includes "combien," which translates to "how much" or "how many." It is very clear that financial concerns are important within IT organizations, hence the addition of a seventh column by us. Interestingly, in German all the columns can be labeled with single-word interrogatives starting with the letter "w"—was, wie, wo, wer, wann, warum, and wieviel, respectively.

- **Refocusing the first column:** The first column is really a structural issue, not a data issue. This simple generalization helps remove the data-oriented bias of the framework, making it clear that you have more options available than just data-oriented artifacts.

- **Cells describe the issues to address:** Each cell indicates the potential issue(s) to address, if any, and suggests a potential artifact to explore those issue(s). Some cells are left blank because the column isn't applicable to the discipline.

It's important to recognize that using the Zachman Framework is optional within the EUP. We believe it provides very good guidance for your modeling and development efforts because it reminds you of the critical issues you need to address. First, keep it simple. You don't need to create artifacts for all the cells; the important thing is that you at least consider the issues for each cell. You can in fact be quite agile with the framework if you choose (McGovern et al 2004). The secret is to avoid documentation-heavy, bureaucratic processes centered on the framework. Remember, your goal is to develop working software, not to create lots of fancy models and documentation. Second, remember that you have choices. Each cell indicates the required perspective, not suggested models. For example, in the Structure column, David Hay (2003) suggests that you create a language-divergent data model in row 2, a convergent entity/relationship model in row 3, and a database design in row 4 of Figure 3-6. Moriarty (2001) suggests a business class diagram, a class diagram, and a schema data model, respectively, in the same rows. Object developers would probably suggest a component model, a class diagram, and another class diagram for these rows. All three approaches are valid, but all three represent the experiences and prejudices of the individual methodologists. Far better advice would be to understand the perspective represented by each box, understand the strengths and weaknesses of each type of modeling artifact, and then apply the right artifact(s).

COMMON THREADS THROUGHOUT THIS BOOK

Throughout this book, we will discuss several common themes, techniques, and concepts:

- **Keep things simple:** One potential problem with implementing the EUP disciplines is that you can create huge bureaucracies as you implement them. Application teams should want to work *with* enterprise staff, not *around* them.

- **Communication:** Communication is the act of sharing information. The need to communicate effectively pervades all aspects of the IT lifecycle—developers and enterprise staff must communicate with one another, IT professionals and end users must communicate, senior management and developers must communicate, and so on. Cockburn (2002) contends that software development is a communication game and that if communication breaks down, so will your IT efforts. He compares the various approaches to communication, depicted in Figure 3-7, arguing that the "richer" the channel, the greater its communication effectiveness. Effective IT professionals actively seek to ensure the most effective communication possible.

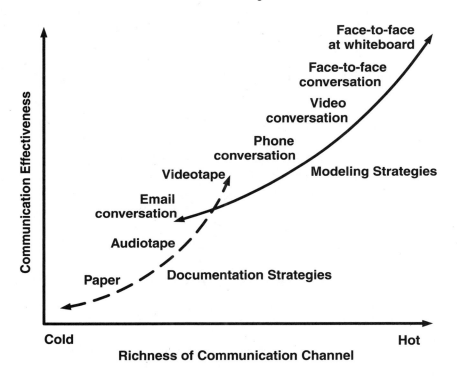

FIGURE 3-7   *Comparing the effectiveness of different communication channels.*

■ **RUP diagrams:** We follow the workflow diagramming approach used in the RUP product, which conforms to the Software Process Engineering Metamodel (SPEM), when we explain the phases and disciplines (Object Management Group 2002). For disciplines, this entails a high-level workflow diagram depicting the steps taken during the discipline and the workflow details for each step, including the individual activities, inputs, and outputs. For phases, we provide a sample iteration workflow (first introduced in RUP 2003) to depict the typical activities undertaken during the phase.

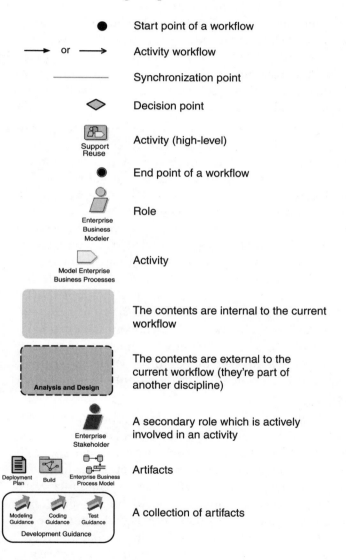

	Start point of a workflow
	Activity workflow
	Synchronization point
	Decision point
	Activity (high-level)
	End point of a workflow
	Role
	Activity
	The contents are internal to the current workflow
	The contents are external to the current workflow (they're part of another discipline)
	A secondary role which is actively involved in an activity
	Artifacts
	A collection of artifacts

FIGURE 3-8 *Workflow diagram symbols.*

- **Collaboration:** Collaboration and communication go hand in hand. Highsmith (2004) reflects that most communication is basically one-way and that you need to take the next step to focus on collaborative two-way communication where people are working together to achieve a common result. Enterprise professionals should actively support project teams by working side by side with them as members of the team. This high level of collaboration may seem strange, and even impossible, within traditional organizations, but our experience is that this teamwork is required if you want to truly succeed at the EUP.

- **Mentoring:** Mentoring is a process where one person transfers her skills to another person. Our experience is that mentoring is critical to the success of the proliferation of new processes and techniques within an organization. We've developed a four-step approach to mentoring: First, people need training from an experienced instructor, preferably the person who will be doing the mentoring, to gain the fundamental requisite knowledge. Second, the mentor demonstrates the technique so that the "mentee" can see how the concepts are actually applied. Third, the mentor guides and assists the mentee in applying the concepts, giving the mentee hands-on experience. Fourth, the mentee does the work on his own, with the mentor reviewing his work and providing feedback as appropriate. The goal in the final stage of mentoring is for the mentor to reduce her involvement over time until she is no longer needed.

- **Guidance:** We use the term guidance to represent both standards (established rules that everyone *must* adhere to) and guidelines (established indications of how things *should* be done). Common guidelines across project teams lead to consistency and quality throughout teams. Guidance can be defined for many areas, including modeling, coding, and user documentation. Our philosophy is that enterprise professionals should be responsible for developing and then supporting their own guidance; for example, enterprise architects are responsible for developing architecture-related guidance and then sharing that with project teams.

- **Supporting project teams:** Supporting project teams is a critical aspect of each of the seven EUP enterprise management disciplines. Enterprise professionals need to train and educate project teams on the techniques and vision of their appropriate disciplines. A good part of this is communication with the project teams and mentoring team members, as well as supporting the relevant guidance in an agile and effective manner. Enterprise professionals will often get actively involved with project teams—for example, enterprise architects will help work on the project architecture, and reuse engineers will help the team develop robust artifacts—to help the team with enterprise-related activities.

- **Generalizing specialists:** The best IT professionals are "generalizing specialists" who are willing and able to take on a wide variety of roles. A generalizing specialist is someone who is very good in one or two IT specialties, such as domain modeling or project management, and who also has a good understanding of the entire IT lifecycle and hopefully of your business domain as well (Ambler 2004). These individuals will have a good grasp of how everything fits together and as a result will typically have a greater understanding and appreciation of what their teammates are working on. They are willing to listen to and work with others because they know that they'll likely learn something new. In many ways, a generalizing specialist is simply a software craftsperson (McBreen 2001). However, we've found "craftsperson" to be an offensive term to traditional IT professionals; similarly, the term "software engineer" is often offensive to agile IT professionals.

- **Reviews:** Reviews are one of several ways to validate the quality of your work, but unfortunately not a very good one. Reviews compensate for overly serial processes and for a lack of collaboration during the development of an artifact. If you don't make those mistakes, you don't need to compensate by holding a review. To avoid these mistakes, you should take an evolutionary and highly collaborative approach to development; adopt agile practices such as pair programming, collective ownership, modeling with others, and active stakeholder participation; and follow accepted guidance within your organization. When you do so, you'll discover that reviews offer very little value and that you can safely reduce the number you hold (Ambler 2003c). We've kept the reviews in the workflow diagrams— as with all activities in the EUP, you are free to tailor them out of your version of the process if appropriate. To reduce clutter and to conform to the RUP approach, though, our diagrams don't show that the review logs (which record the findings of the review) need to be fed back into the activities that created the artifacts in the first place. If you're going to hold a review, you should act on the results.

- **IT governance:** IT governance is the act of specifying the decision rights and accountability framework to encourage desirable behavior in using IT (Weill and Ross 2004). IT governance can take many forms. One extreme is to have a corporate governance board that reviews all relevant efforts and ensures that work products are in compliance and that proper process and procedures are followed. At the other end of the spectrum is a hands-off approach for senior management, where organizational guidance is published with the expectation that teams will govern themselves to ensure compliance. Having a governance board oversee all efforts provides significant insight for executives into what is happening (assuming that everyone is telling the board the truth). However, a governance board reduces your flexibility considerably. An attempt to examine all aspects of efforts leads to disruption, time delays, and fear, where people are afraid of doing something that violates policy, which can get them in trouble. On the other hand, a hands-off approach may well lead to people taking inappropriate liberties. Our advice is to find the balance somewhere between the two extremes, although we've found that the most effective organizations seem to be closer to the hands-off approach.

- **Anti-patterns:** Anti-patterns are common approaches that are proven to not work very well in practice. Each discipline (discussed in Chapters 6 through 13) presents a collection of anti-patterns common to that discipline that you should avoid, as well as a recommended solution to apply if you do fall into the anti-pattern. Understanding a problem is the first step in addressing it.

- **Tools:** A wide range of tools is available from a wide variety of vendors to help you apply the EUP, from simple tools such as whiteboards to very complex software-based tools. Each of the discipline chapters includes a section describing tools that support the concepts discussed for that discipline.

- **Documentation:** The need to write and maintain documentation is a reality within IT; it behooves you to improve your ability to write effective documentation. You should strive to develop agile documents (Ambler 2002; Rueping 2004) that are just barely good enough in order to maximize stakeholder investment, because any additional investment beyond "good enough" is clearly wasted effort.

- **Stakeholders:** We use the term stakeholder to refer to anyone directly involved with, or affected by, an activity. For example, a development project stakeholder is anyone who is a direct user, indirect user, manager of users, senior manager, operations staff member, support (help desk) staff member, developers working on other systems that integrate or interact with the one under development, or maintenance professionals potentially affected by its development, upkeep, and/or deployment. Active stakeholder participation in an activity is usually critical to its success to ensure that you meet their needs; remember that whatever your role is, you are just another stakeholder on the project team.

- **Metrics:** "Metric" is another word for measurement. The fundamental goal with any metrics effort is to take critical measurements of an activity so that you can identify potential areas for improvement. It is critical to recognize that you don't need perfect figures for your metrics to be effective. Fay (2004a) discusses the concept of "good enough metrics (GEMs)," which use a combination of actual data captured within your organization and estimates based on industry information, which you use to fill in the blanks until you have your own data. Effective managers do not manage solely by the numbers; instead, metrics are just one of many information sources on which they act. Be careful when using metrics. Reporting the wrong information based on metrics or interpreting them incorrectly can do significantly more harm than good. Know, understand, and be able to effectively communicate each metric you select; if you cannot do this, ask yourself why that particular metric is needed. Use metrics in combination. For example, if system A has 20 defects and system B has 40 defects, which is the higher quality of the two systems? Sounds like system B. But if system A delivers 10 units of functionality and system B delivers 100 units, now which is better quality? Sounds like system A—system A has 2 defects per unit, and system B has 0.4 per unit.

THE EUP IN PRACTICE

The goal of the EUP is to augment the RUP to include both the overall system and IT perspectives. Thus, the rest of this book gives you more details on extending the lifecycle beyond development to meet your real-world needs. The EUP is an augmentation of the RUP, not a replacement. The principles and practices of the RUP remain the same; the EUP simply adds new phases and disciplines to help organizations think about and execute projects strategically. Before starting any adoption process of the EUP, first adopt the RUP, tailor it to your environment, and then tailor the EUP extensions on top of the RUP. One of the reasons why we started with a discussion of the system lifecycle is that it's a good place for you to stasrt extending the RUP with concepts from EUP. After you're successful with a full system lifecycle, consider adopting the enterprise management disciplines on a priority basis (as defined by your specific needs). Chapter 14 discusses adoption issues in detail. As with RUP, you do not need to use every phase and discipline within the EUP—mix and match them according to your needs. It is extremely important to understand how the RUP fits within your organization before embarking on the journey to adopt and implement the EUP.

SUMMARY

The RUP lifecycle focuses on the development of one system release. Because your organization must contend with running multiple systems, you must extend the RUP to reflect this reality. The EUP includes two new phases and eight new disciplines to complete the view of the overall system and IT perspectives. The operations and support discipline—which encompasses most of the Production phase—has been added to help an organization operate and support its systems. Two new phases of the EUP are Production and Retirement. The Production phase addresses supporting a product after it has been released into production. The Retirement phase has been added to address the real-world needs of sunsetting (or retiring) a product from production. Finally, seven new enterprise management disciplines have been added to address multiple areas within your organization to support cross-project issues.

Suggested Reading

The best resource for up-to-date information about the EUP is the EUP Web site, `www.enterpriseunifiedprocess.com`.

Part II

Beyond Development

Chapter 4

The Production Phase

Reader ROI

- The Production phase is composed of the activities executed when release of a system is deployed.

- Systems must be operated and supported after they are deployed. This includes ensuring that they are up and running, that data is backed up and restored as necessary, and that user questions and error reports are addressed.

- Defect fixes and collections of fixes are developed and applied to deployed systems in a production environment.

- Operations and support efforts need to be managed according to business needs.

The RUP project lifecycle ends with the Transition phase's Product Release (PR) milestone when the release of a system has been deployed to users. However, that's not the end of the story. A complete system lifecycle must take into consideration the issues associated with operating and supporting systems after deployment. There is more to information technology (IT) than just building and deploying systems; they must be operated and supported after they are deployed. This happens during the Production phase, as depicted in Figure 4-1.

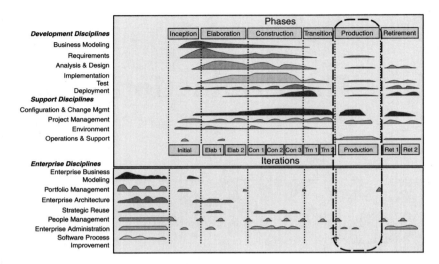

FIGURE 4-1   *The Production phase.*

This chapter explores the following topics:

- The objectives of the Production phase
- Essential activities
- Handling concurrent releases
- Support strategies
- The Release Retirement milestone

OBJECTIVES

The goal of the Production phase is to keep systems useful and productive after they have been deployed to the user community. This process will differ from organization to organization and perhaps even from system to system, but the fundamental goal remains the same—keep the system running and help users use it. Shrink-wrapped software, for example, will not require operational support but will typically require a help desk to assist users. Organizations that implement systems for internal use will usually require an operational staff to run and monitor systems. The Production phase, like the rest of the EUP, requires each organization to tailor it to meet their specific needs.

The Production phase ends when the release of a system has been slated for retirement or when support for that release has ended. The latter may occur immediately upon the release of a newer version, some time after the release of a newer version, or simply on a date that the business has decided to end support. The Release Replacement milestone, described in detail in a later section, is the final approval for a release to exit the production phase.

This phase typically has one iteration because it applies to the operational lifetime of a single release of your software. There may be multiple iterations, however, if you defined multiple levels of support that your software will have over time.

TIP   **It Isn't *Just* Maintenance or *Just* Operations and Support**

The Production phase encompasses "emergency maintenance" of systems, operations, support, and change management. In the EUP, maintenance of a system is done either as emergency hot fixes during the Production phase or during development of a future release of the system.

This phase could have been called *Maintenance*, but that clearly wouldn't have been right. Similarly, it could have been called *Operations and Support*, but that wouldn't be right either—the efforts of your operations and support team(s) occur throughout the entire lifecycle, not just after a system has been deployed.

ESSENTIAL ACTIVITIES

A typical iteration workflow for the Production phase is depicted in Figure 4-2.

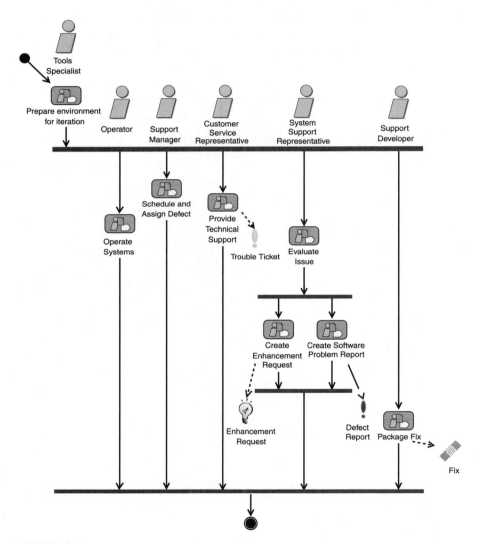

FIGURE 4-2   *Typical Production phase workflow.*

Most of these tasks occur in the Operations and Support discipline (Chapter 6), a new discipline introduced by the EUP. A brief description of the activities follows:

- Operators monitor the system to make sure it is running properly, to start jobs and processes as appropriate, to back up and restore data, and to generally look after the system and operating environment.

- A support manager is responsible for managing the overall support efforts. The support manager prioritizes work, schedules and assigns tasks, ensures that support personnel have the resources to complete their tasks, and ensures that work is completed in a timely fashion.

- Customer support representatives communicate directly with users and assist them in the use of the system. They provide advice and guidance to users and record enhancement requests and problem reports. They maintain contact with users who have reported problems and keep them informed of their progress.

- System support representatives investigate problem reports and act on them. If they are caused by the system behaving improperly, they create defects that are then handled by support engineers. If they are enhancement requests, they create enhancement requests that go to the Enterprise Configuration Control Board for consideration (Chapter 8).

- Support developers address critical defects (errors) in system behavior. They are responsible for making changes to the system to correct incorrect behavior. They are also responsible for packaging fixes to be applied and, if fixes are applied internally, for applying those fixes to deployed systems.

- Preparations are made for recovery from a disaster such as a hardware power outage or a network error that disrupts processing. If a disaster occurs, the disaster recovery plan is executed.

Other activities that take place during Production include the following:

- **Requirements:** During the Production phase, user enhancement requests are received. These new requests must be documented and analyzed.

- **Analysis and Design:** Initial analysis of user enhancement requests takes place, as well as analysis and design required to resolve high-priority defects.

- **Test:** Testing of fixes must be done before they are deployed. These may take the form of hot fixes (a code update to address a specific problem) or service packs (a collection of individual fixes). Regression tests that can be rerun when a fix has been made are crucial to the continuity of deployed software.

- **Configuration and Change Management:** Change requests and defect reports will be accepted and managed during the Production phase. Configuration of the system needs to be tracked and updated as fixes are created and applied.

- **Project Management:** Activities in the Production phase are managed, just like any other activities. Operational activities are managed by an Operations Manager; support activities are managed by a Support Manager. They are responsible for assigning tasks and monitoring and reporting progress.

- **Environment:** Support environments are modified as needed during the Production phase, as are operational monitoring tools, runtime environments, and backup and recovery setups.

- **Enterprise Administration:** While systems are running, enterprise administrators maintain networks and hardware. They also ensure that the underlying security and data infrastructure is stable. When necessary, they troubleshoot any problems that arise with capacity and upgrades, and they assist in testing and applying fixes.

The Configuration and Change Management discipline in RUP defines the processes for use within a project. When a release moves to the Production phase, changes to it must still be maintained outside the scope of any new development projects. Requests will still come in for enhancements; defects will be reported, reviewed, and fixed; and other change requests will be received. If you are implementing the Portfolio Management discipline, change requests will be handled by an Enterprise Configuration Control Board (Chapter 8). This board will review all types of change requests, including enhancements and low-severity defects, determine which ones should be acted on, and then assign them to the appropriate teams. High-severity defects, as identified by a support manager, are assigned to support developers to address immediately (Chapter 6).

Although a configuration management (CM) plan is developed as part of the Configuration and Change Management discipline during a development project, CM plans should not be developed anew for each release. Instead, they should be developed for each *product* and only updated by project efforts as needed. Your configuration management strategy will likely not change significantly between versions 2.2 and 2.3, for instance; there is no need to create a new one each time. There is a need, however, to extend CM plans beyond projects. You need to define how to manage changes and configurations not just during a project but also while systems are in production.

HANDLING CONCURRENT RELEASES

The Production phase for a release does not necessarily end when a new development project for a subsequent release of that product begins. As Figure 4-3 shows, you will have to operate and support earlier releases in parallel to development efforts. In fact, you may have multiple releases in production at the same time. In this example, you see that operations and support for both versions 1.0 and 1.1 continues for a short period after version 1.1 is released. It is not until version 2.0 is released that support for version 1.0 is discontinued.

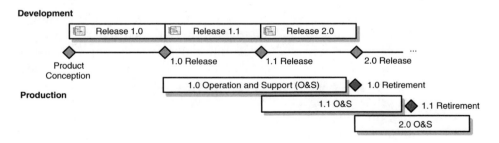

FIGURE 4-3 *Sample timeline of development and production efforts.*

In reality, you will probably have multiple releases in development concurrently. It is not uncommon to begin the software development for release $n+1$ before release n has been completed and deployed, as depicted in Figure 4-4. This may speed up the rate at which new releases are deployed and retired but will complicate your development efforts because you will have two teams updating the same code base.

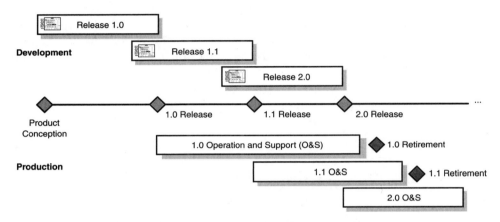

FIGURE 4-4 *Sample timeline of overlapping development and production efforts.*

When you release a new version of a product, support for the older version(s) does not normally end immediately. When you release version 2.0 of your Whizbang product to the general public, for example, you will still support Whizbang v1.1 for a period of time (say 18 months) and Whizbang 1.0 for a lesser period (say six more months). You will dedicate more resources to supporting v2.0 than the older versions, and you may even charge for support for the really old version, but you can't cut off support for clients who haven't upgraded until they've had a reasonable period of time to do so (or are willing to pay for continued support).

There are many different approaches to phasing out operations and support for systems. You should define in advance how long you will support major and minor versions of systems after new releases are available. Explaining your support policy to customers in advance is crucial; no one likes to find out at the last minute that she must upgrade or go without support for a critical software system.

Supporting multiple versions of a system can become messy if it's not managed properly. In most cases, subsequent releases of a product evolve from the work products of an earlier release. Older versions often need to be supported and updated separately from the new release effort. This is often accomplished with a technique called "branch and merge," which starts when the project team for the new release selects its development base for the new effort. You create a copy of all the relevant artifacts (use cases, design model, code, test cases, and so on) that they will work on. This is known as the "branch." You base all their efforts on evolving their copy of these artifacts to create the new release—for example, updating or adding use cases, evolving the design, or updating the code. The original artifacts are maintained separately. This needs to happen to allow the original release to be supported independently of the development effort.

Operations and support of the current version of the product must still happen while new development is progressing. If a critical error is found in production, customers will want it fixed. The support team must be able to make and deploy fixes to the current version without impacting the development effort (and vice versa). For a period of time, there are two copies of the code base and other artifacts as the two efforts support different goals.

At some point, a "merge" takes place. When the development effort for the new release nears completion, you must merge in the changes that the support team has made this to incorporate as many fixes as possible. This may be done late during the Construction phase when new code is being written, or it may happen during the Transition phase. They do this by reviewing the changes that were made to the artifacts after the branch occurred and merging them into their base code. The old code base can be archived and removed if support for the older version is being discontinued; otherwise, both code bases must continue to be supported and evolved.

SUPPORT STRATEGIES

Your organization may opt to offer different levels of support to your customers. Tourniaire and Farrell (1997) describe two basic strategies for delivering support—an escalation strategy and a touch-and-hold strategy. The escalation strategy is based on the idea that most support requests are fairly basic and therefore can be handled quickly, whereas small minorities of requests are complicated and must be assigned or escalated to more knowledgeable staff members. The touch-and-hold strategy combines two roles into a single role and requires a higher level of skill sets than the escalation strategy. This is discussed in detail in the Operations and Support discipline (Chapter 6).

THE RELEASE RETIREMENT MILESTONE

As you can see in Figure 4-5, the Production phase ends with the Release Retirement milestone. The Release Retirement milestone determines whether the operations and support for a release of a system are to be ended. At this milestone, you must answer the following questions:

- Is the functionality provided by this release of the system no longer needed?
- Are the stakeholders ready for the retirement of the release?

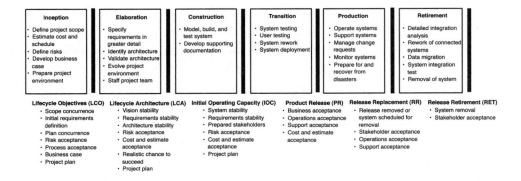

FIGURE 4-5 *EUP phases and milestones.*

During this milestone review, the stakeholders determine if the functionality provided by the release of the system will no longer be provided. This may be due to any of several reasons—replacement by a later version of the system, replacement by another system, the business moving in a different direction, and so on. To pass this milestone, the stakeholders must agree that this functionality should be removed. Transition to the Retirement phase may be postponed if the project fails to pass the milestone review.

CASE STUDIES

This section describes two case studies. One discusses a client's experiences hosting and operating business application software. The other describes Microsoft's approach to application support.

Hosting and Operating Business Applications

Accounting Co. builds, deploys, and operates a large number of accounting applications for its clients, running them in a dedicated operations center. The operations center is equipped with multiple backup systems in case power is lost, as well as additional hardware in case individual machines experience problems. In the event of a larger disaster, they keep copies of systems and data at another location that they can bring up in short order.

Accounting rules and regulations change fairly frequently, so they are constantly updating their applications. Most of their applications are updated on a quarterly basis. They take a time-boxed approach to releases—they collect new requirements, enhancement requests, and defects; prioritize them; and implement them in priority order. They implement as many as they can without missing their quarterly deadline. Customers are assured of receiving their highest-priority items first at the quarterly deployment date. High-priority defects are fixed and deployed as "hot fixes" if they are deemed by a review board to be critical to clients.

The company has a dedicated operations staff to run the applications. These people make sure that the applications are up and running so that clients can access them. They also monitor automated job scheduling to be sure that batch jobs start and finish correctly. The staff works closely with development teams, both to ensure that they understand what is expected of them and to resolve any issues that arise. Their attention to detail is reflected in their high customer satisfaction ratings.

However, their attention to individual customers has sometimes caused them problems. They occasionally customized an application for a particular client to reflect individual needs by deploying a customized version of the application just for that customer. Eventually they had to curtail this practice because they became overwhelmed with too many customized versions of applications; it was a configuration management nightmare. The operation and maintenance of these "one-off" systems became too onerous to justify. They still do this for large customers, but for the most part, they collect customization requests and build them into the application as options instead of spinning off a customized application. This means that the company now cannot offer as many individual customizations as it could in the past, but this was a necessary step to make the production activities manageable.

Microsoft Support

Microsoft supports many versions of its software at any given time. In addition to the many flavors of Windows (Windows 95/98/NT/2000/XP), there also are multiple versions of each one (XP Home, XP Pro). Some of these are evolutions of older systems (Windows 95 to Windows 98), while some maintain backward compatibility but essentially are rewrites of large portions of the system (Windows NT). Microsoft has to support them all, even while it's developing new versions.

Just because Microsoft has a later version of Windows does not mean it stops supporting the previous versions. It supports them even if newer versions of Windows have been developed. When a security vulnerability is discovered (an all-to-common occurrence these days, unfortunately), Microsoft must update every code base for the versions of Windows it still supports, including creating and deploying hot fixes for critical problems.

Microsoft has developed a three-tier support system. The first five years after a product is generally available, Microsoft offers what it calls Mainstream Support. During this period, customers receive Microsoft's highest level of support, including free incident reporting, paid incident reporting, fee-based support, and others. After five years, customers enjoy Extended Support. Extended Support includes security-related patches at no charge and all paid support options. This level of support is available for two years after Mainstream Support ends. After that, products are supported solely by Microsoft's Web site, including FAQs, a searchable knowledge base, and other online resources, for a period of eight years after the product was first released.

SUMMARY

The Production phase begins after the Product Release milestone at the end of the Transition phase. During Production, the system is operated and supported: the software is run, monitored, and backed up; user questions about the system are answered; user defect reports and enhancement requests are recorded and managed; and fixes are made and applied.

Multiple versions of a single system may have to be supported at the same time. In addition, multiple levels of support may be implemented, sometimes depending on the support a client is willing to pay for. The Production phase for a system ends when support for that release of the system has been withdrawn.

Suggested Reading

Information Technology Infrastructure Library (ITIL 2003) is a comprehensive process that focuses on post-development activities.

Chapter 5

The Retirement Phase

> **Reader ROI**
>
> - The Retirement phase defines the activities executed to remove a system (or an older release of the system) from your production environment.
>
> - Retirement of a system can be a complex endeavor that is often treated as a project in its own right.
>
> - Systems can be retired all at once or piecemeal over time.
>
> - It is often useful to run new and old systems in parallel for a length of time to ensure that the new system is operating properly.
>
> - Retirement efforts are often executed in conjunction with the implementation of systems that replace them; they must be coordinated closely.

The final phase of the EUP lifecycle is the Retirement phase, depicted in Figure 5-1. The goal of this phase is the removal of a system release (and occasionally the complete system itself) from production, an activity also known as decommissioning or sunsetting. The problems associated with system retirement comprise a serious issue for many organizations today as legacy systems are removed and replaced by new systems. You must strive to complete this effort with minimal impact to business operations. If you have tried this in the past, you know how complex it can be.

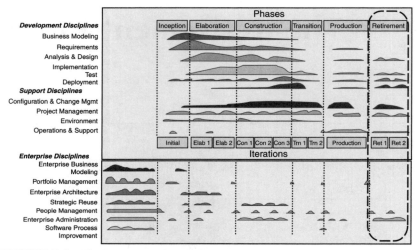

FIGURE 5-1   *The Retirement phase.*

It is important to note that the Retirement phase focuses on the removal of a *release* of a system and not necessarily the entire product. Figure 5-2 provides an example of a system in which multiple releases are being supported and subsequently retired at various points. Version 1.0 moves to the Production phase after it is initially deployed. It remains in Production while version 1.1 undergoes development and even after v1.1 is deployed. It is only when v2.0 is fully deployed that v1.0 is retired; it must then go through the Retirement phase.

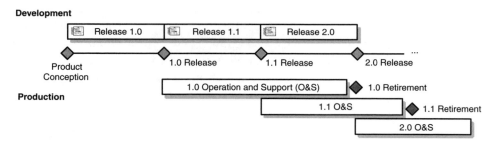

FIGURE 5-2   *Multiple releases in development and production.*

In most cases, the retirement of older releases is handled during the deployment of a newer version of the system and is a relatively simple exercise. Typically, the deployment of the new release includes steps to remove the previous release. There are times, however, when you do not retire a release simply because you deploy a newer version. This may happen if you cannot require users to migrate to the new release or if you must maintain an older system for backward compatibility.

The final retirement of a system can be a different matter. In this case you cannot rely on a newer version of your system being available to supply the functionality that you are retiring. Instead, this functionality and the data that supports it are either implemented by another system (often in a very different manner to the end user) or are completely removed. The implication is that there may be significant rework to update the other systems that interface with this functionality. Final retirement of a system is typically executed in parallel with the implementation of other system(s) that are replacing it, such as when an internally developed system is replaced by a commercial off-the-shelf (COTS) system. In these situations the two efforts must be closely coordinated and may even be executed by the same personnel.

This chapter explores the following topics:

- The objectives of the Retirement phase
- Essential activities
- Managing retirement efforts
- The System Retirement milestone

OBJECTIVES

The goal of the Retirement phase is to remove the release of a system from production with minimal impact to your stakeholders and their normal business operations. System releases are removed from production for several reasons:

- **Complete replacement:** It is not uncommon to see home-grown systems for human resources functions being replaced by COTS systems such as SAP (`www.sap.com`) or Oracle Financials (`www.oracle.com`). Sometimes a legacy system needs to be replaced by a COTS system for competitive reasons.

- **The release will no longer be supported:** Sometimes organizations have several releases in production at the same time, often to support different user bases. Over time, older releases are dropped.

- **The system is no longer needed to support the current business model:** An organization may explore a new business area by developing new systems, only to discover that this is not cost-effective.

- **The system is redundant:** Organizations that grow by merger and acquisitions often end up with redundant systems as they consolidate their operations.

- **The system has become obsolete:** This may be planned obsolescence—for example, systems created to temporarily integrate other systems until a merger or acquisition is completed. An example of unplanned obsolescence is a system built to satisfy legislation that was recently repealed.

Several critical stakeholders are involved in the process of retiring a system:

- **Business owners:** These people do not want the business to be unduly impacted by the removal of the release.

- **End users:** Resistance to change is natural. However, it is unacceptable for users to be surprised by the removal of a system. If they are notified properly in advance and given time to implement alternative solutions, their complaints can be given the credence they are due. The alternative solution is often another system being developed or deployed in parallel with the retiring system.

- **Operations and support groups:** These teams are major stakeholders in the retirement of a system. They are the ones that run jobs and monitor systems; they are the caretakers while the system is active. Their daily activities will most likely be impacted by the retirement of a system.

- **Sales and marketing team(s):** They must be aware that systems are going away so that they do not make promises to potential users that cannot be met.

The end of the Retirement phase marks the complete removal of a release of a system. No vestiges of it should remain when the Release Retirement milestone is complete.

ESSENTIAL ACTIVITIES

A typical iteration workflow for the Retirement phase is depicted in Figure 5-3. Activities in EUP disciplines that take place during Retirement include the following:

- **Analysis and Design:** If the functionality of the system is to be provided by other system(s), analysis and design of that effort takes place. This typically includes a comprehensive analysis of the existing system, often called legacy analysis, to identify its coupling to other systems. Existing systems are redesigned and reworked so that they no longer rely on the system being retired. In addition, programs to remove the system and its data are designed.

- **Implementation:** Programs to remove the system and its data are developed. As necessary, changes are made to other systems that interface with the system to be retired, and data is archived or migrated to other locations.

- **Test:** Programs used to retire the system, and any systems interfaced to the retired system, are tested.

- **Deployment:** One of the final steps in the Retirement phase is the actual removal of the system. This entails removing the code and the data, translating remaining legacy data as appropriate, and deleting any scheduled jobs (including backups).

- **Configuration and Change Management:** Change requests and defect reports received during the Retirement phase against the outgoing system typically are not accepted, although they may be reassigned to alternative systems. Fixes are rarely applied to a system that is slated to be removed, and enhancement requests may be rejected entirely. The final configuration of the system to be retired is archived appropriately.

- **Project Management:** Activities in the Retirement phase are managed, just as with other phases.

- **Environment:** Support environments are modified as needed during the Retirement phase.

- **Operations and Support:** The release to be retired must still be operated and supported until it is finally removed. Support is reduced during this phase because users are encouraged to discontinue use of the system.

- **Portfolio Management:** Portfolio managers assess the impact of the removal of a system on the overall enterprise portfolio and react accordingly. They may examine the loss of major functionality and approve projects that provide something similar.

- **Enterprise Architecture:** The enterprise architects update their "as is" models to reflect the fact that the system has been removed.

- **Enterprise Administration:** Retiring a system often requires configuration changes to the enterprise to reflect the removal of the system.

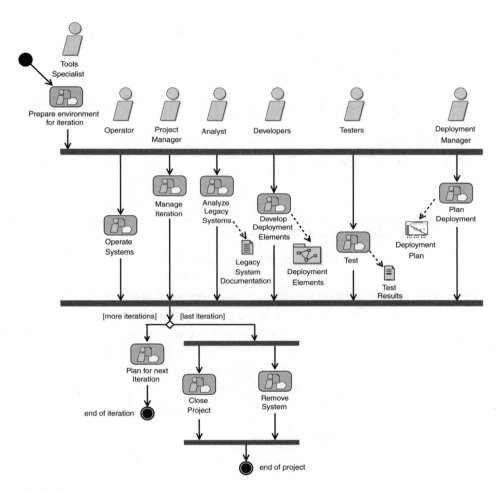

FIGURE 5-3   *Typical Retirement phase workflow.*

In this section we'll describe the worst-case scenario: the complete retirement of a system. The effort required to retire a release is much less and can be tailored down from the advice provided in the following sections. Retiring a system involves several activities; you must do the following:

- Analyze system interactions
- Determine retirement strategy

- Update the documentation
- Test
- Migrate users
- Remove the system

Analyze System Interactions

Most systems interact with other systems in some fashion. As part of your retirement effort, you must identify, analyze, and address each of these interactions. The first step is to identify the legacy assets your system interacts with and the interfaces it provides to other systems (Ulrich 2002). You do this by identifying the "interaction perimeter" of your system, depicted in Figure 5-4. As you can see, there are five interaction possibilities:

1. **Reads from external data source(s):** Your system may read from external data sources such as files or databases. This is rarely a problem when it comes to system retirement.

2. **Updates to external data source(s):** Other systems may depend on the updates your system makes—although if several systems are making the same updates, the loss of your system may have little effect.

3. **External system interface(s):** Your system may interact with other systems through provided systems interfaces such as web services or an application programming interface (API). This can be a problem if your system controls or invokes behavior, such as a batch job that updates an external database, on which other systems depend.

4. **Your data source(s):** Other systems may read or write to data sources "owned" by your system. Either a new source for the data needs to be provided (a source that supports the same informational semantics as your system does), or the external systems must be reworked to accept the remaining data that is available to them.

5. **Your system interface(s):** Other systems may interact with yours by accessing your data sources or through system interface(s). This functionality either must be provided by a new system or new release, or the external systems must be reworked to no longer use the provided functionality.

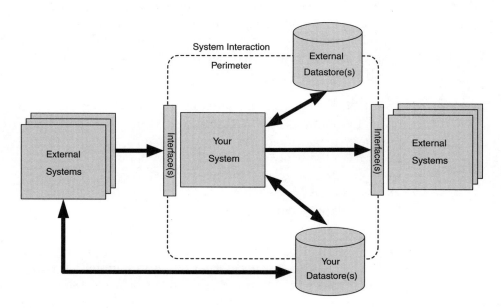

FIGURE 5-4   *System interaction perimeter.*

There are several ways to identify your system interaction perimeter:

- **Read your system documentation:** Your existing documentation, if any, should indicate how your system interfaces with other legacy assets and how they interact with it. Unfortunately in many organizations, legacy systems are poorly documented (if they're documented at all), which means that the first team to come along will have to update the documentation at least to the level they require (Liu, Alderson, and Qureshi 1999). Furthermore, don't assume that any documentation you do have is complete or correct.

- **Seek help from others:** Enterprise architects (Chapter 9), enterprise administrators (Chapter 12), and operations staff (Chapter 6) work with multiple systems on a daily basis. Your enterprise administrators, particularly information and network administrators, may be your best bet because they're responsible for managing production assets.

- **Analyze the code:** Without accurate documentation or access to knowledgeable people, your last resort may be to analyze the source code for your system, including the code that invokes your system, such as Job Control Language (JCL).

TIP	**Keep Your System Overview Documentation Current**
	As you deploy new releases and retire older ones throughout the life of a system, you should keep the system's documentation current. You will need current system documentation to support your continuing development efforts anyway, and it will clearly come in handy when your organization eventually retires your system from production.

Let's assume you can overcome any technical or political obstacles and have full access to everything and everyone you need. The second step is to identify the external systems that interact with assets that comprise the interaction perimeter of your system. Your goal is to identify how these systems are coupled to your system. You must realize that your system is part of the interaction perimeters of each of the external systems, so you must look for the sort of interactions listed earlier from the viewpoint of those systems. It isn't hard, but it is usually tedious and time-consuming. Issues to look for during your analysis include the following:

- **Direction of the interaction:** As noted previously, the direction of the interaction has different potential impacts.

- **Information being exchanged:** You need to identify which data (often down to the data element level) is being accessed and how it is being used. This will help you identify potential replacement data sources and their effectiveness at covering the original need. For example, an external system may access your database to obtain a complete list of products offered within the city of Atlanta. If all other data sources relate products to only the states in which they're sold, the external system will no longer have the precision it had before.

- **Functionality being invoked:** You need to identify the exact services (operations, procedures, functions, and so on) that are invoked at the interaction perimeter.

■ **Frequency and volume:** The frequency and volume of interaction are important. They indicate the load that you will put on the new sources for those interactions—these sources may not be able to handle the additional stress without infrastructure upgrades. Or, in the case of removing load, the new sources may be over-powered, motivating your enterprise administrators to reconfigure the hardware and/or network resources for those systems.

This is not always straightforward. Although you may be able to readily identify the systems that feed data directly to your system, other interactions can be more subtle. You must track down systems (or users) that take an occasional data extract from your system (perhaps for a quarterly report), including the ones that send an infrequent data feed, all systems that invoke functionality from the retiring system (and vice versa), and all links to your system, even if it's just a URL from a web page.

TIP	**Expect to Break a Few Systems**
	You will always miss a few system interactions, particularly the infrequent ones. Your support people (Chapter 6) will get a call late at night about a batch job that has just failed because your system has been retired. Be prepared to install a hot fix for these "stragglers" when they're found.

Data analysis is usually the most difficult task. The data structures, database vendors, and even the types of data sources (for example, relational databases versus XML files versus IMS) of the retiring system and the new systems will vary. Worse yet, the informational semantics are also likely to be different. For example, consider an ice cream company. One database maintains a flavors table, which contains rows for chocolate, strawberry, and vanilla. The replacement data source contains a table with the exact same layout, which maintains the flavors mocha fudge, ultimate chocolate, double chocolate, wild strawberry, winter strawberry, French vanilla, and old-fashioned vanilla. The new table arguably supports chocolate, strawberry, and vanilla, yet there is clearly a semantics problem. Table 5-1 summarizes the types of technical challenges, particularly data-oriented ones, that you may face when retiring a system.

TABLE 5-1 *Potential Technical Challenges in System Interactions*

Challenge	Description
Data quality problems	There is a wide range of potential quality problems when it comes to data. These include a column or table that is used for more than one purpose, missing or inconsistent data, incorrect data formatting, multiple sources for the same data, important entities or relationships that are stored as text fields, data values that stray from their field descriptions and business rules, several key strategies for the same type of entity, different data types for similar columns, and varying default values (Ambler 2003b). This list is not complete, but it should give you a feeling for the challenges you will face.
Code quality Problems	Similarly, you are likely to find problems in legacy code, such as inconsistent naming conventions, inconsistent or missing internal documentation, inconsistent operation semantics and/or signatures, highly coupled and brittle code, low cohesion operations that do several unrelated things, and code that is simply difficult to read.
Design problems	Your legacy assets may suffer from significant design problems. For example, access to data sources may not be well encapsulated, or the encapsulation strategies may be difficult to use. Applications may be poorly layered, with the user interface directly accessing the database, for example. An asset may be of high quality, but its original design goals may be at odds with current project needs. For example, it may be a batch system, but you need real-time access.
Architecture problems	Architecture problems are also a serious issue with many legacy assets. Common problems include applications that are responsible for data cleansing (instead of the database having this responsibility), incompatible or difficult-to-integrate (often proprietary) platforms, fragmented and/or redundant data sources, inflexible architectures that are difficult to change, lack of event notification making it difficult to support real-time integration, and insufficient security.
Architecture impedance mismatch	Each system is built based on its own set of architectural requirements. For example, systems won't necessarily be synchronized: one database may be updated weekly, whereas another may be updated daily. One system may be built to validate data in the application source code, whereas another does it in the database. It is quite common for systems to be architected with the assumption that they will be the primary controller of the interactions, yet this clearly can't be the case after they're integrated. Thus, systems that perform essentially the same services as your system may do so in an incompatible manner, and therefore they can't be considered as potential replacement sources.

The third step is to identify which interactions must be migrated to other systems and which ones can be removed completely. This can be a contentious issue; no one likes to lose access to information that he or she had previously. Stakeholder involvement is important to your success. Follow the activities of the Requirements discipline to determine stakeholders' true needs (the system you are retiring may not implement them properly; this is often the case with older systems).

TIP	**Retirement of Your System May Motivate Simplification of Another** The system you are retiring from production may be the only client of a service provided by another system. When this is the case, you should consider removing this service from the other system, particularly if it isn't likely that anyone else will need it in the immediate future. This will help keep your production systems as simple as possible, reducing your maintenance burden.

Determine Retirement Strategy

After you have identified the interactions that must be migrated and the extent to which they must be migrated, you must architect and implement a method for doing so. How you do this depends greatly on whether you have a replacement for the retiring system and what form it will take:

- **New release of your system:** This is the simplest and most common case. You may need to perform simple data conversions, perhaps applying the collection of database refactorings (www.databaserefactoring.com) implemented during the development cycle for this release, as well as the new version of the application code. Systems that interface with yours will need to be refactored (www.refactoring.com) to work with the new version of your system.

- **In-house replacement system:** The team developing the replacement system will be responsible for architecting, designing, and implementing the interactions. They should do so following the advice of your enterprise architects and the results of the legacy analysis, and they should seek to minimize the impact on other systems.

■ **COTS replacement system:** You might be able to extend the COTS product (if the vendor allows it); however, the amount of functionality you can provide may be limited. You may opt to engage the COTS vendor to develop the additional functionality you need.

■ **Complete system retirement:** This is the hardest case because you need to rework the external systems, which may cause the retirement of other systems that depend on the functionality you removed. You must work with the owners of the other systems and assist them in finding other sources for the information they need.

You will need a strategy to migrate your data. The most common strategy is a three-stage approach called extract-transform-load (ETL) (Kimball and Caserta 2004). The first stage is a simple extraction of the required data into a neutral format such as XML or into a staging database. The second stage is the difficult one—this is where you convert the source data into the required target data as best you can. As you saw in the preceding section, it may not be possible to perfectly convert the data due to incompatible semantics or simply because some source data is missing. The third stage is to load the transformed data into the target database (or file, as the case may be).

TIP	**Be Pragmatic**
	Keep in mind that migrations are usually a one-time event. You most likely do not have to develop or purchase tools that must be maintained or even used again after the migration takes place. For one migration we worked on, we developed tools that would work for 95% of the data files we had to deal with. For the rest, we sent an error message to a log and handled them manually.

If few data transformations must be made, you should consider developing your own migration scripts. If there are many transformations, you should consider purchasing an ETL tool such as Informatica (www.informatica.com) or Ascential Enterprise Integration Suite (www.ascential.com). Even with an ETL tool, you may find that you need to write specific code to handle a few extremely difficult data transformations.

Finally, you may need to develop tools to allow you to remove the system itself. This includes executables, data stores, directory entries, security controls, links from other systems (including web sites), and so on. We strongly recommend that you develop programs or scripts to do this; doing so will greatly assist in testing efforts.

TIP   Remember Operations, Support, and Security
All scheduled jobs must be removed from scheduling systems. All backup procedures must be updated to remove backups done for the retiring system. Systems that monitor applications and processes must be updated to remove references to the retiring system. User IDs granted to people specifically for the purpose of accessing your system should be revoked (U.S. Department of Energy 2002).

Update the Documentation

When a system is retired, you will need to update the following documentation to reflect the fact that your system is no longer in production:

- **Operations and support procedures (Chapter 6):** The backup, archiving, system operation, and support escalation procedures for your system should be archived.

- **Enterprise architecture (Chapter 9):** Your "as is" models, if any, should no longer refer to your system.

- **Administration documentation (Chapter 12):** The metadata maintained about your systems by your enterprise administrators should be archived.

- **Portfolio (Chapter 8):** Your system portfolio should no longer include the retired system, or it should indicate the date on which the system was officially retired.

- **System overview documentation:** The written documentation for your system should be updated to note that it has been retired.

Test

You must test your migration tools just as you would test a system during the Transition phase (Chapter 2). If you are following the evolutionary approach of the EUP, you will be testing your migration and removal tools as you develop them. Although this is desirable, you may not have the luxury of a test environment that supports all of your system, including all your data. If that is the case, make sure that the data you do have is a representative sample of the entire system. Use live data if at all possible instead of fabricated data; after all, this is a test run of the real migration.

TIP   **Have a Backout Plan Ready**

Do not assume that everything will proceed according to plan every step of the way. Have a backout plan in place to turn the system on again if circumstances require it. A common approach is to turn off access to the system for a short period of time and be ready to redeploy it.

Make sure that you test your backout plan ahead of time—you want to be confident that it will work correctly if things go wrong.

Migrate Users

You must give your users advance notice that a system is being retired. Depending on your user base, you can do this via postal mail, e-mail, an announcement that appears when users access the system, or a press release. Most users understand that all systems become obsolete eventually. What they do not like is being surprised by the removal of a system.

Give your users ample time to make other arrangements and, where appropriate, help them do so. If you are replacing your retiring system, you should give your users a period of time during which they can transition to the new system or release (refer to Figure 5-2). Depending on the complexity of the systems involved, this may be from as short as several weeks to as long as several months.

Remove the System

This is often a complex task, as you must migrate and convert data, turn off access, remove all vestiges of the retiring system, and update all the others systems that interact with the retiring system. It's a good idea to make a complete backup of your system before you begin, just in case you need to re-create the system in a hurry. You should consider one of three deployment strategies, summarized in Table 5-2.

TABLE 5-2 *Comparing Deployment Strategies*

Approach	Advantages	Disadvantages
"Big bang" retirement: With this approach, you convert the data, install the system updates, and remove the old system in one fell swoop.	Gets it over with. May be the only way to retire the system due to internal coupling.	"All or nothing" strategy can be very risky.
Staged retirement: With this approach, you select portions of the system and retire them one at a time. At each stage, you convert the relevant data and migrate the subset of the inter-actions, leaving the rest of the system intact.	Potentially less risky because you've orga-nized the retirement effort into smaller, more manageable efforts.	Increased complexity because you need to divide the system into "retirable" portions, which likely have over-lapping data. Stretches out the timeline, increas-ing user frustration.
Parallel system: With this approach, you install the replacement system and moni-tor the two systems for a period of time to ensure that they work in the same manner before removing the old system.	Mitigates the risk of the replacement system not working as intended.	A strategy is required to ensure that both systems are working with the same data (external systems may need to be reworked to work with both systems during the parallel run period). Original system still needs to be retired via one of the other two strategies.

When you're retiring a system, remember the following:

- **Hardware:** You may also need to retire hardware that is no longer required.

- **Licenses:** If your retiring system uses licensed COTS software, you should ensure that you are no longer paying for the software or any associated maintenance fees. Software licensing is discussed in detail in the Enterprise Administration discipline (Chapter 12).

- **Archival:** You should also archive the system just to be safe. This includes creating backups of the system software, its data, all system documentation associated with it, and any proprietary hardware. This will allow you to restore it in case an emergency requires you to reactivate it. The British Association of Research Quality Assurance (BARQA) makes it very clear that the controlled retirement of a system should include steps necessary to assure that records generated by the system are retrievable for the duration of your organization's defined archive period (BARQA 2002).

TIP   **Beware of Security Risks When Retiring Hardware**
When disposing of computer equipment, you must ensure that it has been sanitized (Lunsford, Robbins, and Bizarro 2004). Sanitization is the process of wiping clean all data stored on computer storage media. There are three methods for sanitizing a computer: media shredding, media degaussing, and media wiping. Shredding physically destroys the media to render it unusable. Degaussing exposes the media to strong magnetic fields to destroy its contents. Wiping replaces the current data with random characters. For extra security, you should remove any add-in hardware related to your organization's network and security systems before disposing of computer equipment.

MANAGING RETIREMENT EFFORTS

Although retirement is a phase in the EUP, most retirement efforts are managed as a separate project in their own right. Simple systems are usually retired within a single iteration (during which the stakeholders are notified that the system is going away), access is turned off in an orderly fashion, and the system and documentation are removed. Large, complex, or heavily used systems may require multiple iterations. It's not uncommon to retire systems that handle critical business functionality by running the system to be retired and the system that is replacing it in parallel for awhile to ensure that the functionality is working properly in the new system. Only when the stakeholders are satisfied that the new system is satisfactory can the old system be shut down. This provides the ability to verify that the new system is functioning appropriately by comparing it to the results of the old systems, and it also provides the option to quickly revert to the old system if something goes wrong. It may add significant costs, however, in terms of hardware, support, and time spent running multiple systems in parallel; thus, it is often done only for crucial systems.

Another variation is to retire the system incrementally—just as systems are developed incrementally, they can be retired incrementally too. Portions of the systems are removed in parallel with the addition of similar functionality in other system(s). This can be much easier to manage than attempting to do it all at once, although it may take longer.

Many systems that are retired are replaced by a different system or systems. In that case, two separately yet tightly coupled efforts occur simultaneously—retiring the old system and implementing the new one. Depending on the scope, you may decide to have one team handle both efforts, or you may staff them separately. How you handle this depends on many factors:

- **Staffing:** Is the current system complex enough to warrant having people dedicated only to the retirement effort? Or is it small enough in scope to be addressed as minor tasks of the new system implementation effort? Don't underestimate the effort to retire systems, especially for systems that have been running for a long time. Unless they are completely isolated applications (of which there are very few), tracking down and handling all the interfaces is usually a significant effort.

- **System expertise:** Do you have people who are experts in the old system who don't have the skills required to implement the new system? If so, you may need to focus them solely on the retirement effort.

- **Skills:** Do you have people with skills only in the new system? If so, they may need to be focused only on the new system effort.

- **Retirement strategy:** Will the old system be removed completely, or will some part of it be migrated to the new system? If the latter, it is usually beneficial to have at least some people on both efforts.

No matter how you staff it, the two efforts must be well coordinated.

THE RELEASE RETIREMENT MILESTONE

Figure 5-5 shows that the Retirement phase ends with the Release Retirement milestone. The Release Retirement milestone determines whether the system has been successfully removed. At this milestone, you must have answers to the following questions:

- What are the impacts to the business resulting from the system removal? Are they acceptable to the stakeholders?

- Was the system successfully removed?

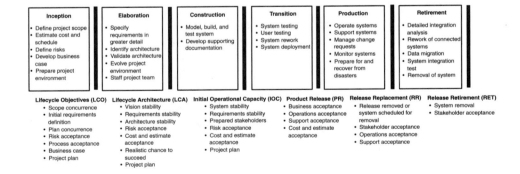

FIGURE 5-5   *EUP phases and milestones.*

For this milestone review, the stakeholders determine if the removal of the system has negatively impacted the business operations. This should have been analyzed and determined before the decision was made to remove the system during the Release Replacement milestone at the end of the Production phase. It is possible, however, that removing a release will have an unforeseen impact. In that case, a decision may be made to either reinstall the release or to begin a new iteration to address the issue.

CASE STUDIES

The first case study describes the retirement of a mainframe system that was replaced with a client/server-based system. The second describes the retirement of a PC-based suite of applications.

Migration off the Mainframe

When working with a large healthcare IT customer in the late 1990s, one of the efforts we worked on was migrating mainframe systems to a client/server model. As systems were migrated off of mainframes, they had to be seamlessly implemented on alternate platforms (usually client/server).

This customer ran the majority of its systems on the mainframe. The systems were business-critical; the customer's main income stream was derived from them. Most were written in COBOL and maintained by mainframe-oriented operations and support staff.

From a hardware perspective, the client was well positioned. It had a brand new data center with plenty of space for the new systems. A plan was put into place to start converting a few of the non-mission–critical systems to the new platform. A new team was assembled to start the design and conversion of these systems. Retirement plans were put into action for the mainframe-based systems.

The migration, however, was not well received by the old team. The COBOL programmers and operations and support staff were afraid of losing the jobs that they had been doing for over 20 years. The migration was slowed considerably by their resistance.

The lessons we learned include the following:

1. The support of the data center operations, support, and development teams is required. This was the number one reason for the difficulties we encountered in retiring the first few systems. The data center team was blindsided by the news that their new state-of-the-art data center would be supporting systems different from the ones they had supported in the past. The goals of the effort were not properly communicated to the teams, and more importantly, buy-in was never obtained from all the stakeholders.

2. Running systems in parallel works. After the initial resistance was overcome, the migration began in earnest. One of the early success stories came as the initial systems were built and put into production in the new client/server environment with consistently positive results. The new systems were run in parallel with the old systems during a transition period. We found out a few times that after the original mainframe system was retired, we would get calls from various customers—both internal and external—about broken data feeds.

3. Training and mentoring are vital. One of the reasons for the resistance from the data center was that they did not understand how to use the new systems. Although the various teams were given manuals and received training on the new systems, system support was a failure until experts were brought in to help provide further mentoring on the new systems.

4. Marketing, sales, and other departments need to be involved when decommissioning legacy systems. The sales and marketing teams were not kept up-to-date on the migration efforts and could not market or sell properly. In some cases, the sales team was not kept up-to-date on the additional capabilities of the new systems, so sales opportunities were missed.

Retirement of an Office Suite

At one time, we worked on supporting a suite of office applications. A new product had come out to replace the old suite we had been using (both purchased products), complete with a new architecture, new interface, and new file formats. After the decision to upgrade was made, we started two efforts—the first to prototype the new suite and work out the kinks in our environment, and the second to retire the old system. Both efforts were staffed with the same people.

The first effort turned out to be the easier of the two. The vendor was helpful in assisting us in installing it and resolving problems. The vendor had a sincere interest in seeing us succeed. For the second effort, however, we were basically on our own. The retirement of the old system and deployment of the new system was a lengthy process, as we needed to convert data files to a new format. We did this on a weekend in order to minimize the disruption to users. Our backout plan was simple—we took a full backup before we started and then shut down access to the system. If we needed to bring the old system back, we would simply restore everything from backup. And this turned out to be useful, too, as the first time we retired the old system and brought up the new one, the operating system crashed multiple times. Although it was unrelated to our effort (our client had been making changes to the OS at the same time—not a good idea), we had to back out our work until the issue was resolved.

After the OS issues were resolved, we were able to proceed smoothly. We had written programs to execute on behalf of each user to convert their data files to the new format. The programs communicated to a central logging program, which alerted us to any unresolved issues. We handled these issues by hand and were able to complete the entire process within our specified timeframe. The prototyping of our migration tools had given us an accurate estimate of the time it would take to convert everyone. We kept the backup files around for a while just to be safe, but after the new system was up and running for a while with minimal problems, we were able to remove all traces of the old system.

SUMMARY

Systems are retired for various reasons: they are replaced by new ones, they become redundant, or they simply become obsolete and are no longer needed. During the Retirement phase, stakeholders are notified that the release is to be removed, a replacement to the release is made available (optional), and all vestiges of the release are removed. Retirement may be a complex endeavor for large releases that implement critical functionality that must be migrated to new or existing releases or systems.

Suggested Reading

Computer System Retirement Guidelines Version 3 (U.S. Department of Energy 2002). This document describes a detailed process for retiring systems and is one of the few such documents available on the Web. Go to `http://cio.doe.gov/ITReform/ sqse/download/ SR-V3-G1-0902.pdf`.

The ISO/IEC 12207 standard (ISO 1998) describes a full system lifecycle, including a retirement phase.

Legacy Systems: Transformation Strategies (Ulrich 2002). This book details how to apply transformation techniques to legacy systems and discusses how to evolve them into useful systems instead of having to retire them.

Chapter 6

The Operations and Support Discipline

Reader ROI

- You must plan how systems are deployed into your operations and support environments.

- This discipline adopts many of the best practices of the Information Technology Infrastructure Library (ITIL).

- Service-level agreements (SLAs) are needed by both operations and support teams.

- Support developers may need to apply hot fixes to your production environment to address high-severity defects.

- You must plan for disasters and be prepared to execute your plans.

As the name implies, the primary goal of the Operations and Support discipline is to operate and support your software in a production environment. The focus of operations is to ensure that software is running properly, that the network is available and monitored, and that the appropriate data is backed up and restored as needed. Disaster planning and recovery are also critical activities. The focus of support is to assist end users by answering their questions, analyzing the problems they are encountering with production systems, recording requests for new functionality, and making and applying fixes.

WORKFLOW

The workflow for the Operations and Support discipline is depicted in Figure 6-1. Like any phase or discipline within the EUP, your organization will apply the activities contained within this discipline in a manner that reflects your environment. Organizations that develop and deploy systems in-house do more in terms of operational support than companies that produce shrink-wrapped software. The latter may spend more time and effort on support terms to keep their diversified base of paying customers satisfied and therefore have no operational staff, while the former may have an entire team dedicated just to operations.

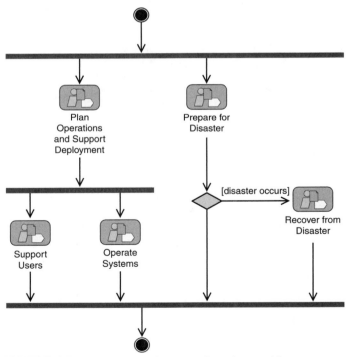

FIGURE 6-1   *Operations and Support discipline workflow.*

Plan Operations and Support Deployment

A critical success factor within this discipline is planning the deployment of a system into your production environment, the activities for which are depicted in Figure 6-2. This effort augments the Deployment discipline to include planning how a system will be operated and supported while in production.

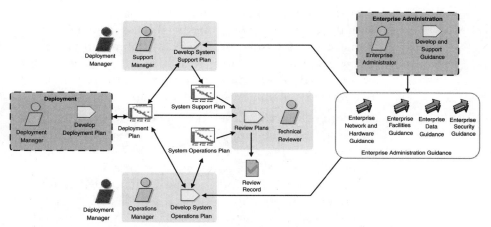

FIGURE 6-2 *Plan Operations and Support Deployment workflow detail.*

The support manager must define the support plan prior to deploying a system into production. The system support plan should address the following:

- **How support will be provided:** There are several methods you can use to implement support, as described in Table 6-1. You should consider how support will be paid for by customers (either internal or external)—will you bill to a specific cost center or to credit cards? You must also define how different types, or tiers, of support for paying and non-paying customers will be implemented. For example, e-mail–based support would be charged at a different rate than telephone-based support.

- **System contact personnel:** It is crucial to keep contact information up-to-date because without a current list, the calls at 2 a.m. may go unanswered, leaving you in a bind. Contact lists should include
  – Who should be contacted

- What times the person should and should not be contacted
- Under what circumstances the person should be contacted
- How the person should be contacted—telephone, pager, or other specific means

■ **Defect reporting and enhancement request strategy:** Support staff are the ones who take the initial call and work with the end user throughout the process. Enhancement requests and low-severity defects are submitted to the Enterprise Change Control Board (ECCB), which is a part of your Portfolio Management discipline efforts (Chapter 8). See the next section for more details about this.

■ **The support Service-Level Agreement (SLA):** The support SLA addresses the support issues for a system within a production environment. These include the following:
  - **Defect prioritization and resolution time periods:** As the severity levels for defects (or enhancements) are already defined in the support plan, the organization must establish what constraints (time, money, and other resources) are put into each severity level to meet SLA requirements.
  - **Defect escalation criteria:** Define the proper escalation path based on the severity and agreed-upon resolution time periods.

■ **How to deliver fixes into production outside the scope of an official release:** For each system, you must determine the following: the release schedule (defined date or on a per-customer basis), deployment approach (via e-mail, web, physical media, or a combination thereof), and the priority order (if any) in which clients receive fixes.

TABLE 6-1   *Advantages and Disadvantages of Different Support Options*

Support Type	Advantages	Disadvantages
E-mail	• Allows support personnel to analyze the situation before answering • Relatively inexpensive • Can be automated with auto-responder systems	• Time delay from viewpoint of end users, even when staffed 24/7 • Can be construed as one-way communication
Online web-based chat service	• Allows support personnel to analyze the situation with the end users while online with them • Can be automated with auto-responder system	• Time delay from point of view of end users, even when staffed 24/7 • Can be construed as ineffective and not working if an end user system is not actually working • Relatively expensive
Live call center	• Enables support personnel to analyze the situation with the end users while on the telephone with them • Allows empathy to come across if the support engineer is trained to do so	• Requires support staff with great patience and people skills • Must be able to multitask with different callers and problems from end users • Expensive

The operations manager, working closely with the project teams, creates the operations plan. The system operations plan defines how the system will be operated while it is in production; it includes

■ **Contact personnel:** As with the support people, it is crucial to have the contact personnel information defined and up to date.

■ **The operations SLA:** The operations SLA defines what is needed when operating systems in a production environment; these include the following:

– **System uptime commitments:** Details what is expected in terms of system uptime. Remember, "five nines" (99.999%) uptime only allows for about five minutes of downtime per year. This can become an extremely expensive goal in terms of monetary, computing, and human resources. Would 95% actually work for the system in your organization? Do the math and determine a realistic and acceptable strategy.

– **Scheduled system maintenance windows:** Include special system maintenance windows that are not included in the SLA. This will allow for normal production updates, such as database updates that occur during the lifetime of a system.

– **Failover strategy:** Things to consider here include the following: What must happen if the system totally—or partially—fails in a production environment? Does the system automatically fail over to a new machine and backup system? Is this failover system on-site or at a hot site (a duplicate data center) in another physical location? See the section "Prepare for Disaster" later in this chapter, which describes disaster recovery planning in detail.

– **Repercussions for missing SLA items:** Issues to consider for repercussions include determining the cost associated with system downtime, defining who pays for the downtime if a cost is associated with it, and communicating to the operations staff that their compensation could be tied to meeting these SLA goals.

■ **System operating procedures:** The operating procedures define how to operate systems and how to escalate issues when they occur. Escalation procedures can be as simple as, "For this type of problem, first take this action; if that does not work, take that action. If the problem still exists after X minutes, take this action." Actions may include commands such as "Restart this process" or "Enter the command XXX." They may also entail contacting people on the system contact list. If at all possible, you should set things up such that contacting the technical personnel on the maintenance team is the last recourse. The operations staff should be the first line of defense for fixing any operational problems.

■ **Backup and restore procedures:** This allows the system to
be protected if a problem should occur—either a relatively
minor one (hard drive crashing) or a major one (loss of the
entire facility—this is disaster recovery). Although backup
and restore procedures are sometimes associated with
disaster recovery, they can also be something as simple as
recovering an accidentally deleted or overwritten file. Your
organization may also simply be required by law or regula-
tion to provide backup and restore procedures. Here are
some items your organization should consider:

– What data needs to be backed up in order for your system
  to be restored to full functionality? Work with your enterprise administrator(s) (Chapter 12) to help define and
  execute these requirements.
– What data that can be deleted might users want to roll
  back?
– How will backups be used to recover systems in case of
  disasters?
– Where will the data be stored? Off-site storage is recommended for disaster recovery.
– How often will backups be created?
– How long will backup data be kept?
– Will the backups be incremental, data only, or full? What
  medium will you use for backups? Will you use tape drive
  systems with automated robotic storage and retrieval,
  off-site virtual storage systems, or other means?
– How long will backups take?
– Will backups be disruptive? For example, will you have to
  bring the system or a portion of it down in order to create
  the backups?

Utilize the Best Strategy for Backups

There are several styles to use when backing up data:

- **Incremental backup:** Backs up only items that have changed since the last backup. The main advantage is decreased time required to back up the system, which is good for environments that change regularly.
- **Full backup:** Backs up an entire system (including all of the data) in full every time a backup is completed. The main advantage to this is that you get an exact copy each time a system backup is run.
- **Data backup:** This is a backup of just the application data. System files, like executable code, are not included. The advantage of this is speed, which is good for an environment where data is centralized and changes often but where the executable code does not change.

When choosing a backup strategy, you need to consider the costs, the amount of storage that is needed, the time it takes to do a backup, and other specific implications within your operating environment. For example, restoring a system that was backed up with incremental backups means restoring the system in the same order that the backups were done. You will likely choose to implement a combination of these solutions to balance issues such as doing a full backup once a week and incremental backups nightly, as well as an off-site monthly backup.

Support Users

Tourniaire and Farrell (1997) describe two basic strategies for delivering support—an escalation strategy and a touch-and-hold strategy. The escalation strategy is based on the idea that most support requests are fairly basic and therefore can be handled quickly, whereas small minorities of requests are complicated and must be assigned or escalated to more knowledgeable staff members. This approach scales well, although hand-offs between support staff can prove to be frustrating for the person being supported. With the touch-and-hold strategy, the initial person who took the support request follows it through to the end, although this person may have to work with other people to fulfill the request. The touch-and-hold strategy typically results in greater customer satisfaction because the support requester needs to deal with only one support engineer. However, this approach requires highly skilled support people and is difficult to scale because it can be hard to hire and retain such staff. More information about incident management, problem reporting, and service desks can be found in the associated ITIL Fact Sheets (ITIL 2003).

Escalation Strategy
Figure 6-3 depicts how the Support Users workflow works with an escalation strategy. As you can see, four roles are associated with this approach:

1. **Customer Support Representative (CSR):** This is the primary contact point with the user for providing technical support and escalating issues if required. This is often referred to as "level one" (the first level) of support.

2. **System Support Representative (SSR):** This person is responsible for evaluating issues (triage), which includes reproducing the problem, determining if the issue is a defect in the system or an enhancement request, evaluating the severity, evaluating the complexity, and identifying and documenting the system or module where the error exists.

3. **Support Manager:** This person is responsible for prioritizing work, assigning work to people, and then managing work activities. This person will also monitor how SSRs evaluate trouble tickets to ensure consistency.

4. **Support Developer:** This person will resolve a high-severity defect by updating existing code, rejecting the defect (perhaps it's a known issue), deferring the defect to a later release, or documenting a workaround for the issue. After the fix is developed and tested, it is reviewed, packaged, put under configuration management (CM) control, scheduled, announced, and then deployed into production.

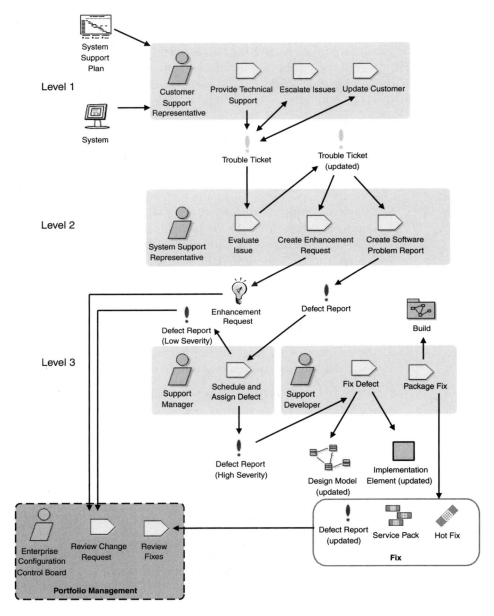

FIGURE 6-3   *Support Users workflow detail.*

Figure 6-3 differentiates between a defect and an enhancement request. Both defects and enhancements are change requests. In the RUP, a change request is defined as an artifact used to document and track requests for a change to a product. The EUP looks at the change request as the concrete artifact, with both defect reports and enhancement requests being specializations of that artifact. A defect report defines a problem; that is, the system is not working the way it should. An enhancement request is a request to add or change functionality. This is often a point of contention; a good CSR must be able to make this distinction and convince customers that their judgment is correct. More information about how to manage multiple releases of systems, including fix/patch releases, can be found in the Production phase (Chapter 4).

Touch-and-Hold Strategy
The main difference between the escalation strategy and the touch-and-hold strategy is that the CSR and SSR (levels one and two) roles are both customer-facing; changes throughout this process, such as technical support, evaluation, and updates to the customer, are handled by one person. Unlike the escalation approach, there is no concept of a specific systems support role; instead, CSRs must be highly skilled. The level three support personnel can be considered internal support because they do not have any direct customer contact.

Making Support Work
We have found the following strategies to be effective for system support:

1. **Keep the customer updated:** It's critical to let people know that you are actively working on their problem. This can be done via status updates from the CSR or automatically via e-mails generated by your help desk.

2. **Be service-oriented:** CSRs are responsible for calling back and updating customers on a periodic basis to report status; they also work with others (system support, the support manager, and developers) within the organization to ensure timely and accurate reports to customers. It is critical that CSRs have people skills, excellent communication skills, and patience.

3. **Train support specialists:** It is unrealistic to expect CSRs to be knowledgeable about all of your systems, particularly in large organizations. Some CSRs may specialize in certain systems, or you may hire people with excellent communication skills who simply record customer issues and then pass them to the appropriate specialist(s).

4. **Consider outsourcing:** Many organizations today outsource support to third-party organizations. The current trend is to utilize "offshore" organizations that potentially offer a large cost savings. The trade-offs involved in offshoring include the potential loss of intellectual capital and the difficulty of bringing support back into your organization if outsourcing doesn't work out. Before outsourcing, try to test both your existing and (potentially) outsourced departments to follow some actual problem cases through the system—the results may be very enlightening.

> **TIP   Use a Process for Support**
> Some organizations new to system support believe they can do it without a formal process. Then they discover that they waste more time and money supporting and losing customers as a result. We recommend putting a process in place with a well defined, tested, and proven escalation path.

Operate Systems

The goal of this activity, depicted in Figure 6-4, is to operate systems in a production environment. Two main roles are associated with this activity:

1. **Operator:** This person is responsible for keeping systems running, backing up and restoring data based on the operations plan and requirements of the system, managing any problems, performing periodic cleanup, performing fine-tuning and any system reconfigurations, monitoring systems, and redeploying systems as necessary. Because operations support is usually a 24/7 activity, a hand-off protocol should be defined and followed to address the problem of transferring a problem between shifts, along with a definition of what each team is responsible for completing both prior to and at the completion of a shift.

2. **Support Developer:** This person is responsible for applying maintenance fixes to the system via hot fixes (also known as service packs or patches). This is often a member of the development team. As with your development environment, always test any fine-tuning or reconfiguration of programs or systems in a test area prior to deploying it to the production environment—and have your back-out plan ready to put into place if serious system problems occur.

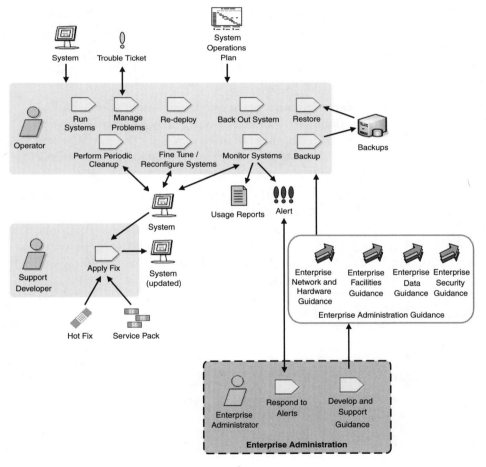

FIGURE 6-4 *Operate Systems workflow detail.*

Making Operations Work

Operations should not be viewed as an extension to your development team because operations activities require different skills and a mind-set that differs from development:

- **Perspectives:** Developers are concerned with building their individual systems and releasing them into production, whereas the operations team is concerned with keeping all systems running safely. For example, a developer may want to use MySQL (`www.mysql.com`), but the production environment requires all systems to run on the enterprise version of Oracle they support today.

- **Open communication:** Both teams should work closely with each other during each EUP phase to reduce conflicts due to different perspectives.

- **Working hours:** Operations teams often work on a 24/7 basis and cover multiple systems by working in several shifts. Development teams often work the day shift and will have at least one person responsible for on-call support to the operations team if needed.

- **SLAs:** The operations team is responsible for meeting the SLAs to the end user—you will need to both monitor systems and measure their effectiveness against the SLAs. The development team is responsible for delivering a working system that meets the needs of their stakeholders in a timely and cost-effective manner.

TIP	**Get Help with SLAs**

You should consider reviewing both the support and operations plans before putting the system into a production environment. Naomi Karten has some excellent content regarding SLAs at `www.nkarten.com/sla.html` (Karten 2003). More information about SLAs can be found in their associated ITIL Fact Sheet (ITIL 2003). Finally, as with any legal contract, make sure that the appropriate legal people who are familiar with this topic and its associated pitfalls review these documents.

Prepare for Disaster

Disaster recovery defines the steps you will follow to get your critical systems back up and running in case something catastrophic happens (Barnes 2001). Disasters in this context could be a natural disaster such as a hurricane or a tornado that destroys your entire Network Operations Center (NOC). It also includes man-made disasters like the blackout that struck the American northeast in the autumn of 2003. Figure 6-5 depicts the activities associated with disaster recovery planning. More information about IT Service Continuity Management can be found in the associated ITIL Fact Sheet (ITIL 2003).

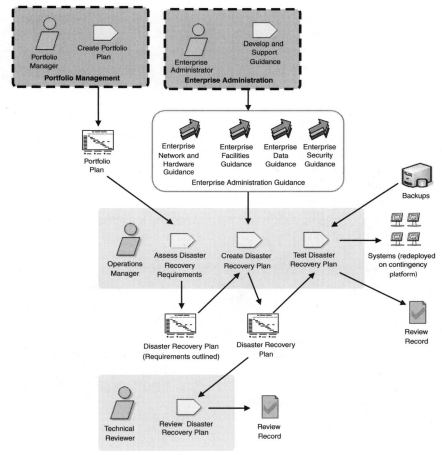

FIGURE 6-5 *Plan for Disaster Recovery workflow detail.*

Ensuring 100% system recovery at a moment's notice would require doubling (at a *minimum*) your cost for things like hardware, communications, leasing, and other items. This is a very expensive proposition. Instead, many organizations invest in the infrastructure to get just the critical functionality up and running long enough to buy or rebuild the rest if a disaster occurs.

You do not want to discover that your disaster recovery strategy fails the first time a disaster occurs. Simulating a disaster and implementing your disaster recovery plan may be expensive and disruptive, but that is the only way to truly know if it will work. When validating your plan, you need to keep in mind the realities of a disaster and act accordingly. For example, in your simulation, did you rely on cell phones as a backup communication medium for all your employees, only to find out that all the cell phone towers in your region were put out of commission during the hurricane? Incorporate these lessons into your disaster recovery plan.

One disaster recover strategy is to run systems in several locations. Ideally, each location would have the capacity to run the critical functionality of the other site if another one goes down. Building extra capacity at geographically diverse locations can both support disaster recovery and assist future expansion. Having your backup operations center in the same city will not help you if a disaster impacts a large region. In the fall of 2003, having both operations centers in the American northeast would not have been enough. You are better served by having multiple locations separated geographically as far apart as feasible to lessen the chance of a disaster impacting both locations.

TIP   Minimize Disruption When Testing Your Disaster Recovery Plan
Not everyone has the luxury of simulating a disaster by cutting off the power (or flooding the operations center, or burning it to the ground) and working under true disaster conditions. You can minimize the disruption by testing your recovery plan incrementally. You can take backups one day and then restart one system on an alternative platform the next day, another one the next day, and so on over the course of a week until you have executed your entire recovery plan.

Recover from Disaster

Your organization may ultimately have to execute the disaster recovery plan, as depicted in Figure 6-6. Be sure to give the disaster recovery plan in hard-copy form to multiple people in multiple locations. When a disaster occurs, you may not have access to the electronic versions.

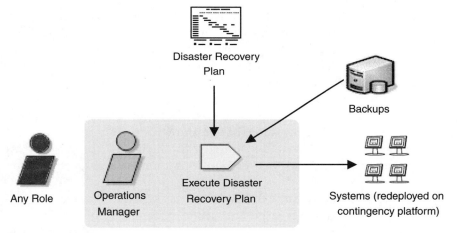

FIGURE 6-6   *Recover from Disaster workflow detail.*

The Operations Manager is responsible for executing the disaster recovery plan, and that person will work with the various project teams when necessary in order to recover the systems. The final output of a successful disaster recovery is to have your systems running—according to the plan—on a contingency platform. The operations manager is also responsible for reviewing the recovery effort to identify and then act on the lessons learned.

CASE STUDIES

The two case studies presented next discuss the different challenges you can run into when performing both operations and support activities. The first describes a situation where senior management hobbled a support department because they wouldn't let them follow their process. The second is a situation where a large software organization succeeded with an escalation-based support process.

Operations

The operations centers at Outsource Company each had a beautifully bound operation and support manual—professionally completed by MBAs, outside consultants, and non-practitioners. It was even touted as a competitive advantage to prospective clients during the pre-sales cycle. Unfortunately, when severe problems occurred, the operations center would become completely disorganized and ineffective.

Everything was documented. Very specific timeframes were listed, down to the number of minutes in a response window. Contacts and escalation details were intimately defined (and were kept up to date). The process looked great on paper. When "severity one" problems came up, though, people would follow the operations plan for a short time before degenerating into total chaos. Why was this happening? After a little bit of research, we found out that when the president of Outsource Company received a call from an irate client, after notifying the help desk, he would then personally create a SWAT team to work on this "high-profile" issue on his own.

Things finally came to a halt one day when a "severity one" issue brought down a large number of systems. While in his office with the team of operations and support people all around, he screamed, "How did this [insert expletives here] happen?" We took him aside and explained the situation; when he realized what was happening, he stopped interfering and let the process work as defined. It took some getting used to on his part, and sometimes he would still revert to his old ways, but a few months later, productivity and morale were up within operations and support.

Support

At Software Corp., we were involved in multiple levels of support for mass-marketed operating systems. The support teams utilized a three-level support escalation strategy successfully. The support teams worked seamlessly enough—sometimes in multiple geographic locations—to perform weekly builds of more than 20 million line systems. Level one personnel were responsible for logging the call and troubleshooting questions with the end user; if the issue could not be resolved by the level one team, they opened a defect report and escalated the issue to the level two support team—which was then responsible for duplicating the problem. If the problem could not be duplicated, it was up to the level two personnel to actually troubleshoot it with the client for resolution. When a defect was found and duplicated, it was escalated to the level three change team for fixing the code within the operating system.

Although this may seem like a lot of overhead, the teams worked together successfully to do the weekly builds and keep customer satisfaction levels at a high level. A strong change control management system was used, with multiple levels of checks and balances and multiple code bases and releases being managed for different clients.

ANTI-PATTERNS

You need to be aware of the following process anti-patterns (approaches that do not work very well in practice) to avoid common mistakes:

- **Untested Recovery Plan(s):** Many organizations believe plans will work without any testing, only to find out that the plan fails miserably when something needs to be rolled back out either after a bad deployment into their production environment or after a disaster. The solution is to recognize that you need to build testing into your culture and test incrementally if you cannot test all at once.

- **Service Level Disagreement:** Organizations that do not require SLAs from their vendors find out the hard way that their customers expect them to have them with their own vendors. The solution is to create, negotiate, and enforce SLAs for all vendors with whom your organization works in a production environment. Read the fine print and test often.

- **Silver Bullet Contractor:** This is analogous to the "Silver Bullet" (Brooks 1995) promised by tool vendors, where companies fawn at the feet of a contractor with a well-known name or who is from a well-known company. The solution is to always check references, but do not always believe them. If a person looks too good to be true, trust your instincts and pass on that person. Do not believe that anyone is right for you just because of what he or she has done for others in the past.

TIMING

Planning operations and support activities happens while a project is being developed—mainly in the Inception and Elaboration phases—before the system is deployed. The rest of the activities happen while the project is leaving the Transition phase and is in the Production phase (but some may happen during an alpha or beta test). Finally, operations and support must also take place during the Retirement phase to ensure proper shutdown of any outdated or unnecessary databases or other materials.

TIP   **Get Involved with Alpha and Beta Testing**
An enterprise needs to test its operations and support processes; therefore, these staff members need to be included in the testing efforts. Support people know what issues the end users see and feel; therefore, they're often good candidates to be alpha/beta testers.

TOOLS

There are several excellent sources of operations and support tools, including but not limited to the following:

- **IBM Tivoli** (`www.tivoli.com`): This is a suite of system monitoring products, including application, database, network, middleware, and operating system monitoring.

- **Opsware, Inc.** (`www.opsware.com`): Opsware produces operations-oriented tools for provisioning, configuration tracking, deployment, rollback, operations reporting, disaster recovery, and asset tracking.

- **Remedy** (`www.remedy.com`): Remedy produces a service management package and help desk suite for the small business to enterprise-level clients.

- **Revelation Help Desk** (`http://gg1.revelation helpdesk.com`): This is a modularized, web-based help desk product for logging, managing, and reporting on support requests.

A valuable resource is `http://tools.itsmportal.net`, which lists a wide range of operations and support tools.

RELATION TO OTHER DISCIPLINES

The Operations and Support discipline is related to other disciplines:

- **Deployment:** Operations and support managers work with deployment managers to plan the deployment, operations, and support of a system release.

- **Portfolio Management:** This discipline provides a review of all enhancement requests and low-severity defects to be addressed by the ECCB to be later assigned to individual systems as appropriate. It also provides input into the disaster recovery planning process.

- **Enterprise Administration:** This discipline provides guidance relevant to operations and support and aids in monitoring operations.

SUMMARY

The Operations and Support discipline covers essential processes for operating and supporting your systems within a production environment. This discipline includes planning the deployment of a system, supporting users and operating systems, preparing for disasters, and, if required, executing the disaster recovery plan. There is no value in developing a system if you can't keep it up and running after you've done so—thus, this discipline is critical for your overall success.

Suggested Reading

Practical Software Maintenance (Pigoski 1997). This book provides a very good overview of common practices for maintaining software after it is in production, including the issues surrounding the development of "hot fixes" for ailing systems.

The Art of Software Support (Tourniaire and Farrell 1997). This book is the classic text for software support, covering in detail how to set up and then manage a successful support operation.

Information Technology Infrastructure Library (ITIL 2003). The ITIL is developed and owned by the Office of Government Commerce (OGC) in the UK. It claims to be the most widely accepted foundation for quality IT Service Management in the world. ITIL is continually evolving and may be worth a look if you're serious about operations and support.

Part III

The Enterprise Management Disciplines

Chapter 7

The Enterprise Business Modeling Discipline

> **Reader ROI**
>
> ■ Enterprise business models should provide high-level overviews, not onerous details.
>
> ■ Enterprise business modeling should occur on a regular basis throughout the life of your organization.
>
> ■ Enterprise business models explore the businesses processes, external environment, organization structure, and critical business entities pertinent to your organization.
>
> ■ Your enterprise stakeholders must be active participants in the development of your models.
>
> ■ Involve the actual stakeholders for your enterprise business models when you're developing them to ensure that the models reflect their requirements.

Business modeling is an integral part of the RUP. The existing RUP business modeling discipline provides a view of the business structures and processes of the organization relative to a specific project, identifying the proper scope of the project and showing how the system fits into and supports the business. This is incredibly important for a project, but it isn't sufficient for the enterprise;

the enterprise business modeling discipline encompasses the same activities as the business modeling discipline but does so at the enterprise level. To be fair, the RUP product (IBM 2004) does describe the need to model at the enterprise level, but because there is no mechanism within RUP to depict cross-system issues adequately, it doesn't do the concept justice, nor does it provide an explicit way to share information between projects—hence the need for this discipline within the Enterprise Unified Process (EUP).

Carr (2004) makes a very good case that most information technology (IT) investments do not provide competitive advantages for the organization implementing them. He points out that if all of your competitors implement or buy a customer relationship management (CRM) system or an enterprise resource planning (ERP) system, there is very little chance that you will gain a competitive advantage by doing so. And you know what? He's right. To succeed, you need to look beyond IT and consider the larger picture—that of the entire business process (Smith and Fingar 2003). This is why enterprise business modeling is required for your organization to succeed—it takes an organization-wide viewpoint when modeling the processes, structure, and external environment of your business. Your goal is to provide the context that your IT department supports and works within—fundamentally, all business software is embedded within business processes, and a business system isn't successful unless the business is (Poppendieck and Poppendieck 2003).

TIP	**Executive Buy-In Is Crucial to Your Success**
	Isn't it always?

Your enterprise business modeling efforts should explore a wide range of issues. As a result, your enterprise business model is actually composed of a collection of smaller artifacts (see Table 7-1). The business issues that you should explore include the following:

- **Business entity types:** Something of interest to your enterprise, such as a person, place, thing, or concept. Business entities within a bank would include *Account*, *Customer*, and *Branch*. Business entity types will typically be captured within your enterprise domain model.

- **Business environment:** Your external business environment includes your customers, suppliers, partners, and competitors. Note that these are not mutually exclusive groups, for you may find yourself competing against some of your customers. Your business environment is also defined by the rules and regulations (which are defined by government legislation and industry governance bodies) that constrain your activities. Examples of such legislation within the United States include the *Sarbanes-Oxley (Sarbox) Compliance Act* (U.S. Government 2002) and the *Health Insurance Portability and Accountability Act (HIPAA)* (U.S. Government 2004). Your business environment will affect all aspects of your enterprise business model, although it will be most explicitly depicted by your enterprise business process model.

- **Business processes:** A collection of coordinated activities, either manual or automated, that provides value to one or more internal or external clients. Business processes within a bank would include generation of account statements and fulfillment of retail banking transactions such as deposits and withdrawals. Business processes should be described within your enterprise business model.

- **Business rules:** Constraints that influence or guide the everyday workings of an organization. Within a bank, a potential business rule would be that monthly interest for a checking account is calculated by multiplying the interest rate by the lowest balance within the account that month. This is captured within your enterprise business rules specification.

- **Locations:** An enterprise must know both the physical and virtual territories where it does business. For a bank, this would include places such as Canada, Germany, the state of Alaska, the British Isles, and the Internet. This is depicted by your organization model.

- **Management concerns:** This includes a definition of the mission and vision for the organization as well as associated long-term plans. They are captured within your enterprise mission statement and enterprise vision.

- **Organization structure:** This consists of the organizational units (teams, groups, divisions, and so on), the people or positions within the organization, the roles that the people and organizational units fulfill, and the relationships between them all. The organization structure of a bank would indicate the various divisions (for example, retail banking and corporate banking), the international groups within the bank (for example, North America and Continental Europe), and the senior executives within each division. This is captured within your organization model.

TABLE 7-1   *Components of an Enterprise Business Model*

Artifact	Description
Enterprise business rules specification	The definition of the constraints that influence or guide the everyday workings of an organization.
Enterprise business process model	Captures the fundamental business processes, the external entities (customers, suppliers, partners, or competitors), and the major workflows between them.
Enterprise domain model	Depicts the main business entities of interest to an organization and their relationships.
Enterprise mission statement	A statement of the strategies to be followed to achieve the enterprise vision.
Enterprise vision	A statement of the primary goal(s) of an organization.
Organization model	A definition of the location, positions, organizational units, and their interrelationships within an enterprise.

Development of the enterprise business model starts with a broad view of the entire business. This doesn't mean that you'll model your entire business—for example, you may choose to ignore the accounting aspects of your organization because it's stable—but it does mean that your model will go beyond the scope of a single project. Your goal should be to capture the fundamentals of your business by working with your stakeholders in an all-encompassing yet shallow model—you don't need much detail, but you do need breadth. You need to identify and prioritize areas of importance so that they can be explored in detail by the business modeling efforts of individual project teams. Your enterprise business model should define an accurate, high-level overview of the business and should contain information that is relatively stable over time. For example, within a bank, the need to process retail banking transactions has existed for centuries, yet the way in which this occurs has changed dramatically over time—the high-level need is stable, whereas the details are very fluid.

TIP	**Good Enterprise Business Models Are Stable**

Because the scope is your entire enterprise, the only way an enterprise business model can be relatively stable is if it does not go into detail and is technology-independent. These models still have significant value to development teams because they should address important high-level issues, such as how the overall organization functions and what the main business entities are. Furthermore, because they will be short and ideally well written, they are likely to be read. Nobody is likely to read a 500 page document, but people may be willing to read five pages.

Enterprise business modeling is important to the success of your IT organization for several reasons. First, it helps facilitate a common understanding of the business that your organization is engaged in. Although this may seem superfluous to some, formally documenting the business that your organization engages in will lead to many interesting conversations about how things should really work and, ultimately, to a shared understanding of exactly what business you are in and how you execute your work. Second, it helps identify areas of your business that can be improved either through targeted automation or wide-scale business process reengineering. Third, it helps identify business areas that your organization doesn't yet address or that your organization is very weak in. Fourth, it provides important information to project teams that can help them to delimit the scope of their project, in particular helping them to identify how their effort fits into the overall business.

Enterprise business models are used to depict both "as-is" and "to-be" views; this is important for strategic planning because changes in strategic direction can be mapped out and examined before they are implemented. Senior management, not just IT implementers, can benefit greatly from enterprise business modeling that is forward-looking. Because they are developing a shared vision together, it can often be the impetus that gets business and IT executives working together effectively in organizations where a divide exists between the two groups.

From a technical point of view, an enterprise business model can be used to identify common concepts that should be automated and reused repeatedly in systems. Enterprise architects, working with reuse engineers, can examine the domain model within the current and targeted areas of automation to identify potential domain assets, a concept called domain engineering. Implementation of these assets can lead to increased efficiencies in system development efforts by reducing both development and maintenance costs (Chapter 10).

WORKFLOW

The workflow for the Enterprise Business Modeling discipline is shown in Figure 7-1. A critical success factor for this discipline is your relationship with your enterprise stakeholders, which includes senior IT executives, senior business executives, suppliers, customers, and domain experts (often senior business analysts). Agile Modeling (www.agilemodeling.com) promotes a practice called *Active Stakeholder Participation*. Not only should stakeholders be available to make decisions and provide information in a timely manner, but they also should be actively involved with your modeling efforts, something that is possible when you work with inclusive tools and techniques that are easy to learn and work with. Inclusive tools include paper, whiteboards, and word processors; inclusive techniques include essential use cases (Constantine and Lockwood 1999; Ambler 2004) and simplified or reduced versions of common modeling notations for data modeling or process modeling.

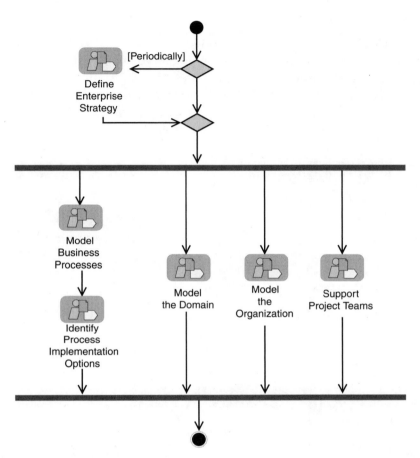

FIGURE 7-1   *The Enterprise Business Modeling discipline workflow.*

Define Enterprise Strategy

A critical aspect of enterprise business modeling is to define your overall business strategy because it guides your business modeling efforts. The workflow diagram is depicted in Figure 7-2. Work closely with your enterprise stakeholders to develop the enterprise business strategy—the strategy must come from and be accepted by the business; it isn't an IT-only strategy.

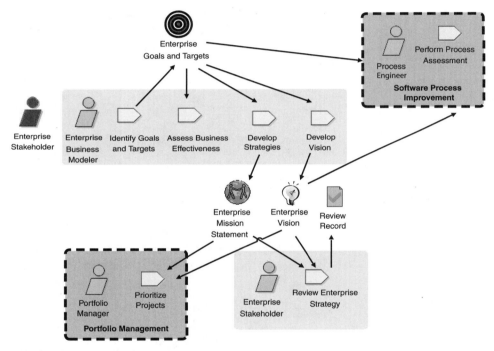

FIGURE 7-2   *Define Enterprise Strategy workflow details.*

Enterprise business modelers will work closely with the enterprise stakeholders to define the goals, targets, and vision for your enterprise. Options for doing this include facilitated modeling sessions such as joint application development (JAD) meetings (Wood and Silver 1995), less-formal agile modeling sessions, or separate one-on-one interviews. Your goals and targets are typically short-term, such as to grow the number of corporate banking customers (the goal) by 2% this quarter (the target), and are therefore likely to change on a regular basis. Your vision, such as to become the largest retail and corporate bank in North America as measured by managed assets, is typically longer-term and therefore less likely to change over time. It's important to have an overall vision—if you don't know where you're going, you'll never get there.

There is more to this effort than simple brainstorming—you must assess your organization's capability to fulfill your goals. One aspect of this capability analysis should be to simply ask the appropriate people what your organization is capable of achieving, what its core competencies are, and what its overall weaknesses include. This approach works in an organization that has a culture of open and honest communication, but it will often result in an overly optimistic (and grossly inaccurate) assessment when this isn't the case. Facilitation by an outsider, usually a consultant, should be considered when you are unable to assess yourselves accurately. An outsider can lead you through politically sensitive challenges without fear of political repercussions.

You will then need to develop strategies to address the gap between what you can do and your vision for what you want to achieve. Your strategies, which will change over time, will be captured within your enterprise mission statement. An enterprise mission statement defines the ongoing operation activity of your organization and is the means to achieving your enterprise vision (Hay 2003). Your enterprise vision and mission statements should be concise—often a paragraph and a collection of five to eight points.

For example, consider a company that is a collection of martial arts studios. The vision might read, "The XYZ Schools will help their students improve their minds, bodies, and spirits through training in the martial arts." The mission statement may contain the following points:

- XYZ Schools will offer training in Goju Ryu karate, Kobudo, Ju Jitsu, and Taoist Tai Chi.
- Both adults and children (at least six years of age) will be encouraged to train.
- Martial arts philosophies and history will be intertwined into training classes.
- Respect for family, self, and country will be encouraged in training classes.

- XYZ Schools will work with external experts to bring specialized skills to their students.

- Camaraderie between students will be encouraged. We should be able to have fun while we're learning.

Figure 7-2 indicates that you should review your enterprise strategy, but this is only one way to validate the quality of your work. Reviews compensate for overly serial processes and for a lack of collaboration during the development of an artifact (Chapter 3). If you follow a more agile approach, you don't need to compensate by holding a review.

A strategy map (Kaplan and Norton 2004) is a style of flow chart that is a useful technique for validating your enterprise strategies. Strategy maps model specific processes, competencies, cultural attributes, and technologies, showing how these elements are connected to satisfying customers and increasing long-term shareholder value. By creating strategy maps, you approach the issue from a different angle, providing opportunities to validate and hopefully improve your enterprise mission statement.

Model Business Processes

The modeling of business processes is one of several modeling activities within this discipline, the workflow details of which are presented in Figure 7-3. Your business process modeling efforts address the How (Function) column within the Zachman Framework (ZF) (Chapter 3) and should reflect both your enterprise mission and vision. Your business process model should describe the following:

- **Your external environment:** Before you can effectively model a business process, you need to understand the environment it exists within. You must identify your customers, in particular their needs (some of which are perceived and some of which may be motivated by your sales and marketing efforts). You must also identify the suppliers/vendors/partners of services and materials to your organization—perhaps you work with courier companies as part of your order fulfillment process. An important part of your environment is your competition—your rivals will be doing their best to lure your customers away from you by offering better value. Your competitors may not always be obvious, and who they are will change over time. For example, Wal-Mart was seen as a primary competitor of department stores and smaller specialty shops for years, yet it was not perceived by grocery stores to be much of a threat. Then in the late 1990s, Wal-Mart entered the grocery business with its superstores and has put hundreds of grocery stores out of business as a result.

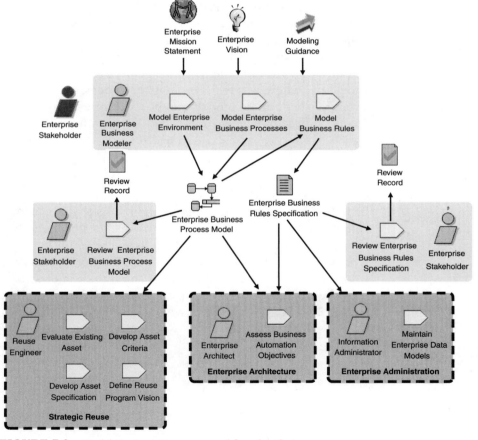

FIGURE 7-3 *Model Business Processes workflow details.*

■ **Business processes:** The business processes of an online retailer would include marketing, sales, order fulfillment, inventory management, and government reporting. An important part of enterprise business process modeling is identifying the offerings (services and products) your organization provides to your customers, what you want to provide, and what you would like to stop providing. The next step is to identify, at least at a high level, how you go about (or should go about) doing so. Although the RUP product suggests that use case models should be used for business process modeling, the fact is that many options are available to you, as summarized in Table 7-2, and you should choose the ones that are best suited for your environment. Some models are good for logical process modeling, where you focus on what you need to accomplish but not how you'll do it; others are well-suited for physical modeling, where you focus on how the processes are accomplished. Some models can be used for either. Many of these models are described, with examples, at `www.agilemodeling.com/artifacts/`.

■ **Critical business rules:** As you explore the business processes within your organization, you will also identify critical business rules that you should capture. Your goal should be to focus on capturing the fundamental idea, such as the rule that a bank will charge a monthly fee for checking accounts, but to not go into the details (for example, specify what to charge for each type of account but not how to do it). Enterprise business rules should stand the test of time—they should describe business policies that will very likely still be in effect years from now.

TABLE 7-2 *Potential Business Process Modeling Artifacts*

Potential Business Process Models	Description	Trade-Offs
Data flow diagram (DFD)	A diagram that shows the movement of data between processes, entities, and data stores (Gane and Sarson 1979).	Useful for logical and physical modeling. DFDs are the mainstay of traditional project-level process modeling and are often used for enterprise modeling activities. DFDs are typically supported by traditional modeling tools, although because this technique fell out of favor in the early 1990s, many IT professionals are not familiar with it.
Integrated Computer-Aided Manufacturing Definition (IDEF0) diagram	IDEF0 is a business process model that shows the processes and the flows between processes. There are syntactic rules—inputs enter the left side of a process, outputs leave the right side, and controls enter at the top—that enable the creation of sophisticated models via a simple notation (Hay 2003).	Detailed logical process and/or workflow modeling. Supported by high-end business process modeling tools, although this notation gained little acceptance outside the American military establishment.
Unified Modeling Language (UML) 2.0 Activity diagram	An industry-standard diagram that shows activities/processes and the control flow between them (Object Management Group 2003). The workflow detail diagrams, such as Figure 7-2, are UML activity diagrams with visual stereotypes applied to improve their appearance.	Can be used to model high-level business processes or the complex logic within a system. Although this is an industry standard, the current tool support for this diagram is questionable at best.

continues

TABLE 7-2   *Potential Business Process Modeling Artifacts (Continued)*

Potential Business Procvess Models	Description	Trade-Offs
Use case model	A use case model comprises zero or more use case diagrams (which depict actors and use cases) and specifications describing the actors and use cases (Jacobson, Christerson, Jonsson, and Overgaard 1992). Use case diagrams are one of the standard UML 2 diagrams.	Very good at exploring how people interact with your organization but not very good at depicting true process flow.
Value stream map	A value stream map lists the steps/activities of a business process across the top as a collection of serial boxes. Below the boxes is a simple timing diagram depicting two actions: the work time it takes to accomplish a process step and the wait time within and between steps (Poppendieck and Poppendieck 2003).	Used to analyze the effectiveness of a business process, identifying potential loss of value (wait time) to the customer of a process. A very simple diagram, which can be quickly drawn on paper or a whiteboard. Very useful when you need to compare different physical implementations of a logical process. This technique is not well known within the IT industry.

Our experience is that effective enterprise process models are mostly if not completely logical in nature. This is because the fundamentals of what your enterprise is trying to accomplish change slowly over time, whereas the physical aspects of what you do can change quite rapidly. Furthermore, enterprise models, including both business and architecture models (Chapter 9), should be very high-level. Details, although important, are better left to specific project teams. If you find yourself documenting the specifics of a business rule or business process, perhaps in something like business process execution language (BPEL) or object constraint language (OCL) (www.omg.org), you're definitely going into too much detail at this level.

An emerging standard is the Business Process Modeling Notation (BPMN) from the Business Process Management Initiative (BPMI) (`www.bpmi.org`). The BPMN specification defines a (potentially) standard graphical notation for expressing business processes. Figure 7-4 applies BPMN to depict the business processes of managing XYZ Schools. Figure 7-4 is a simple model; a good enterprise business process model should capture the fundamental processes. The objective of BPMN is to define a notation that is intuitive to business users yet still sophisticated enough to represent complex process semantics for the developers. In addition to the basic process flow and activities depicted in Figure 7-4, it is also possible with BPMN to depict swimlanes (which indicate who/what performs activities), data flows, and message sends. At the time of this writing, BPMN v1.0 had just been released, and many people within the business modeling community seem to be accepting it. Our suggestion is that you keep an eye on this emerging standard but beware of the hype. The important thing is that IT and business stakeholders work together—the shapes of the bubbles and lines they draw when doing so aren't nearly as important.

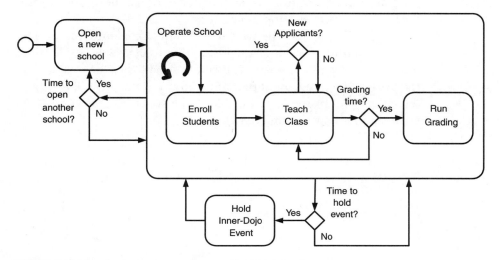

FIGURE 7-4 *A business process diagram for XYZ Schools.*

> **TIP   Take an Iterative Approach to Modeling**
>
> A challenge with enterprise business modeling is that IT profes-
> sionals often have a bottom-up view of business modeling, be-
> cause they're modeling within the context of a single project,
> whereas businesspeople often have a top-down viewpoint. Both
> are important, but when it comes to enterprise modeling, you
> need to find a way to work together effectively. This implies that
> you need to cycle back and forth between the two viewpoints.

Identify Process Implementation Options

Identifying areas for process automation is a key component of enterprise business modeling because it helps put your IT efforts into
the context of the overall organization. IT must be viewed as an
enabler of your business, not an end unto itself. Putting automation in the context of the business ensures that technology is not
implemented for its own sake. Some processes will be fully automated, and some will be fully manual, but the vast majority will be
somewhere in between. Our philosophy is that the term "process
automation" can bias people toward IT solutions when manual
ones are not only viable but also better options; therefore, we prefer the term "process implementation."

Figure 7-5 depicts the workflow details for identifying process
implementation options. New ideas for projects will be identified
during the discussions, and information will then be provided to
the portfolio management planning efforts in the form of a very informal project proposal (which could be something as simple as a
few sentences on a whiteboard).

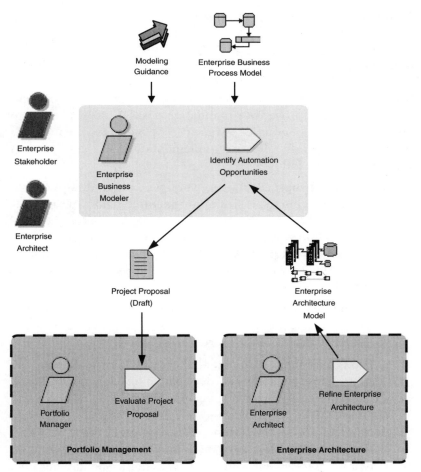

FIGURE 7-5 *Identify Process Implementation Options workflow details.*

TIP   Capture Technical Requirements

Enterprise-level technical requirements, such as hardware platform strategies or volume estimates, will often be identified and captured during the discussions of what to automate. This is critical information for your enterprise architects (Chapter 9).

Identifying potential ways to implement a business process is an art. If it weren't, every bookstore chain in the world would have seen the opportunity presented by the Internet and would have built its own version of Amazon.com. Furthermore, determining implementation strategies can be very difficult: the goal is to identify what to automate, what to perform manually (you'll still want to find ways to improve your manual processes), and what style of business process interactions you need between the various subprocesses. To identify effective implementation strategies, we advise you to do the following:

- **Leverage people:** People are very good at handling situations involving inconsistent or incomplete information, situations where computer systems struggle. Therefore, you want to find ways to provide good-enough information (even if it's not perfect) to help people make informed decisions. Don't try to automate things at which people are well suited.

- **Automate repetitive tasks:** Computer systems are good at processing vast quantities of information and relatively straightforward tasks; therefore, automate these things.

- **Focus on financial return:** The tasks that you automate should have both a positive return on investment (ROI) and a relatively short payback period. As a general rule, if it will take more than two years to recoup your investment, you should consider a different strategy, because your business environment likely changes too fast to allow you more than two years to benefit from the new system. Spend what is required but no more to achieve essential differentiation via business processes and the IT systems that support them. Estimating, at least roughly, the actual ROI, payback period, and other financial statistics is an activity of the portfolio management discipline (Chapter 8). However, effective business modelers will always consider financial implications to ensure that they invest their time wisely.

Model the Domain

An important part of enterprise business modeling is the creation of a high-level domain/conceptual model that depicts the main business entities and their relationships that are of interest to your organization. This model, which does not need to be very detailed, is valuable input into the enterprise data modeling efforts of your information administration group (Chapter 12) as well as the requirements and business modeling efforts of project teams. In both cases the enterprise domain model provides a basis from which to begin more-detailed modeling efforts—the project teams won't have to reinvent your domain model each time. In parallel you will also create an enterprise business glossary, which defines a common vocabulary within your organization. This enterprise business glossary is a valuable resource that should be shared with all your project teams. It doesn't make sense for individual project teams to define common business terms such as "customer" over and over again because this can lead to wrong assumptions and incorrect data. Instead, teams should reference the commonly accepted enterprise business glossary and then focus on the terminology that is unique to their effort. This is an example of artifact reuse (Chapter 10). The workflow details for enterprise domain modeling are shown in Figure 7-6.

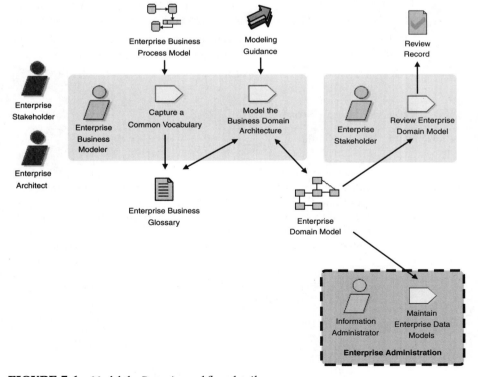

FIGURE 7-6 *Model the Domain workflow details.*

You have several options for enterprise domain modeling, as summarized in Table 7-3. Although several types of models are described, the bottom line is that at this level of modeling it really doesn't matter which one you choose, as long as it gets the job done. Your enterprise domain model should be very slim, showing boxes representing business entities that are connected by lines that represent relationships. The boxes should be labeled with the name of the business entity (for example, *Customer* and *Order* within an e-commerce organization), and the lines should have a label representing the relationship between the entities (for example, *places*) as well as the multiplicity of the relationship to indicate how many of each entity is involved (for example, a customer places *one or more* orders). That's it. Any more detail, such as an indication of data attributes or operations of an entity, is better left to the more-detailed modeling efforts described in Chapter 12. Figure 7-7 depicts a slim domain model for XYZ Schools, which uses the UML 2 class diagram notation. Because the model is so simple, which notation you choose doesn't really matter, as long as the model's audience understands it. Furthermore, you can and should take liberties with the notation to make your diagrams inclusive for non-technical stakeholders. Note that it is very common for diagrams like this to include more than 100 entity types. Figure 7-7 is smaller because the domain is limited in scope.

TABLE 7-3   *Potential Enterprise Domain Modeling Artifacts*

Potential Domain Models	Description	Trade-Offs
Class Responsibility Collaborator (CRC) cards	CRC cards are standard paper index cards that have been divided into three sections: the name of the class, a list of responsibilities (what the class knows or does), and the collaborators (other classes) it interacts with to fulfill its responsibilities (Beck and Cunningham 1989; Ambler 2004).	Because CRC cards are inclusive—they're simple and use simple technology—they are very useful as an interim modeling tool to work with enterprise stakeholders. However, they are not suitable for long-term documentation, so you will need to use a more formal approach such as a UML diagram. CRC cards are a primary artifact of Extreme Programming (XP) (Beck 2000.)

continues

TABLE 7-3   *Potential Enterprise Domain Modeling Artifacts (Continued)*

Potential Domain Models	Description	Trade-Offs
Logical Data Model	Depicts data entities, their interrelationships, and optionally their data attributes.	A very common technique for domain modeling. Unfortunately, there isn't a commonly accepted single notation for data modeling, so some people within your IT department may not understand the notation. Agile Database Techniques (Ambler 2003b) includes a chart comparing common data modeling notations. Good tool support is available.
UML 2 Class Diagram	Depicts classes, their interrelationships, and optionally their operations and data attributes.	An industry-standard notation that many people within the IT industry understand. Good tool support is available.
UML 2 Component Diagram	Depicts components, their interdependences, and the interfaces (collections of operations) that the components implement	An industry-standard notation, although not as commonly understood as class diagram notation. Tool support is spotty at best.

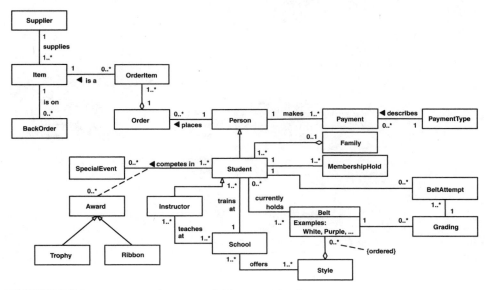

FIGURE 7-7   *An enterprise domain model for XYZ Schools.*

Model the Organization

Your organizational structure is what enables you to implement your business processes, and the two must be aligned if your organization is to succeed. Most people think of organization modeling as the creation of an organization chart, which depicts the reporting structure of your senior executives. That's important information, but it's just a start. A true organization model describes your organizational units (teams, groups, divisions, and so on), the primary positions, the senior people, the roles and responsibilities that the people and organizational units fulfill, and the relationships (potentially including both reporting and flow of control) between them all. The workflow diagram for organization modeling is depicted in Figure 7-8.

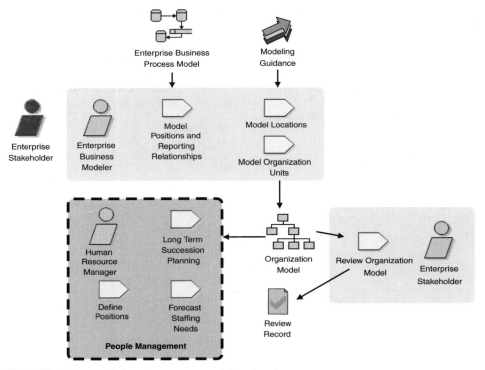

FIGURE 7-8   *Model the Organization workflow details.*

Your enterprise business process model identifies what your organization wants to achieve. This is valuable information when you're modeling the structures that will help you do so. The following list includes our advice for each aspect of the model:

- **People/position reporting structures:** You don't need to model each and every position and person within your organization; however, you do need to identify the fundamental roles and reporting structures. Keep your models simple and concise; you probably need a lot less documentation than you think.

- **Location modeling:** You need to identify the territories in which you're doing business because the regulations and customs within those territories will constrain the way in which you do so. Note that territories may be physical, such as the Canadian Maritime Provinces, or they may be virtual, such as the Internet. You will also need to know where all your main offices or manufacturing plants are, but in the case of organizations with many stores (for example, Starbucks locations) or branches (for example, HSBC bank branches), an estimated count by territory is likely sufficient. Model to the level of detail that is appropriate to your audience, and no more.

- **Organization units:** Organization units may cross-cut both your reporting structures and location structure. For example, a business development team may be made up of people from around the world, each reporting to a different director. This aspect of your model may simply be a list of major teams within your organization, a brief description of the team's charter, and an indication of who is sponsoring and/or leading the team. This information will help provide insight into the tactical working infrastructure of your organization.

- **Organizational relationships:** Model the high-level relationships between your organizational units. Limit your models to the relationships that define your overall business goals. For example, in your organization, your Marketing unit may be chartered to identify new product opportunities that the IT or Development unit will produce. Approval of that product development would result in a notification to the Sales unit and the Operations and Support unit so that they can begin preparing for the eventual delivery and support of the product. We recommend that you not model low-level, tactical relationships between these organizations; for example, do not include the acceptance criteria that Quality Assurance presents to IT for all products submitted to system and acceptance testing.

Figure 7-9 depicts an organization model for XYZ Schools. The diagram is simple—the company is small, after all—but it captures critical concepts. Various roles exist—external experts who teach additional seminars to students, senseis (senior martial arts instructors) who run their own schools, and a pool of instructors who teach classes at one or more dojos (martial arts schools)—and various relationships exist between them. Remember that one person can fill more than one role.

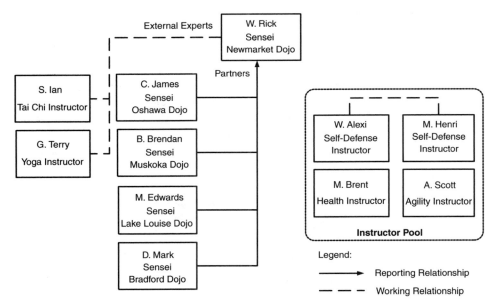

FIGURE 7-9   *An organization model for XYZ Schools.*

Support Project Teams

It isn't sufficient to simply create enterprise business models and give them to your project teams because they probably will simply ignore the models. We've worked on development projects in several organizations where we discovered that many times an enterprise business model is available but the teams never think to take advantage of it, if they even know it exists. Successful enterprise business modelers communicate their work to development teams and are willing to support the teams in taking advantage of the enterprise business models.

Figure 7-10 depicts how enterprise business modelers will support project teams. It is quite common for them to mentor or train business analysts in process modeling skills and all developers in general analysis and modeling skills (Chapter 3). It is also common for enterprise business modelers to take an active part on development teams, often in the role of business analyst. They will also develop and maintain appropriate modeling guidelines and standards (guidance) for enterprise business modeling. This guidance is often something as simple as the selection of standard modeling notation, such as BPMN or UML 2, as well as guidelines for effective models (visit `www.agilemodeling.com/style/` for a collection of suggested modeling guidelines). Your enterprise stakeholders should be part of the review process for your modeling guidance because they are an important part of the audience for your enterprise business models. In addition, you need to ensure that your guidance describes how to develop models that stakeholders will understand so that they can be actively involved in modeling.

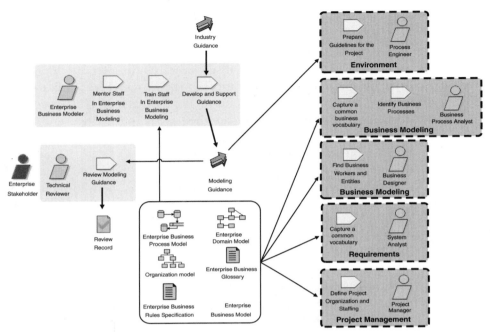

FIGURE 7-10   *Support Project Teams workflow details.*

CASE STUDY

Several years ago, two of the authors were involved with a very large software development program—over 300 people working on a portfolio of related software projects. This program had been in progress for several years by the time we became involved; however, the team hadn't yet delivered anything of substance, and everyone was getting worried. We were asked to provide mentoring to the team responsible for coordinating the overall technical effort. We were involved with three aspects: overall software process improvement (SPI) to help them to become effective with object technology, enterprise business modeling, and enterprise architecture (Chapter 9). All three of these efforts needed to be in sync with each other and needed to evolve in parallel; otherwise it was feared that the development effort would become even more chaotic.

The enterprise process modeling effort focused on the development of a high-level use case model, which depicted 10 main actors and 25 use cases. The actors were each described with a short paragraph and the use cases with a one- or two-page formal use case specification. The model needed to be reviewed by an outside agency, and the team felt we needed to ensure that the use cases were well written (point-form descriptions wouldn't be sufficient in this case). The team had originally developed a detailed IDEF0 process model, which had been previously reviewed and accepted, but we discovered that the project teams weren't using it in practice, even though it was available to them (it was even posted on the wall). This was more a reflection of the prejudices of the developers; their perception was that if something wasn't object-oriented, it wasn't any good.

The organization model focused on the three different types of sites on which the systems were to be deployed—small sites with fewer than 10 users, large sites with more than 10 users, and disconnected users who may not have network access for days or even weeks at a time. The reporting structure was well known, relatively rigid, and well documented already.

The high-level domain model was captured as a UML component diagram, which reflected our desire to take a domain engineering approach to the enterprise architecture (Chapter 9). Each domain component was then described with a UML class diagram showing the main business entities within the component and the relationships between them. In all, about 150 entity types captured were within the model. Similar to the process model, the team had originally developed a detailed enterprise data model, a model that was openly derided by the object developers (although it was actually pretty good). The bottom line is that it doesn't matter how good your models are if their audience isn't interested in them.

The enterprise business models were initially developed on a part-time basis, two to three hours a day over a period of six weeks by a team of 10 people (not everyone was involved at all points, however). The team included some of the original enterprise data and process modelers, several business stakeholders, a couple of technical project leads, and a mentor skilled in the new modeling techniques. The models were then updated over time as we discovered that we had either missed or misunderstood a few concepts.

The enterprise architecture team, which included several of the enterprise business modelers, used our models to formulate the enterprise architecture. The project management office (PMO)—which was responsible for portfolio management (Chapter 8)—used the models to help them define and prioritize the projects within the program. Individual development teams used the models as the starting point for their requirements and business modeling efforts, providing feedback, which we used to update our models.

To communicate and support our models, we were actively involved with both the enterprise architecture and project development teams. The models were made available within a shared documentation repository, and the diagrams were printed and tacked to the walls of well-traveled hallways. When we did this, we announced via e-mail to everyone on the project that the models were available and whom to contact if they needed help or wanted to provide any additional input. Our open approach was well received by our coworkers and helped us help them do their jobs.

ANTI-PATTERNS

Over the years we've seen the enterprise business modeling efforts of several organizations run into trouble because they inadvertently adopted one or more of the following anti-patterns:

- **Modeling for Modeling's Sake:** Too many enterprise modeling efforts are started because a modeler thought it would be a good idea to develop the model. The modeler was probably right—it is a good idea to have an enterprise business model, but if the intended audience doesn't recognize the need for the model, it will be ignored. The solution is to first garner support for enterprise business modeling and then model only enough to add immediate and obvious value to your IT organization.

- **Detailed Enterprise Model:** A common misconception is that people need a lot of details in enterprise models. The reality is that what is typically needed is a solid overview and vision of what is required. People rarely read the details, often because they're not interested in them or because they don't trust them to be accurate. The solution is to model with a purpose, to know the audience for your model(s), and to model just enough. Better yet, work with your audience to develop the models. They're the best judges of what they need, not you.

- **Yesterday's Enterprise Model:** Many organizations make the mistake of developing an enterprise business model and then declaring it finished. Businesses constantly change, which means that your "finished model" becomes out of date, resulting either in its being ignored or, worse yet, used to make strategic business decisions because it is believed to be accurate. The solution is to update your models on a regular basis as the business changes.

- **Tomorrow Suffers from Today:** While attempting to improve business processes, it is a common mistake to describe how things are *currently* done without exploring how things *could be* done. The solution is simple: explore new possibilities while keeping today's realities in mind.

- **Ungrounded Future:** Ignoring the current approach can be damaging as well because we don't exist in a Utopian world. Like it or not, we are constrained by organizational culture, human imperfections, and resource restrictions. The solution is to understand the current situation before attempting to improve it. Although the current processes may not be optimal, there are probably reasons why things are done the way they are. Understanding those reasons will help you formulate realistic processes.

- **Real-World Disconnect:** Modeling the entire business model for the enterprise can be a daunting task. The modeler may do things differently than other people or may completely misunderstand what is actually happening. The solution is to involve the people who actually execute the business processes and get their perspective on the modeling process.

TIMING

Enterprise business modeling efforts will slowly increase in parallel with your enterprise architecture modeling efforts because the architects need to base their work on the needs of the enterprise. When the enterprise architecture stabilizes, efforts will diminish. From that point on, you should update your models as project teams discover deficiencies in them. This often happens because your models don't reflect recent changes within your environment, such as the adoption of new technologies or the introduction of new offerings by your competitors.

On project teams, enterprise business modelers will be involved in the latter part of Inception and throughout Elaboration as they assist, review, and mentor the modeling efforts.

TOOLS

Enterprise business modelers have several categories of tools to assist them in their efforts:

- **Whiteboards:** An enterprise business modeler's most valuable day-to-day tool is a whiteboard. With a whiteboard, you can sketch ideas with others, invite them to review these ideas, and then quickly and easily modify them. With a digital camera, it's easy to snap a picture of a whiteboard sketch and send it to coworkers.

- **Modeling tools:** Software-based modeling tools like System Architect from Popkin (`www.popkin.com`) and Enterprise Modeller (`www.enterprisemodeller.com`) are excellent business process modeling tools.

- **Diagramming tools:** Tools such as Microsoft Visio (`www.microsoft.com`), Tablet UML (`www.tabletuml.com`), and CorelDraw (`www.corel.com`) let you draw diagrams freehand and present them in a fashion that makes the most sense to their audience.

- **Business activity monitoring (BAM) software:** BAM software monitors transactions between various systems within your organization, providing insight into the amount of business processing that is currently going on. Examples of such tools include webMethods Optimize (`www.webmethods.com`), which is an add-on to web-Methods enterprise application integration (EAI) software, and Halo (`www.ispheres.com`), which works with a wide range of transaction-based products.

RELATION TO OTHER DISCIPLINES

As you've seen throughout this chapter, the enterprise modeling discipline affects many of the other EUP disciplines:

- **Business modeling:** The enterprise business process model, enterprise business rule specification, and enterprise business glossary are important input for identifying business processes that are applicable to the development project. Similarly, the enterprise domain model and organization model can be leveraged to help identify applicable business workers and entities.

- **Requirements:** Capturing a common vocabulary is an important part of this discipline, and the enterprise business glossary should be the starting point for this effort.

- **Project management:** The organization model should be used by project managers to guide their own organization and staffing efforts.

- **Environment:** Process engineers should adopt the existing business modeling guidance, where applicable, for the various project teams.

- **Portfolio management:** Your enterprise business modeling efforts will help identify potential new projects, and projects that are accepted should be prioritized so that they reflect both your enterprise mission and vision.

- **Enterprise architecture:** Your enterprise architecture must reflect your enterprise business process models; in particular, the enterprise technical requirements you identify are used as input for assessing business automation objectives.

- **Strategic reuse:** Part of evaluating potential assets as to their reusability should be a check against the enterprise business process model to verify that upcoming projects may need the asset.

- **People management:** Your organization model is an input into your staff forecasting, position definition, and long-term succession planning efforts.

- **Enterprise administration:** Your enterprise data model, if any, should cover the details missing from your enterprise domain model and should reflect the policies defined within your enterprise business rule specification.

It is important to recognize that your enterprise business models will be used both within your IT department and within the business areas. For example, the people in charge of business development will want to use the models to help explore a particular business area or to assist in their strategic planning for your enterprise as a whole.

SUMMARY

Your enterprise business model describes your enterprise and its environment, including your enterprise mission and vision, critical business processes, your main business entities and the relationships between them, your organization structure, and the locations at which you do business. Your enterprise business models should be concise, providing a high-level overview of your enterprise without getting into a lot of unnecessary (and usually unwanted) detail. Enterprise business modeling provides the foundation for much of your other enterprise management efforts, including enterprise architecture (Chapter 9), portfolio management (Chapter 8), and enterprise administration (Chapter 12). A solid understanding of your enterprise is a success factor for system development efforts, making your enterprise business models a valuable resource for project teams.

Suggested Reading

We've found the following books to be valuable business modeling resources:

Business Process Modeling, Simulation, and Design (Laguna and Marklund 2004). This textbook covers the fundamental skills required to be a successful business modeler.

Enterprise Modeling with UML (Marshall 2000). This book describes how to use the diagrams of the UML to model an enterprise and is arguably *the* book on this topic.

Does IT Matter? (Carr 2004). In the May 2003 issue of *Harvard Business Review*, Nicolas Carr published an article questioning whether investment in information technology truly provides competitive advantage. He expanded this article into the book *Does IT Matter?* This book highlights the need to truly understand your business when implementing new technologies and is a must-read for any enterprise modeler.

Requirements Analysis (Hay 2003). This book provides a very good description of how to model within an organization that has adopted the Zachman Framework.

The Object Primer, 3rd Edition (Ambler 2004). This book summarizes 35 modeling techniques, including most of the techniques suggested in this chapter.

Chapter 8

The Portfolio
Management
Discipline

Reader ROI

■ Portfolio management exists throughout a system's entire lifecycle—from its inception and initial vision through the end of the Retirement phase.

■ Portfolio management enables you to identify, and then effectively manage, the highest-value projects.

■ Major contracts with service vendors are managed at the portfolio level.

■ Small risks associated with the project level can compound to become huge risks at the program level—and spell disaster for your organization.

The goal of the Portfolio Management discipline is to help improve the overall efficiency and effectiveness of information technology (IT) within an organization by selecting and then managing viable software development projects. You do this by ensuring that all are visible, planned for, and aligned to the goals of the business. Successful IT departments look beyond the needs of a single system; studies have shown that organizations that manage their IT investments most successfully generate as much as a 40% higher return than their competitors (Ross and Weill 2002). It is critical to recognize that portfolio management must happen throughout the entire lifecycle of a system—from its inception and initial vision through the end of retirement. Figure 8-1 depicts the full lifecycle of a system.

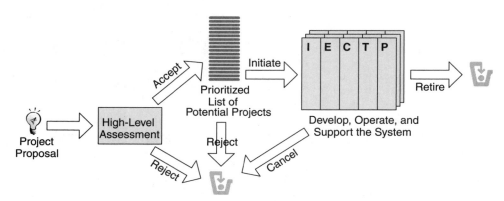

FIGURE 8-1   *The complete lifecycle of a system.*

A software portfolio is a collection of IT projects, both proposed and in progress, as well as the deployed systems within your organization. Your IT portfolio should be a diversified mix of highest-value elements, just like your personal investment portfolio, all leading to the creation of systems to support a strategic business goal.

Large organizations will often choose to organize related groups of projects or systems into programs. For example, a financial institution may have banking, insurance, online brokerage, and private banking programs within its portfolio. Doing so can help create synergy between similar efforts and provide a more efficient mechanism for managing and reporting projects. When projects are not coordinated and managed, IT can turn into a barrier for an organization—instead of an enabler—to becoming strongly integrated with the strategic context (Weill and Broadbent 1998).

Figure 8-2 shows how the concepts of projects, programs, and portfolios relate to one another. Portfolio management addresses the greatest scope, including the management of all your organizational projects—including potential, planned, underway, and in production—and the management of the various programs. Program management includes the management of a subset of project within your portfolio. Finally, the scope of project management is that of a single project; a project may exist outside of any particular program, but it still should be identified by the portfolio manager.

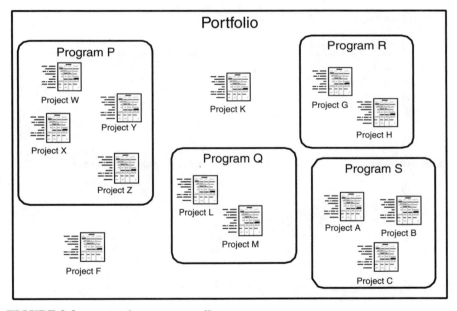

FIGURE 8-2   *Scope of management efforts.*

WORKFLOW

The workflow for the Portfolio Management discipline is shown in Figure 8-3. The first two activities—Inventory Current Systems and Plan Portfolio—are periodic, but the remaining four can be almost daily activities.

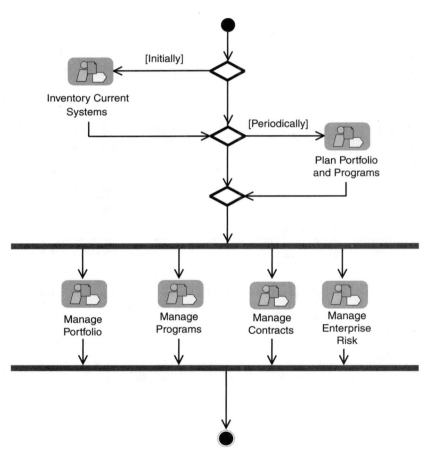

FIGURE 8-3   *Portfolio Management workflow.*

Inventory Current Systems

Before creating a portfolio plan, you must take an inventory of the current systems—sometimes called assets—within the enterprise. The goal of this activity is to find out what already exists in the enterprise, as well as what is currently being worked on. Every system—from the "side projects" to mission-critical enterprise systems—should be identified. This often is easier said than done; however, it can be as simple as creating a checklist of projects and programs to bringing in a third-party vendor to assess the situation and give you a detailed report of their findings.

The usual reaction to this activity is surprising; you may find out that your organization is currently supporting versions of effectively the same application on different platforms (the mainframe, the web, or client/server) or within different departments (your Toronto office has its own version, as does your San Diego office, as does your Denver office). Senior management will often suspect that this is the case before you do your system inventory, but they rarely understand the true extent of the problem until you actually do this work. Your system inventory will provide the base from which to plan potential system consolidations, and it will help you avoid the development of new versions of applications that you already own. Remember, you're not going to get a fully accurate inventory, and you don't need one—it just needs to be good enough to start the planning process, because you can update it over time.

TIP   Take Inventory with Caution

This inventory task can be challenging. Some people are not always comfortable sharing the information about all their applications. This can be intensified if this process is done by an outside consultant. Sometimes the staff members get a feeling that the consultant will try to eventually re-create all of their systems. Unfortunately (for the current staff), this is sometimes true.

Plan Portfolio and Programs

The planning cycle, depicted in Figure 8-4, usually takes place on a yearly or quarterly basis. It is important to plan your portfolio, because without a plan in place to meet the business objectives, you cannot accurately align programs and projects to meet the strategic goals of the enterprise. As Ken Orr (2003a) states, "Project management in IT is not a science; not yet, anyway." From a portfolio perspective, it can become even less precise because you are dealing with multiple projects—some included within a program—that make up the entire IT portfolio.

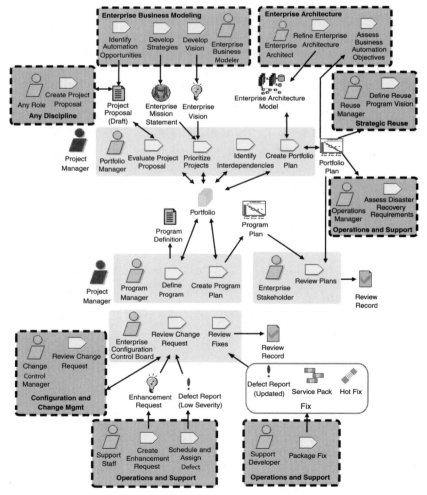

FIGURE 8-4   *Plan Portfolio and Programs workflow details.*

The portfolio manager role can be filled by either a single person or a board composed of senior business and IT management. Project managers are involved throughout the planning process. A large part of the portfolio manager's responsibilities is to evaluate and prioritize potential projects. A project proposal can be produced by any role in any of the disciplines, although they most commonly come from product management and marketing people. The portfolio manager must analyze the business impact of each program and project to help determine the priority within the portfolio; non-political, objective measurement criteria are critical to your long-term success. Your priority list should be posted publicly so that people on the various project teams know how their project impacts the larger program and the portfolio; this increases the level of accountability, which may cause people to become uncomfortable. Ultimately, your priority list is changed and updated by the appropriate project managers with input from their teams according to an accepted priority update policy.

Interdependencies between projects should be identified, understood, and accepted within the portfolio in order to ensure the delivery of systems that meet the overall business objectives of the organization. The interdependencies can include deliverables such as common architectures (which may emerge when the plan comes together), important release dates, arrival of new infrastructure hardware, plans for database or other system upgrades, or a myriad of other project-related issues. You can also take this time to identify overlapping or redundant resource dependencies and skills. Another benefit is that people can synchronize their activities between projects and even programs.

The primary artifact created during this effort is the portfolio plan. The plan consists of what is required to fulfill the overall business goals of your organization (Chapter 7). The projects in your portfolio plan need to contain a mix of risky versus safe projects, just like an investment portfolio. Some projects will fail. Not all projects can be (or necessarily should be) completed. Priorities can shift over the planned period; some initiatives may be eclipsed by new opportunities and their resources may become reallocated. It is OK to cancel a project if doing so makes sense. The list contains the programs and projects that should be taken on during the upcoming period of time. After the portfolio plan is created and accepted, it must be periodically reviewed as part of your IT governance efforts (Weill and Ross 2004).

You may also need to define any program(s) and corresponding program plans. To define a program, you need to go through the process of identifying the related projects and bundle them together. A program plan defines the strategy for implementing the similar or related projects in a program in the most efficient manner possible. This plan also helps show the portfolio manager the dependencies between the other programs and projects being run outside of a program.

Finally, your Enterprise Configuration Control Board (ECCB) is responsible for reviewing unassigned (as of yet) change requests, including both enhancements and defects. Change requests are first identified by support staff (see Chapter 6) in response to a user request. They perform triage on the requests, assigning most to project teams working on new releases of existing systems or to operations staff who develop quick fixes to resolve serious problems. The change requests that apply to several systems, or to systems which do not exist yet, are handled by your ECCB. This is where enterprise change management differs from the single system change management covered by the Configuration and Change Management (C&CM) discipline within the RUP. The change request is either processed appropriately by the individual project team in the case of systems currently being worked on or is put in a queue for future consideration.

The ECCB will review hot fixes to systems made in the production environment to ensure that the support team addressed the defect appropriately. The defect and accompanying hot fix must then be assigned to the appropriate project team(s) so that it may be properly addressed in future releases of the system (Chapter 6).

TIP   Even Small Companies Need Portfolio Management
If your organization is big enough to have several projects under way, or at least under consideration, you effectively have a project portfolio, which needs to be managed. "We're too small for this" is rarely a valid excuse for not adopting at least some portfolio management techniques.

Manage Portfolio

The portfolio manager executes to the portfolio plan, as depicted in Figure 8-5. Projects that fall outside the scope of a program are initiated as part of this activity; otherwise, they are initiated within the scope of program management (see the next section). The initial version of the vision document is created by the portfolio manager; quite possibly this could be in bullet point form. The only way to get projects funded is to make sure the project's outcome adds to the business goals. A funded project should then get added to the portfolio plan so that it can be monitored. From the point of view of the RUP this is "pre-Inception" work to get the project under way. There is an implicit assumption within the RUP that this work occurs; the EUP makes it explicit.

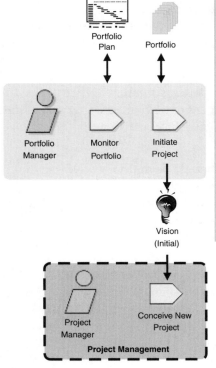

TIP   `Remain Agile:` The potential exists to write a significant amount of documentation, including plans and funding requests, while managing a software portfolio. Write concise, agile documents that are good enough to fulfill your goal. Visit `www.agilemodeling.com/ essays/agile Documentation.htm` for pointers on writing agile documentation.

FIGURE 8-46 *Manage Portfolio workflow detail.*

In practice, some projects that are critical to your organization may not fall within with a specific program. They still have visibility to the portfolio manager but are managed directly by a project manager. Some organizations simply choose to create a "Special Projects" program to which they assign such projects so that every project falls within the scope of a program.

Things change, so the portfolio manager must monitor the status of programs and projects. When the portfolio manager sees that two projects share the same goal, either one project needs to be eliminated or the two projects need to be merged. This sort of problem shouldn't occur if your portfolio management efforts are effective; therefore, you should identify how this situation happened and why. Retrospectives, described in Chapter 13, are a good option. Also, if a program is dependent on some external project for functionality and that project runs into trouble, the main program will need to adjust accordingly.

The portfolio manager monitors the portfolio against the metrics defined within the portfolio plan (metrics advice is provided in Chapter 3). Fundamentally you want to ensure that you're investing your money wisely (from a business perspective), to validate and improve your estimates, and to track the ability of specific project managers to help ensure that you assign the right person to a new project. Here are some potential metrics to consider:

- **Schedule deviation:** A schedule deviation is anything that materially alters the original project schedule within a portfolio. This is used to measure the ability to deliver projects according to the original baseline schedule.

- **Total cost of ownership (TCO) and ROI:** TCO is a current buzzword that defines the cost of developing, supporting, and retiring a system throughout its lifetime. ROI is defined as (Value-Cost)/Cost. Costs and benefits need to be specified with equal precision (DeMarco and Lister 2003). Use a combination of these two metrics in order to validate the original project justification.

- **Earned Value Management (EVM):** EVM is "an integrated program management technique that integrates technical performance requirements, resource planning, with schedules, while taking risk into consideration" (`www.valuebasedmanagement.net`). This metric is used to monitor project finances.

As with all metrics, do not manage solely by the numbers. At best you have a collection of heuristics that you apply when you're managing; the metrics are one of many inputs. In order to use these metrics effectively, the portfolio manager must combine the numbers to reveal an overall picture, quantify it so that senior management (and project teams) can understand it, and then start the process of measuring the portfolio against these metrics.

Manage Programs

The activities for managing programs are depicted in Figure 8-6.

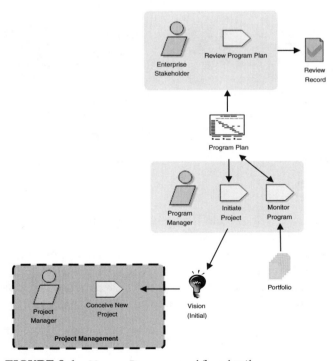

FIGURE 8-6   *Manage Programs workflow detail.*

The activities for this are very similar to the Manage Portfolio activities described previously; however, although a program has a smaller scope and focus, it is often just as complex to manage as your entire portfolio. The main goal of program management is to manage a specific group of projects with similar scope and business goals. The main effort of initiating a project will happen here (or in Manage Portfolio, the preceding section), and then the program manager will monitor the project against the program plan. A key difference is that program reviews take place at regular intervals to monitor the progress of the program. The responsibilities of a program manager include

- Ensuring that the projects within the program align with the goals of the program.

- Ensuring that individual projects are on track according to the program plan.

- Taking corrective action if a program appears to be in trouble.

TIP   Grow Your Project Managers

The project managers of today are potentially the program and portfolio managers of tomorrow within your organization. Stretch their limits and see how they perform at a project level. Evaluate how they create value for specific programs and how they add value to the portfolio for the enterprise. Make this evaluation visible within your project, program, and portfolio management circles.

Manage Contracts

Vendor managers are responsible for identifying external contractors and awarding the contract at the end of the process, as depicted in Figure 8-7. Both the portfolio and vendor managers work together with the HR manager in monitoring the awarded contract from a different viewpoint. Each project or program within the portfolio requires different staffing levels.

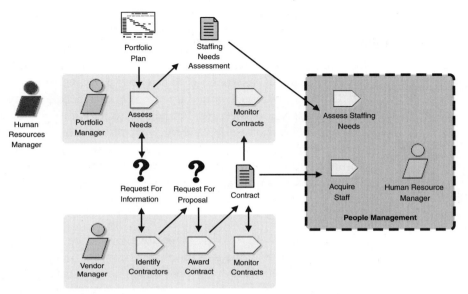

FIGURE 8-7 *Manage Contracts workflow detail.*

The portfolio manager manages *contracts*, and the vendor relations manager administers the *contractors* on any given project. The portfolio manager can help the enterprise realize an increased business value by lowering contracting costs and increasing the overall productivity of your development and maintenance teams by managing the resources required across the various programs and projects. It is effective to organize the management of contracts for any staffing activity at the enterprise level because some projects can impact others and span several years. Efficiencies can be achieved by reducing duplication of effort (for example, contact with legal and strategic sourcing can be centralized), and service vendors are willing to give you substantial discounts on long-term and large contracts.

The portfolio manager must assess the needs for individual projects or programs, following one of two approaches (or something in between):

1. **Formal approach:** Working together with the vendor manager (often someone from the purchasing department), a formal Request for Information (RFI) is created, which is typically issued and sent to different vendors. The vendors are expected to provide information based on what is requested within the RFI. Based on the responses from the

RFI, a Request for Proposal (RFP) is then issued to the responding parties who fulfilled the initial requirements. When goods instead of services are being requested, a Request for Quote (RFQ) is used in place of the RFP. The advantage of this approach is that many of the requirements for a project are stated up front, and a formal question-and-answer session can help clear up any ambiguities. This approach is often utilized in government projects. The disadvantages of this approach include missed—or changed—requirements from the project team after the RFP has been issued; as we have seen with clients in the past, this can lead to a no-win situation for everyone involved.

2. **Informal approach:** Selecting a contractor can be as simple as picking up the phone to a referenced contact or someone you have worked with in the past and who you trust. The evaluation process can be as simple as a checklist for requirements to a detailed specification; remember, do what works best for your organization. The advantage of this approach is that if you know the right people, you can immediately establish a contract with them and have them working on your project quickly. The disadvantage is that your organization may be perceived as bringing in contracts without going through a formal RFP process.

After the contract is awarded, both the portfolio and vendor managers must monitor its progress when project managers acquire staff and other resources. Although project managers are ultimately responsible for managing how subcontractors are used on a daily basis, the portfolio manager is responsible for managing the overall relationship with the contracting organization(s). The portfolio manager should work with the various program and project managers to ensure that all the enterprise issues are being handled and addressed. Here are some critical issues:

- **Favored vendors:** If you decide to use preferred vendors (to save costs in the contracting process) instead of using other experienced vendors, you must consider the possible trade-offs; these include missing out on other vendors who can deliver a higher value to the portfolio and instead receiving familiar but mediocre service from your "favored" vendor.

TIP **Select Vendors Based on Valid Requirements**

When defining vendor evaluation criteria, you must think hard about the requirements of the various program or portfolio teams. Make sure the requirements make sense and are not defined so that they sway the selection process toward one vendor over another. For example, one requirement we saw in the past was "A process expert who can define Model Driven Architecture (MDA)-compliant methodologies." This is nonsense, because although the Object Management Group (OMG) is pushing this as a new standard, most tool vendors interpret the requirements differently, and the skills for implementing this from a people perspective can be sketchy. For more information about Model Driven Architecture, visit
`www.agilemode ing.com/essays/mda.htm`.

- **Contractor quality:** Large IT service vendors can typically supply large numbers of relatively good people. However, these vendors are rarely leading-edge, and their staff are typically given several weeks of training on the company way of doing things and then are assigned to client work. Smaller boutique vendors typically can supply smaller numbers of very highly skilled people. Small vendors are typically staffed with experienced people who have left the larger vendors and are the primary source of leading-edge techniques. As a case in point, you learned in Chapter 1 that the RUP is based on the work of Objectory AB, a company that was purchased by Rational Corporation, which in turn was purchased by IBM, and the EUP comes from a small services vendor as well. Staff of larger vendors will often tell you what you *want* to hear; staff of smaller vendors may tell you what you *need* to hear—which do you want?

- **Relationship management:** This involves managing and assessing the business relationships with the various vendors (you should keep track of who to send the RFI, RFQ, and RFP to—these people change positions frequently). From the standpoint of your organization, keep current with your vendor list—including who to possibly watch out for when receiving responses from any of the requests you send out.

- **Location:** Which contracted services should be outsourced to another location (or country)? Trade-offs in outsourcing are discussed in detail in the Operations and Support discipline (Chapter 6).

Manage Enterprise Risk

Risk needs to be managed at the enterprise level in order to discover any potential problems with meeting the strategic business goals of your organization. They exist on all projects, so remember, "if a project has no risks, don't do it" (DeMarco and Lister 2003). Just as project managers are responsible for managing project risk, portfolio managers are responsible for managing portfolio risk. Portfolio risk, often referred to as enterprise-level risk, is the aggregated risk of all the different smaller risks at the program and project level that can literally kill successful implementations. The activities for managing enterprise risk are depicted in Figure 8-8.

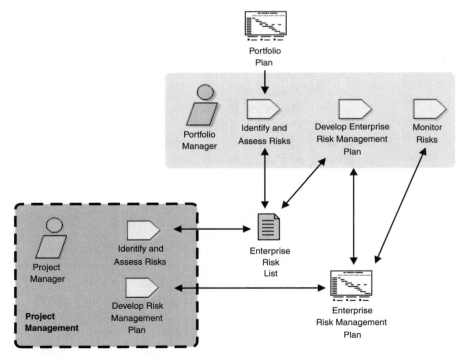

FIGURE 8-8   *Manage Enterprise Risk workflow detail.*

Each project (when looked at solely from the project perspective) may be low-risk, but when examined from a portfolio perspective, all the projects combined can pose high risk to your organization. For example, if your organization is a COBOL shop running mission-critical systems, a majority of your staff may be nearing retirement. Another example is basing all your projects on a new development platform or technology—if that technology or platform fails in the marketplace, so may your entire program. To help mitigate portfolio risk, the portfolio manager may need to help the program and project managers see how their specific project deliverables relate to the overall picture of the enterprise.

Creating a risk list involves identifying and assessing the risks to the enterprise at both a program and portfolio level; this is sometimes referred to as risk discovery (DeMarco and Lister 2003). Portfolio managers should identify programs and projects that are viable and that meet the strategic business goals of the enterprise. Alignment is a key to success for portfolio management. One thing to remember in both the identification and alignment process is that emotions must be put aside in the decision-making process because they are one of the most prevalent reasons for poor project decisions (Hollington 2003). The portfolio manager should steer the organization away from projects that do not meet the strategic business goals while using a fair mix of both perceived risky and safe projects. Any combination of low-risk projects can be a very high risk for the enterprise. For example, if every single application you're building is based on a single vendor's J2EE-based environment and that vendor goes out of business, so could you. Combining the project-level risk lists would provide very little benefit because most of the project-level risks are just that—a risk to a specific project; however, a small minority of project risks might actually reflect enterprise issues.

What kind of risks should you identify and assess at the program and portfolio level? Each project team will manage project-level risk themselves, but low-risk items for a single project team become high-risk if every project encounters the same risk. The RUP tool (IBM 2004) presents a detailed list of project-level risks and examples of what risks to look at from an enterprise perspective, including the following:

- **Possible change in corporate direction:** Is reorganization planned for the near future? At some of our clients, this is a quarterly event and is built into the culture of an organization; the implication here is that the portfolio manager should be aware of what is happening at the corporate level that may have an impact on his or her decision to move forward with a program or project.

- **Acquisitions:** A new organization may be added as a division to the existing enterprise—thus eliminating the need for certain projects that are under way.

- **Aggregate risks:** A collection of common small risks may add up to a large risk for the enterprise. For example, if staff turnover has been defined as a project risk across multiple programs, a large problem exists within your overall IT organization. This is something that should be addressed, and it is discussed more in the People Management discipline (Chapter 11).

- **Dependencies on shared resources:** One person or team may be mission-critical for several projects, and due to lack of resources may drive the projects to a complete halt. Worse yet, what happens if this person leaves your organization or is simply unavailable? Most of the time, the project teams are aware of this, but they might not be willing to document it due to politics. This is a problem we see often because it is very common for organizations to assign their staff too many projects at the same time.

- **IT's inability to deliver projects:** This is a huge risk from the viewpoint of the business community, particularly in light of the Chaos Chronicles (Standish Group 2003), which show failure rates between 65% and 85%. If you suffer from this sort of project failure rate, you will miss key market opportunities and get clobbered by a start-up that looks at the business using a totally different paradigm. To mitigate this risk, you may choose to purchase systems or outsource projects to multiple teams (both internally and offshore).

In addition to the risks listed here, studies have shown that there are five common project-level risks (DeMarco and Lister 2003) that, when aggregated, can have a significant impact on your portfolio. These include an inherent schedule flaw, scope creep, employee turnover, specification breakdown, and poor productivity.

The portfolio manager develops the Enterprise Risk Management plan, which lists the risks and the risk mitigation strategies. The portfolio manager should actively monitor the risks against the enterprise risk management plan and mitigate as needed. Finally, the portfolio manager should develop contingency plans for high-priority risks in case the mitigation doesn't work. There are four basic strategies for dealing with risk (DeMarco and Lister 2003):

1. **Avoid the risk:** This can have negative business results (such as missing a key feature) that your competitors may use to their advantage. Think about how some brick-and-mortar bookstores were impacted by the decision not to enter into the web market that Jeffrey Bezos opened with Amazon.com.

2. **Contain the risk:** You can set aside resources in case the risk—or set of risks—materializes. As the bookstores saw Amazon.com becoming successful, they started implenting own online strategies (often too late).

3. **Mitigate the risk:** Take steps before the risk materializes in order to plan for the containment. Some bookstores saw the advent of Amazon.com and started planning immediately for how to either reposition themselves within the market or how to join with Amazon.

4. **Ignore the risk:** Cross your fingers and hope the risk does not materialize. Even today there are many successful bookstores without an online presence.

Identify Risk Early

We've found the following questions (Orr 2003b) to be effective at identifying risks during project initiation:

1. **Has anyone worked on something like this?** There is a difference between a three-person team and one that is spread across multiple time zones and possible language barriers.

2. **Has anyone used this methodology/technology on a project this big?** If the answer is no, bring in a mentor who can help you through this process (Chapter 3).

3. **Has anyone on the project team been involved in a large system failure?** These people are usually tough to find, but they can bring high value to your team. Look around your organization for people who have been on large system failures—more than three—because they will have a lot to offer your team.

4. **Do the right people have planning, architecture, requirements, and design skills?** After assessing the current skill sets of your available employees, you may want to consider adding new full-time employees or contractors to the team (see the preceding section) or working with the team to help them gain these skills (Chapter 11).

5. **Has anyone thought about contingency plans?** We have found that this question usually goes unanswered, in the hope that a risk never reveals itself during a project.

CASE STUDY

The case study presented here discusses how one of our clients allowed the continuance of pet projects in spite of their portfolio management efforts—along with the dire consequences for the existing IT team. In addition, risk management—or the lack thereof—was also something that, in retrospect, doomed this team.

At Sweet Co., the CEO asked some tough questions about why IT projects seemed totally out of control. To address this problem, an assessment was made, and a portfolio plan was put into action. During this process, risks were assessed at a minimal level, if at all; the standard excuse was, "We do not have time to plan for contingencies, and nothing like that will ever happen anyway." One of those risks included an IT shop that was 100% AS/400 systems—and any new systems would be on entirely different platforms with new proprietary languages.

The CIO decided to purchase a large Enterprise Resource Planning (ERP) package to replace existing systems (which were silos around the organization). Many consultants were brought in. During the inventory of the current systems, it was discovered that the new system overlapped with several existing systems in functionality and usability. Unfortunately, a lot of these duplicated systems were allowed to stay in production during and after the ERP implementation. Because of mainly political reasons—including the allowance of pet projects and ignoring the fact that the current IT staff was not trained to handle the new system—the multimillion-dollar ERP implementation failed.

Eventually the entire IT division was dissolved after a hostile takeover—a purely business-related decision—and the entire IT team was fired. When speaking with the ex-CIO after this happened, it turns out that the root cause was many pet projects running outside the scope of the enterprise portfolio. The prevailing attitude at this company was an unwillingness to reevaluate existing projects for political reasons, which turned out to be its downfall.

ANTI-PATTERNS

You need to be aware of the following process anti-patterns (approaches that do not work very well in practice) in order to avoid common portfolio management mistakes:

- **Unmanaged Portfolio:** Your software portfolio will grow over time. If you do not track it somehow, you may eventually lose track of what systems you have. This configuration management nightmare can lead to inefficiencies and customer relationship problems. The solution is to take the time to document your portfolio. Keep your portfolio up to date and use it to plan your IT efforts.

- **Pet Project Syndrome:** Pet projects will continue to surface within your organization. Remember that from a portfolio management perspective, every IT project must be aligned with a business goal. If your organization has this problem, the solution includes identifying all pet projects and placing them in a "Special Projects" group, where at least you will have exposure to what is happening.

- **Silver Bullet Contractor:** Have you brought in a vendor that promises full delivery of everything for a fixed price, without the specifications even being discussed? This is analogous to the "silver bullet" promised by tool vendors (Chapter 6). The solution is to be skeptical when selecting a contractor to work with your project and program teams.

TIMING

Almost all aspects of portfolio management are ongoing, but from the viewpoint of a project, a lot of the work happens before the Initiation phase.

TOOLS

The tools for supporting portfolio management vary from a simplistic spreadsheet to a full-scale, enterprise-level portfolio management system. An initial approach is to capture your plans and portfolio/program specifications in a spreadsheet or database to help create the plan for the enterprise—most small- to midsize organizations will need nothing more than this. However, larger organizations will want to consider one of the commercial portfolio management tools. Here are some leading tools:

- **Artemis 7** (us.aisc.com): This is a portfolio management tool from Artemis International that helps with investment portfolio, program, and project management, along with resource allocation and time reporting.

- **Primavera Enterprise** (www.primavera.com): Along with project management tools, Primavera offers a flexible enterprise portfolio management product. The product centers on project management, with different aspects of process, resource, work order, and portfolio management, which also supports collaboration among different teams.

- **PMOffice** (www.systemcorp.com): In addition to the products for supporting portfolio management, this web-based solution from Systemcorp promises ease of use by offering simple dragging and dropping of projects within different folders.

- **UMT Portfolio Management Software Suite** (www.umt.com): This suite of products from UMT is made up of four different modules and a central repository; the modules include solutions to create, select, plan, and manage an enterprise portfolio.

As always, our advice is to do your homework and evaluate the available tools against your actual requirements. As with all of our recommendations, we have no official ties to any of the listed tool vendors.

RELATION TO OTHER DISCIPLINES

As with all RUP and EUP disciplines, other disciplines can affect the Portfolio Management discipline. Specifically, the Portfolio Management discipline is directly related to other disciplines:

- **Enterprise architecture:** The enterprise architecture helps identify whether potential assets fit into your portfolio management decisions.

- **Enterprise business modeling:** When prioritizing projects for the portfolio, the Enterprise Business Modeler works with the Portfolio Manager in communicating the enterprise mission statement and enterprise vision.

- **Change and control management:** The ECCB works with the Change Control Manager to review any project-related change requests.

- **People management:** When selecting a vendor to work with your organization on a contract, the Human Resources manager can help throughout that process where needed.

- **Strategic reuse:** The reuse of assets (Chapter 10) across the portfolio is an important input in some of the metrics that the portfolio manager may want to measure. The real issue is that there are potential cost savings due to reuse within a program, and you may want to schedule some projects before others because of the potential for setting a foundation for future projects.

- **Project management:** This is related to the Project Management discipline in that if something negatively affects something else at the project level, it can be compounded across projects and programs and have a negative impact on the enterprise.

SUMMARY

The goal of portfolio management is to ensure that all projects are visible, planned for, and aligned on a strategic level to meet the goals of the business. To accomplish this, you must plan your overall portfolio, plan any programs within the portfolio, execute and evolve those plans, manage contracts at the enterprise level, and manage risk at both the program and portfolio levels. If your organization has multiple projects planned or in development, or systems in production, portfolio management is likely a significant concern for you.

Suggested Reading

Waltzing With Bears: Managing Risk on Software Projects (Demarco, Lister—2003). This book is one of the leading publications on defining enterprise risk, a key component of portfolio management. If you are looking at making the case for risk management within your organization, this is the book to read and share with your team.

`www.portfoliomgt.org`. This site includes many forums and links to articles related to portfolio management.

`www.cio.com`. This site is an excellent resource for metrics and information about overall portfolio management issues.

Project Management Body of Knowledge (Project Management Institute 2004). The PMBoK is an important source of project, program, and portfolio management information.

Chapter 9

The Enterprise Architecture Discipline

Reader ROI

- Enterprise architecture addresses enterprise-wide issues for organizations with multiple systems, including cross-system concerns.

- Your enterprise architecture model addresses both technical and business views.

- Enterprise architects formulate, prove via code, document, and support the enterprise architecture model.

- Enterprise architects develop and then support reference architectures, which show you how to implement aspects of the enterprise architecture.

Organizations that develop and support more than a handful of systems will benefit from taking an enterprise view of architecture. In the Enterprise Unified Process (EUP), an enterprise architecture includes the frameworks, networks, deployment configurations,

173

domain architecture, and supporting infrastructure that form the technical architecture for the enterprise. It comprises the environment within which all applications of an enterprise are deployed.

An effective enterprise architecture promotes consistency across your organization's systems by guiding development teams toward using a common set of proven approaches to application architecture. This enables both reuse (Chapter 10) and system integration through common mechanisms and compatible semantics across systems. Enterprise architects are concerned with how their work impacts multiple systems for both the present, in the form of "as is" models, and for the future, in the form of "to be" models. They look further than the needs of a single application and assess architectural impact on the entire enterprise, laying the foundation for future efforts.

Enterprise architects are responsible for formulating, proving, and then supporting the enterprise architecture. The architecture itself is built out through the efforts of your enterprise administrators (Chapter 12), who are responsible for your data, security, network, and hardware infrastructures. Your enterprise architecture will also be built out by application project teams. Your enterprise architects should not only support these build-out efforts; they also should be actively involved in them.

The main difference between enterprise and application architecture is one of scope. Whereas an application architect on a development project identifies architectural solutions for a system, an enterprise architect defines architectural solutions, frameworks, patterns, and reference architectures for use across multiple systems within the organization. Application architects guide the team of application designers and implementers in their efforts to understand and apply the application architecture; enterprise architects guide application architects in their understanding and applying of the enterprise architecture. Just as application architects take a broader yet generally shallower view than the designers and implementers of a system, enterprise architects take a broader and generally shallower view than application architects. Although the enterprise architect establishes the architecture for your organization, much of the actual implementation of it is done by your application development teams and by enterprise administrators (who often build infrastructure in advance of systems being released).

Instituting an enterprise architecture program does not guarantee that applications will be developed better, faster, and cheaper. It can be a powerful force within your organization and can go a long way toward helping your application development. However, because it has such a broad impact on the IT effort, it can also have a negative impact if implemented inappropriately.

WORKFLOW

The workflow for the Enterprise Architecture discipline is shown in Figure 9-1. Enterprise architecture is not just about modeling the "big picture." Models are an important part of enterprise architecture efforts because they help depict and convey the enterprise architecture, but it is more accurate to say that enterprise architecture is represented in the structure and distribution of technical and business assets of the enterprise.

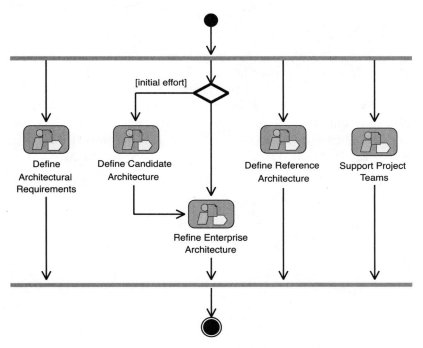

FIGURE 9-1 *Enterprise Architecture discipline workflow.*

TIP   **Take a Multi-View Approach**

Enterprise architectures encompass a wide range of issues, and as a result you should develop the appropriate views/models to address each one (Shaw and Garlan 1996). A popular approach within the Rational Unified Process (RUP) community is the 4+1 view of application architecture (Kruchten 1995), which includes logical, process, implementation, deployment, and use case views. The Zachman Framework (Chapter 3) has been extended to define a multi-view approach for the EUP. Regardless of the approach(es) you adopt, the fundamental point is that you will need several views to describe your enterprise architecture.

Define Architectural Requirements

An architecture, be it an application architecture or your enterprise architecture, must reflect a set of requirements. Figure 9-2 depicts how to identify the technical and business requirements for your enterprise architecture. Some architects want to focus solely on technical issues, but our experience is that this isn't sufficient. Smith and Fingar (2003) say it best: "It isn't about information technology. It's about how business gets done. IT is an enabler of business processes and practices, not a separate and distinct provider of value." The primary goal of your enterprise architecture is to enable the business to meet its IT goals and objectives, not simply to define the "cool technologies" that the IT people get to work with. Hence, you must identify both technical and business requirements.

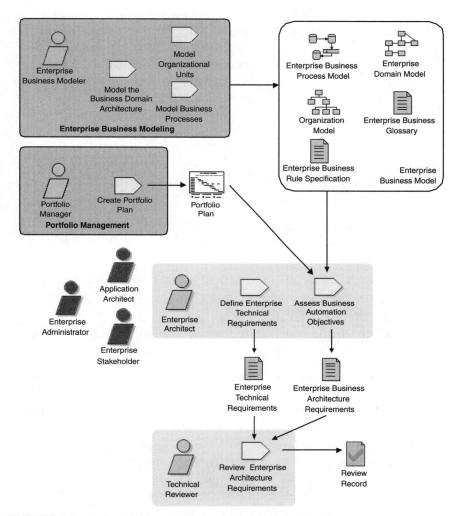

FIGURE 9-2   *Define Architectural Requirements workflow detail.*

Your enterprise business model (Chapter 7) identifies the fundamental business aspects of your organization, including business processes, business rules, and domain entities. This model captures the high-level business requirements to which your enterprise architecture and the systems you develop should conform. Enterprise architects will use this information to ensure that IT solutions keep pace and support the changing business environment.

The portfolio plan, produced as part of your portfolio management efforts (Chapter 8), helps enterprise architects understand the current and future direction of application efforts. The portfolio plan indicates the upcoming projects that are currently identified, as well as when they are expected to start. For example, if you see that more systems are planned for the long term that need historical data for decision support, you may decide to start investigating a data warehouse solution to lay the foundation for such efforts.

You must also identify technical requirements, including those relating to performance or availability, which your enterprise architecture must also reflect. Here are some examples of enterprise technical requirements:

- Applications will log all security violations to a central log by sending the *SecurityViolation* message to the Audits message location.

- Applications will implement a "heartbeat" that indicates to monitors at least once every five minutes that the application is operational.

- Applications will shut down within 30 seconds upon receiving a "shutdown" request from an operator.

Enterprise architects will work closely with application architects, enterprise administrators (network, data, security, and facilities administrators), and enterprise stakeholders (such as senior IT and business management) to identify enterprise technical requirements. In the course of working with project teams, an enterprise architect will often identify a new requirement when he or she hears suggestions or responds to questions from application architects. Enterprise administrators support development teams and operations staff on a daily basis and often have a very good understanding of the common challenges faced by these people—hence they are also a good source of requirements. Finally, enterprise stakeholders will suggest requirements based on their vision of the enterprise.

Define Candidate Architecture

When you are first formulating your enterprise architecture model, it isn't reasonable to try to address all of these issues at once; instead, you should tackle individual aspects of your enterprise architecture one at a time. This strategy is also appropriate for evolving your enterprise architecture—you want to do so gradually so that your organization can successfully adopt a new infrastructure in a low-risk manner. A good approach is to identify and then validate candidate architectures, which are the building blocks from which your enterprise architecture is built. The workflow details for doing so are presented in Figure 9-3.

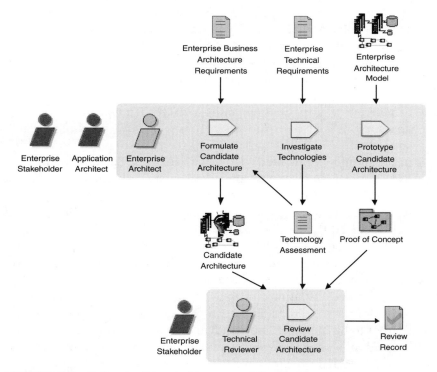

FIGURE 9-3 *Define Candidate Architecture workflow detail.*

A candidate architecture is a proposed addition or change to the enterprise architecture that has not been fully detailed or implemented; it may be as nebulous as the statement "start exposing our applications to a wider audience of users, possibly via web services" or as concrete as the idea that you should adopt a persistence framework such as Hibernate (www.hibernate.org). Candidate architectures can be described in various formats, from something as simple as a paragraph describing the idea to a simple position paper to a detailed white paper describing a new technology. Depending on the scope of the candidate architecture, you may need to investigate it further through online research, attendance at conferences or training sessions, or online discussion groups, or by talking with your peers at other organizations who have experience in the technologies.

The next step is to show that the candidate architecture actually works and fits into your existing enterprise architecture. Of course, every product works perfectly in marketing literature, but you don't want to put your organization at risk by adopting a technological solution that you are not familiar with. Furthermore, technologies such as .NET and J2EE are complex beasts that cannot simply be deployed "out of the box" but instead must be adapted to each environment. .NET supports multiple languages such as C#, Visual Basic, and COBOL, for example. Questions to address include: Which one(s) will work best for the enterprise now and in the future? How will applications built with .NET integrate with legacy applications and data sources? How will .NET be deployed and supported? Which parts of .NET can applications use, and which parts should be avoided? How will security be implemented in .NET? All of these issues, and more, need to be investigated and proven to work within your environment. It's not enough to just say it will work; it must be demonstrated to work (Beedle and Schwaber 2001; Ambler 2002).

You can follow two approaches to prove your candidate architecture—you can initiate a project for the sole purpose of doing so, or you can apply the candidate architecture on a system development project. Initiating a project has the advantage of allowing you to explore a candidate architecture well before project teams require it to be in place. The disadvantage is that you may prove and then adopt a candidate architecture that no team actually needs in practice. Proving a candidate architecture on an actual application development project avoids this problem because you know that at least this application will take advantage of the architecture, but you put the team at risk of schedule slippage if the candidate architecture proves insufficient.

In Chapter 3 we discussed the fact that the RUP promotes the best practice of building systems from component-based architectures but that the EUP generalizes this idea to simply taking an architecture-based approach. Table 9-1 summarizes the leading technical strategies currently available to you that you may want to consider as candidate architectures.

TABLE 9-1   *Architectural Strategies*

Technology	Strengths	Weaknesses
Aspects. Aspect-Oriented Programming (AOP) (`aosd.net`) is based on the idea that some features, such as security or persistence, cut across many classes. These aspects should be easy to add or modify without changing the underlying code.	It's easy to add common functionality to an existing object system.	Few people understand AOP. Few tools support AOP; AspectJ (`eclipse.org/aspectJ`) is one of the few. In practice, few aspects truly cut across a wide portion of your application classes, leading us to believe that AOP is a solution looking for a problem.
Component. A component-oriented architecture, such as Enterprise JavaBeans (EJB), is based on the idea that systems should be built from self-contained bits of functionality called components. Components can be thought of as large objects and are often implemented as a collection of classes.	Offers significant potential for reuse. Most object languages include component libraries or at least have them available for purchase or download.	Component "standards" such as Microsoft's DCOM or Sun's EJB are incompatible. The standards continue to change, requiring applications to be reworked to keep up.
Data. A data-oriented architecture is based on the idea that systems exist to process data, so your focus should first be on the data aspects of your environment.	Well-understood technology. Well-accepted standards such as SQL and XML exist. Many IT professionals are fluent with data technologies.	Limited vision that does not take functionality into account. Each database vendor implements its own version of the standards.
Object. An object-oriented (OO) architecture is based on the concept that systems should be built using objects, which implement both data and behavior. OO languages include Java, C#, and C++.	Object technology is very popular and is arguably the technology of choice for new development projects. Significant experience exists in the marketplace.	Impedance mismatch with relational database technology makes it difficult to truly achieve the object vision. Largely a technology limited to the desktop and application server platforms.

continues

TABLE 9-1 *Architectural Strategies (Continued)*

Technology	Strengths	Weaknesses
Procedural (structural). Procedural architectures are based on the idea that systems should be built from procedures, which process/transform information into a new form. COBOL and C are examples of procedural languages.	Proven languages have existed for decades. Many highly experienced procedural developers are still available. Many legacy assets still exist that were developed in procedural languages.	Procedural languages are steadily being eclipsed by object- and component-based languages. Largely a technology limited to the mainframe and UNIX platforms.
Services. A service-oriented architecture (SOA) is based on the idea that systems should be built from collections of services, which are well-defined and self-contained functions that do not depend on the context or state of other services.	Promotes reuse through system integration. Web services, which are services that use Internet-based technologies and XML, offer a truly cross-platform architecture.	People are still learning to work with this relatively new approach. Significant performance overhead exists with web services.

After you have proven it to work, the final step is to review your candidate architecture (as discussed in Chapter 3, this should be considered optional). When reviewing a candidate architecture, or any software-based artifact for that matter, you should consider the issues summarized in Table 9-2 (Clements, Kazman, and Klein 2002).

TABLE 9-2   *Components of an Enterprise Architecture Model*

Quality Attribute	Issues to Consider
Performance. The ability of a system to allocate computational resources to requests for service in a timely manner.	Arrival pattern of events
	The resources (CPUs, network, and so on) being used
	Resource consumption/load
	Resource arbitration policy (for example, fixed scheduling versus load balancing)
	The latency requirement for each message type
	Consequences for not meeting the latency requirement
Availability. The ability of a system to remain in operation and to recover from faults that cause it to fail.	The provisions to detect hardware or software faults
	Mechanisms to detect and recover from failure
	Redundancy strategies
	Mean time between failures (MTBF)
	Periodicity of various types of faults
	Mean time to recover (MTTR)
	Acceptable levels of reliability
Modifiability. The ability of a system to be changed after it is implemented.	Types of changes anticipated during the lifecycle of the candidate architecture
	Approach to encapsulating functionality
	Separation of concerns
	Use of mediators so that consumers and providers do not have direct knowledge of each other
	Impact of anticipated changes
	Difficulty to trace coupling dependencies

Refine Enterprise Architecture

With a suitable candidate architecture in hand, the enterprise architects integrate it into your enterprise architecture model, as depicted in Figure 9-4. Your enterprise architecture model should reflect accepted enterprise administration guidance, such as security and data standards and guidelines, which is maintained and supported by your enterprise administrators. It should also reflect the modeling and enterprise development guidance that the enterprise architects develop and support for your organization (see the section "Support the Project Teams" later in this chapter).

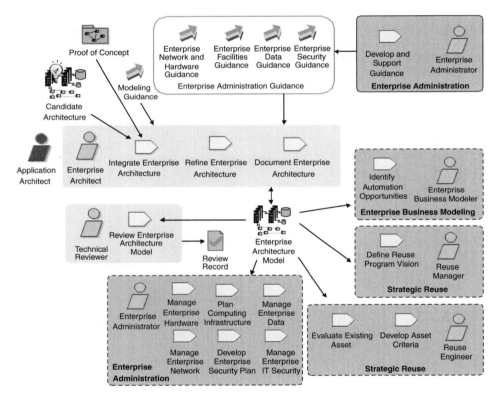

FIGURE 9-4   *Refine Enterprise Architecture workflow detail.*

Your enterprise architecture model is an important artifact used by several of the other enterprise management disciplines. Enterprise business modelers use it to help determine potential opportunities to automate portions of a business process, the end result being a new project proposal. Your enterprise architecture model is used in the Strategic Reuse discipline as an input into setting the vision of your organization's reuse program. It is also used as an input to determine whether an existing asset should be generalized into a robust asset that could potentially be reused and to identify the criteria for assets that are to be developed or purchased. Because your model calls out technical issues such as your network architecture, your data architecture, and your security architecture, it is valuable information for your enterprise administrators who are responsible for building and then managing these portions of your IT infrastructure.

Your enterprise architecture is probably very complex, so you will need several views to adequately model it. Chapter 3 covers the extended Zachman Framework (ZIFA 2002) for the EUP, which defines a collection of views that you need to consider in each EUP discipline. Table 9-3 describes the five views that we believe are applicable to the enterprise architecture discipline

Let's work through examples of the views that may not be so obvious—domain architecture, software architecture, and workflow architecture. When you see how these three views fit together, it should be pretty clear how you can extend them with data architecture and network/deployment architecture diagrams (these views are technical in nature, just like the software architecture view). Figure 9-5 presents a domain architecture diagram for a financial institution that uses the Unified Modeling Language (UML) 2.0 component diagram notation. This diagram depicts a collection of large-scale components, each of which could be built from hundreds of classes, web services, or even procedural COBOL modules. The functionality that the components encapsulate is accessed via interfaces, such as IPortfolio, IBankAccount, and IQuery (a generic interface that provides a standard way to access XML data structures), enabling applications to reuse the functionality in a black-box manner. The goal of domain architecture modeling is to indicate high-level domain components that can be evolved and reused by application development teams. The process of doing so is often called domain engineering or product-line engineering (Atkinson et al. 2002; Weiss and Lai 1999; Clements and Northrop 2002). Chapter 10 discusses architecture-driven reuse such as this in more detail, arguing that it offers great potential for productivity improvement but is very difficult to achieve in practice.

TABLE 9-3   *Components of an Enterprise Architecture Model*

View	Description
Software	This view provides a technical look at the software infrastructure for your organization. It would potentially address your interoperability approach (such as a message bus), the web and application server farms and their deployment to support failover, the enterprise data warehouse and operational data stores, any frameworks (for security, business rules, or even domain components), and the technologies that applications can use, such as Java or Oracle.
Network/ Deployment	This view focuses on the hardware, network, and middleware technologies in place within your organization. This view should depict all major hardware systems, including legacy mainframe systems (which are the dominant hardware still in use within most organizations).
Workflow	This view translates the business processes captured within your enterprise business model into a technology-oriented view that depicts the flow of control between systems to describe your high-level business processes.
Domain	This view depicts the high-level domain components or modules that make up a common business infrastructure that applications can reuse. Just as application teams can take advantage of common reusable technical components such as a security framework, there is no reason why they couldn't take advantage of a common reusable domain component such as a customer framework. In fact, many commercial off-the-shelf (COTS) systems such as Oracle Financials (www.oracle.com) and SAP (www.sap.com) are now sold in the form of modules such as logistics, accounts payable, and customer relationship management (CRM). These modules are effectively domain components.
Data	This view describes the high-level infrastructure that supports data-oriented activities within your organization. It includes data warehouse(s), data marts, operational data stores, extract-transform-load (ETL) tools, and reporting tools. This view should not include a detailed enterprise data model, something that is the purview of the Enterprise Administration discipline (Chapter 12), nor does it include a high-level domain model, which is the purview of the Enterprise Business Modeling discipline (Chapter 7).

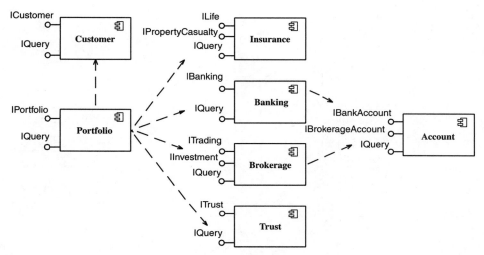

FIGURE 9-5   *Domain architecture diagram for a financial institution.*

Figure 9-6 depicts a free-form diagram for the "to be" software architecture for our financial institution. It indicates the major software technologies—browsers, firewalls, EJB, and so on—and how they should work together. This diagram doesn't go into much detail—for example, it doesn't specify the versions of the technologies or the names of many of the implementing technologies. This information might be maintained in a supporting web page or other form of documentation. Good enterprise models should stand the test of time: too much detail will force you to update your models on a regular basis, resulting in maintenance and versioning burdens, which you want to avoid.

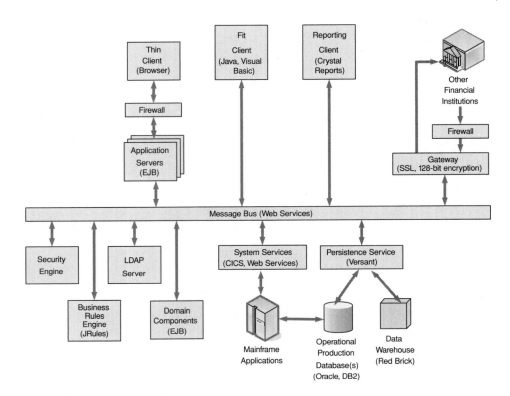

FIGURE 9-6 *Software architecture diagram for a financial institution.*

Now let's consider a workflow view. Figure 9-7 depicts a business workflow diagram for the financial institution, a type of diagram that you could use to depict the internal logic of an enterprise business process (in this case, processing payments). Although this diagram is very useful from a business modeling viewpoint, it doesn't say much about your architecture. Figure 9-8 shows the architectural version of this workflow, depicting the major systems that are involved, the organizations/people involved, and the flows between them. This view effectively shows how the business workflow is supported by the IT infrastructure, which is valuable information for any application teams extending or integrating into this business process.

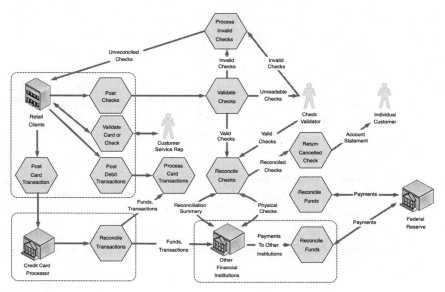

FIGURE 9-7 *Business workflow diagram for payment processing.*

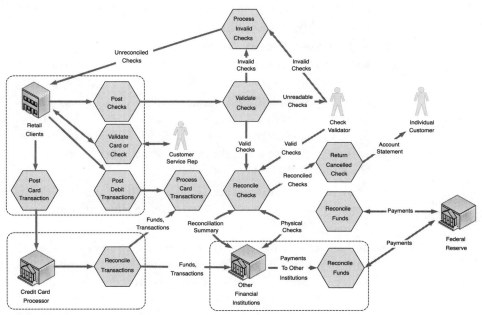

FIGURE 9-8 *Architectural workflow diagram for payment processing.*

Enterprise architecture diagrams can be depicted in various manners. Early in the process, your enterprise architecture model may simply be a whiteboard drawing or an exchange of e-mails. As your enterprise architecture model becomes fully refined, however, it evolves into more formal documentation. Various stakeholders should review the model, and application teams should learn about it and understand it. We believe that the following advice, described in *The Practical Guide to Enterprise Architecture* (McGovern et al. 2004), will help enterprise architects work effectively with project teams:

- **Focus on people, not technology or techniques:** The greatest architecture model in the world has little value if you can't find a way to work with developers effectively and convince them to use it.

- **Keep it simple:** The simpler the architecture, the greater the chance that it will be understood and actually followed by developers.

- **Work iteratively and incrementally:** Your architecture will evolve over time due to new requirements, new technological choices, and greater understanding among your enterprise architecture team.

- **Roll up your sleeves:** Developers won't respect you, and therefore won't accept your architecture, if you aren't willing to get actively involved in their project efforts.

- **Build it before you talk about it:** Everything works in diagrams but can fail miserably in practice. Just like in the RUP, you should prove your application architecture via technical prototyping; there is no reason why you can't do the same at the enterprise level.

- **Look at the whole picture:** This is a primary skill of enterprise architects, which is one of the reasons why a multi-view approach is so important to you.

- **Make architecture attractive to your customers:** If your enterprise architecture artifacts aren't easy to understand, to access, and to work with, your customers (developers and senior managers) will very likely ignore your work.

TIP   **Beware the MDA**

The Object Management Group (OMG) currently promotes the Model-Driven Architecture (MDA) (`http://www.omg.org/mda/`). The MDA is based on the idea that a system or component can be modeled via two categories of models: Platform-Independent Models (PIMs) and Platform-Specific Models (PSMs). PIMs are further divided into Computation-Independent Business Models (CIBMs) and Platform-Independent Component Models (PICMs). As the name implies, PIMs do not take technology-specific considerations into account, a concept that is equivalent to logical models in the structured methodologies (Gane and Sarson 1979; Yourdon 1989) and to essential models within usage-centered techniques (Constantine and Lockwood 1999). The CIBMs represent the business requirements and processes that the system or component supports, and the PICMs are used to model the logical business components, also called domain components. PSMs bring technology issues into account and are effectively transformations of PIMs to reflect platform-specific considerations.

All of this sounds good in theory, but in practice, the MDA may not be appropriate for the majority of projects within your organization. Do you have people on staff with the requisite modeling skills, or can you train them? If so, can you keep them, or will they realize they can make more money consulting? Worse yet, the tools seem insufficient for the job. (Producing 80% of the code and leaving the difficult 20% to you doesn't seem quite right to us.) In short, we think that the MDA will fail for pretty much the same reasons that the Integrated CASE (I-CASE) vision failed in the late 1980s. Don't get sidetracked. The web page `www.agilemodeling.com/essays/mda.htm` provides links to articles exploring the strengths and weaknesses of the MDA.

Define Reference Architecture

A reference architecture is an architectural pattern designed and proven for use in a particular domain, together with supporting artifacts to enable their use; it at least serves as an example and at best provides the basis for creating an application architecture. Reference architectures help application teams craft application architectures that utilize your enterprise architecture. They can greatly speed application development effort and minimize support costs because applications are architected in standard, proven ways. Reference architectures are not theoretical models of how things might work. They are proven patterns of how things do work. Nothing demonstrates that better than working code that teams can inspect to see how to apply it. The workflow detail to define reference architectures is shown in Figure 9-9.

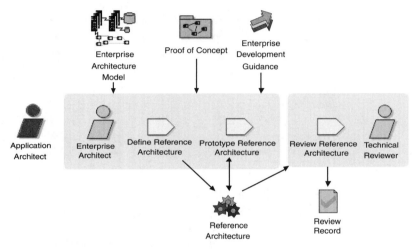

FIGURE 9-9 *Define Reference Architecture workflow detail.*

A reference architecture may be geared toward a particular technology or domain. Examples of technical reference architectures include implementations of the Messaging Gateway and Event-Driven Consumer integration architecture patterns (Hohpe et al. 2003). Although described in pattern form within an existing book, had your enterprise architecture team identified these patterns, you very likely would have presented them as short white papers at first. Later on, if development teams require it, you could extend the white papers by providing working examples of (near) production-ready code with supporting documentation. Reference architectures evolve over time, just as your enterprise architecture does.

The reference architecture should be documented in a manner that is easy to use by application developers. One way to do so is to create a standard RUP Software Architecture Document (SAD). Remember to keep your documentation concise and well written— it is possible to be agile when creating documents (Ambler 2002; Rueping 2004).

Like any other architecture, reference architectures should be reviewed before they are released. In addition to the criteria in Table 9-2, you should also consider whether the following are true:

- It complies with the enterprise architecture
- It has a well-defined context—that is, criteria for when it should be applied
- It is documented well enough to be easily understood by application architects
- It has been proven to work
- It is a long-term solution and not just a quick fix

Support the Project Teams

A vital part of the enterprise architecture discipline, as with the other enterprise management disciplines, is supporting project teams. It does no good to define a great enterprise architecture if application teams cannot understand it or do not adhere to it. As depicted in Figure 9-10, enterprise architects must work with project teams to help them succeed at adopting and following the enterprise architecture.

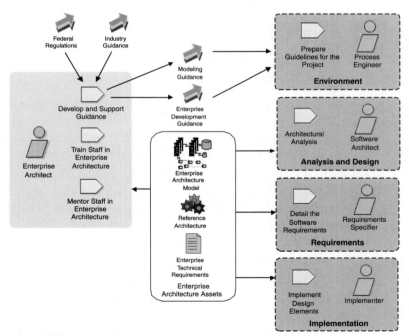

FIGURE 9-10   *Support Project Teams workflow detail.*

Enterprise architects work closely with application architects (the software architect role in RUP) to help them formulate architectures for specific applications. They do this by helping them apply reference architectures and craft application architectures with enterprise needs in mind. A good enterprise architect will spend the majority of his or her time mentoring others.

Enterprise architects will also hold training sessions. This may take the form of formal, classroom-style lectures, brown-bag lunches, or presentations. Training is often called for when a significant change or addition to the enterprise architecture is made that needs to be communicated to the entire IT organization. Enterprise architects can get the word out to the largest audience quickly by presenting some form of training followed up with mentoring to specific application teams or individuals.

Application teams will reflect enterprise technical requirements as goals and/or constraints in the Goals and Constraints section of their Software Architecture Document (or their equivalent application architecture document). Enterprise architects will also review application architectures, fulfilling the role of Technical Reviewer called out in the Refine the Architecture activity within the Analysis and Design discipline.

ANTI-PATTERNS

Our experience is that there are several process anti-patterns that enterprise architects should avoid at all costs.

- **30,000 Feet and Climbing:** The enterprise architecture is so high-level that it is of limited or no practical use to application teams. The solution is to develop reference architectures and get actively involved with the development teams.

- **Stuck in the Weeds:** You are too far into the details, attempting to do all the work for application teams. The solution is to mentor developers in the architecture, work with them as equal partners on the development teams, and, after they've gotten going, focus on providing them with guidance and advice as needed.

- **Ivory Tower Architecture:** Your enterprise architecture looks good on paper but unfortunately doesn't reflect the realities of your actual environment, often because you haven't worked with teams or have chosen to ignore their feedback. The solution to this anti-pattern is the same as for 30,000 Feet and Climbing: develop reference architectures and get actively involved with the develoment teams.

- **Strive for Perfection:** The architects are always prototyping and tinkering but never actually roll anything out because it's not perfect. The solution is to accept the fact that your architecture will need to evolve and then develop a "good enough for now" architecture instead.

- **Bleeding Edge:** The architects are constantly trying out new technologies and techniques before they are mature or stable enough to deploy effectively. The solution is to accept the fact that older technologies do in fact work quite well; the majority of your business may still be batch COBOL running on an IBM mainframe, and that may be acceptable.

- **Technology Above All:** The architects make technology a business driver instead of a business enabler. The solution is to base your enterprise architecture on actual requirements defined by your stakeholders.

- **Goldplating:** The architects overbuild the architecture to implement really cool features that you might need at some point, but these features often are not value-driven. The solution is to consider the big picture but also trust in your ability to solve tomorrow's problems tomorrow.

TIMING

Your planning efforts will occur in parallel with or slightly after your portfolio management efforts and in parallel with or slightly before your strategic reuse planning efforts. The remaining activities will occur on an ongoing basis throughout the lifetime of your organization.

Looking at it from the viewpoint of a development project, during the Inception phase, enterprise architects will support the project team by discussing potential architectural strategies with them. During the Elaboration phase, enterprise architects will mentor and, better yet, actively participate in modeling and then proving the application architecture. In the Construction phase, they will continue to mentor project team members in the enterprise architecture, modeling, and related skills.

TOOLS

Enterprise architects have several categories of tools to assist them in their efforts.

- **Modeling tools:** Software-based modeling tools like System Architect from Popkin (www.popkin.com) and Rational Rose/XDE from IBM Rational (www.ibm.com) can be critical to your success. System Architect is good for enterprise models, whereas Rational Rose/XDE is well suited for software architecture models.

- **Diagramming tools:** Tools such as Microsoft Visio (www.microsoft.com) and CorelDraw (www.corel.com) give you the capability to depict architecture diagrams freehand and present them in a fashion that makes the most sense to their audience.

- **Interactive presentation tools:** One of the main tasks of enterprise architects is to assist application teams in applying the enterprise architecture. Tools such as instant messaging or Webex (www.webex.com) can be invaluable aids for communicating the architecture when the organization is not co-located.

- **Non-interactive communication tools:** Providing a mechanism for others to view and provide feedback or ask questions is crucial. This can be done via an internal web site where the enterprise architecture is presented with a Frequently Asked Questions (FAQ) list with the ability to submit questions or feedback to the enterprise architects. A mechanism for some type of discussion group can also be used to allow teams to have discussions with enterprise architects (and each other) about the enterprise architecture. Software packages like Groove (www.grove.net) or Wikis (www.wiki.org) can also be used in this capacity.

- **Whiteboards:** An enterprise architect's most valuable day-to-day tool is a whiteboard. With a whiteboard, an architect can sketch ideas, invite others to review it, and quickly and easily modify it. Alternative approaches can be created, reviewed, and rejected or accepted with the stroke of a marker or dry eraser and added back in seconds if desired. With PolyVision's Whiteboard Photo

(`www.websterboards.com/products/wbp.html`) and a
digital camera, it's easy to snap a picture of a whiteboard
sketch, clean it up, and send it to coworkers. A whiteboard
has been, and will always remain, an architect's best tool.
Whiteboard tips are available on the Agile Modeling site
(`www.agilemodeling.com`).

RELATION TO OTHER DISCIPLINES

The Enterprise Architecture discipline is related to the following
disciplines:

- **Portfolio Management:** Enterprise architects work with the
  portfolio manager(s) to understand the current and upcoming products.

- **Enterprise Business Modeling:** Enterprise architecture
  must support the overall business goals of the enterprise
  to be effective, and the business process models should
  reflect the opportunities presented by new or emerging
  technologies.

- **Strategic Reuse:** The enterprise architecture provides guidance to the reuse team, helping identify potential assets that
  need to be built or bought, and also provides important
  input into your reuse program plan.

- **Enterprise Administration:** Enterprise administrators will
  supply operation guidance to the enterprise architects,
  guidance that should be reflected in the enterprise architecture. The enterprise administrators will use the enterprise
  architecture model to guide their efforts in building out the
  technical infrastructure ahead of project teams.

- **Analysis and Design:** Enterprise architecture interfaces
  with the Analysis and Design discipline by providing reference architectures, mentoring application architects, and
  reviewing application architectures.

- **Implementation:** Enterprise architects provide reference
  architectures, which implementers will use as examples for
  building to portions of the enterprise architecture.

SUMMARY

The Enterprise Architecture discipline defines the activities necessary to define the enterprise architecture for your organization. It describes the process to craft the enterprise architecture—the frameworks, networks, deployment configurations, domain product lines, and supporting infrastructure that form the architectural infrastructure for your organization. Enterprise architects will also supply reference architectures, the technical requirements, standards, and guidelines that the enterprise architects set for applications to follow.

Suggested Reading

Software Architecture in Practice by Len Bass, Paul Clements, and Rick Kazman (Addison-Wesley 2003). This book describes the fundamental concepts needed for architecting systems, including several well-written case studies.

The Practical Guide to Enterprise Architecture by James McGovern et al. (Pearson Education 2004). This book contains practical advice for effective enterprise architecture and covers current approaches such as component-based and service-oriented architectures.

The Zachman Institute for Framework Advancement at ww.zifa.com. The Zachman Framework (ZF) describes a comprehensive, although potentially overly bureaucratic, multi-view approach to architecture.

A System of Patterns: Pattern-Oriented Software Architecture (Buschmann et al. 1996), *Patterns of Enterprise Application Architecture* (Fowler et al. 2003), and *Enterprise Integration Patterns* (Hohpe and Woolf 2004). Each describes critical architectural patterns that all enterprise architects need to be aware of.

Chapter 10

The Strategic Reuse Discipline

> ## Reader ROI
>
> - It is very difficult to succeed at reuse.
> - You can reuse a wide range of assets, including code, components, and templates.
> - Something must be reused before you can claim that it's reusable.
> - You must communicate, and even market, the fact that an asset has become available for reuse.

Reusability is one of the "holy grails" of the information technology (IT) industry, one that is seldom achieved. Many organizations fail at reuse because they don't understand its scope—reuse between projects is where you get your payback, not reuse within a single project. Many organizations prematurely give up on reuse when they don't see positive returns on their first few projects or even on their very first one. Strategic reuse is a long-term endeavor that has strategic returns instead of tactical ones. This is why it is critical to look beyond the needs of a single project to the needs of your entire organization. Hence, Strategic Reuse is an EUP discipline, the goal of which is to define how organizations

Let's start with some definitions. An asset is a project artifact that is retained at the end of a project. A robust asset is well documented, generalized beyond the needs of a single project, thoroughly tested, and ideally has several examples to show how to work with it. Robust assets are much more likely to be reused than items without these characteristics. A reusable asset is a robust asset that has been used on three separate projects by three separate project teams (at a minimum). You can claim that something is reusable, but it isn't truly reusable until it's actually been reused; reusability is in the eye of the reuser, not in the eye of the creator. As Bertrand Meyer (1997) likes to say, "before a component can be reusable, it must first be usable." Our experience is that three seems to be the magic number: when one team uses the asset of another, it may just be for convenience or because of laziness, but when two other teams do so, chances are very good that the asset is in fact reusable. Throughout most of this chapter we'll use the term robust artifact to help reinforce this philosophy. It is a serious mistake to just declare that something is reusable; it is far better to make it robust and suggest that people reuse it if they see fit.

Reuse is often described as not "reinventing the wheel," and the first step for succeeding at reuse is to understand that you have more than one option at your disposal. You can reuse source code, components, development artifacts, patterns, and templates. Figure 10-1, modified from *A Realistic Look at Object-Oriented Reuse* (Ambler 1998c), shows several categories of reuse (described in Table 10-1), with examples of each. The left arrow indicates the relative effectiveness of each category—pattern reuse is generally more productive than artifact and framework reuse, for example. Similarly, the right arrow indicates the relative difficulty of succeeding at each type of reuse. Code and template reuse are relatively easy to achieve because you simply need to find the asset and work with it. Other forms of reuse become hard to achieve. With framework reuse, you need to learn the frameworks; with pattern reuse, you must learn when (and when not) to apply various patterns; and with architected reuse, you need an effective approach to enterprise architecture (Chapter 9) in place.

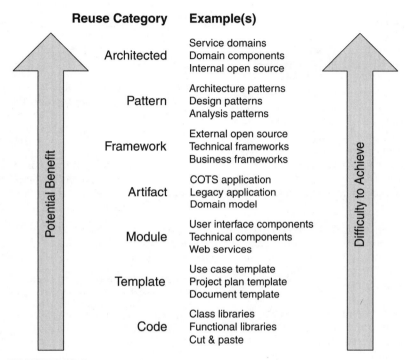

FIGURE 10-1 *Potential approaches to reuse.*

TABLE 10-1 *Categories of Reuse*

Category	Description	Trade-Offs
Architected reuse	The identification, development, and support of large-scale, reusable assets via enterprise architecture (Chapter 9). Your enterprise architecture may define reusable domain components, collections of related domain/business classes that work together to support a cohesive set of responsibilities, or service domains, which bundle a cohesive collection of services together.	Provides a very high level of reuse between applications. Requires a sophisticated approach to enterprise architecture. Requires a reuse team to support and evolve the reusable assets over time.

continues

TABLE 10-1 *Categories of Reuse (Continued)*

Category	Description	Trade-Offs
Pattern reuse	The use of documented approaches to solving common problems within a specified context. With pattern reuse, you're not reusing code; instead you are reusing the concepts behind the code. Patterns can be at multiple levels—analysis, design, and architecture are the most common. Ward Cunningham's site, www.c2.com, is a useful source of patterns on the web.	Can be implemented across multiple languages and multiple platforms. Increases the maintainability and enhanceability of your application by using common approaches to problems that are recognizable by experienced developers. Patterns don't provide an immediate solution—you still have to correctly apply the pattern and implement the code.
Framework reuse	Using collections of classes that together implement the basic functionality of a common technical or business domain. Horizontal frameworks, such as a security framework or user interface framework like the Java Foundation Class (JFC) library, and vertical frameworks, such as a financial services framework, are common.	They provide a good start at developing a solution for a problem domain. They often are a good way to review industry-based best practices. They often encapsulate complex logic that would take years to develop from scratch. The complexity of frameworks makes them difficult to master, requiring a lengthy learning process because of the steep learning curve. They are often platform-specific and tie you into a single vendor, increasing project risk. Although frameworks implement 80% of the required logic, it is often the easiest 80%. The hard part, the business logic and processes that are unique to your organization, is still left for you. Frameworks rarely work together because they are often built on different architectural foundations, unless they come from a common source. Vertical frameworks often require you to change your business to fit them.

TABLE 10-1   *Categories of Reuse (Continued)*

Category	Description	Trade-Offs
Artifact reuse	The use of previously created development artifacts—use cases, standards documents, domain-specific models, procedures and guidelines, and even other applications such as a commercial off-the-shelf (COTS) package—to give you a kick start on a new project. Sometimes you take the artifact as is, and other times you simply use it as an example to give you an idea about how to proceed.	Promotes consistency between projects. You can often purchase or download many artifacts: Coding standards for leading languages are often available, and sample models such as use cases are easy to find as well. It is often perceived as "overhead reuse" by hard-core programmers—you simply move the standards and procedures binders from one desk to another.
Module reuse	The use of pre-built, fully encapsulated "modules"—components, services, or code libraries—in the development of your application. A module is self-sufficient and encapsulates only one concept. Module reuse differs from code reuse in that you don't have access to the source code.	Offers a greater scope of reusability than code reuse because you literally plug the modules in and they work. The widespread use of common platforms and standards provides a market that is large enough for third-party vendors to create and sell modules to you at a low cost. Because modules are often small, you need a large library of them. You often are unable to modify them, although this is changing with the growing popularity of aspect-oriented programming (AOP), and sometimes the licensing arrangements (see Chapter 12, "The Enterprise Administration Discipline") are convoluted.
Template reuse	The practice of using a common set of layouts for key development artifacts—documents, models, and source code—within your organization.	Increases the consistency and quality of your development artifacts. Some people have a tendency to modify templates for their own use and not share their changes with coworkers.

continues

TABLE 10-1   *Categories of Reuse (Continued)*

Category	Description	Trade-Offs
Code reuse	The reuse of source code within sections of an application and potentially across multiple applications. At its best, code reuse is accomplished through the sharing of common classes and/ or collections of functions and procedures. At its worst, code reuse is accomplished by copying and then modifying existing code, causing a maintenance nightmare.	Reduces the amount of actual source code that you need to write, potentially decreasing both development and maintenance efforts. Generic/reusable code is inherently more complex than single-purpose code, making it harder to develop and maintain (from the viewpoint of a single project). Its scope of effect is limited to programming. Can increase the coupling within an application.

You can address these reuse categories simultaneously. Framework reuse often locks you into the architecture of that framework, as well as the standards and guidelines used by the framework, but you can still take advantage of the other approaches to reuse in combination with framework reuse. Artifact and module reuse are the easiest places to start; with a little bit of research, you can find reusable items quickly. However, if your organization doesn't follow a well-accepted development process that is common across projects, you may get little benefit from templates. Pattern reuse is typically the domain of developers with good modeling skills, and your enterprise architects should be publishing and providing pattern-oriented guidance to them (Chapter 9).

TIP   Your Mileage May Vary

Although Figure 10-1 indicates that pattern reuse is generally more effective than artifact reuse, you may discover that within your organization the opposite holds true. This may occur because you have a comprehensive collection of reusable artifacts in place, because your organization's culture is conducive to artifact reuse, or simply because your developers have little experience with patterns.

Workflow

Reuse isn't free; it isn't something that happens simply because you're using certain tools or working with certain technologies. Instead, reuse is something you have to work at very hard, as you can see in the workflow for the Strategic Reuse discipline in Figure 10-2. A key component of reuse is open communication within your organization. In our experience, this is usually the major point of failure in implementing any reuse program.

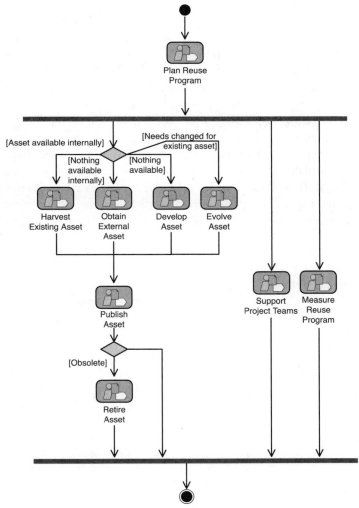

FIGURE 10-2 *Strategic Reuse discipline workflow.*

Plan Reuse Program

You must actively plan and budget for reuse: you need to allocate the time and resources necessary to make reuse a success. You must invest the time to generalize or harvest your work; otherwise, project pressures will motivate you to put that work aside. The bottom line is that you need to plan for and then operate a reuse program within your organization. This is often difficult to do. There is an upfront cost to reuse that may impact early projects. You must be willing to tolerate short-term pain for long-term gain.

Figure 10-3 depicts the workflow details for planning your reuse program. Two roles are shown: reuse manager and program reviewer. The reuse manager role is comparable to the project manager role in the RUP: this person is responsible for allocating resources, shaping priorities (for example, determining whether your reuse team should focus on supporting framework reuse over component reuse), establishing reuse quality practices and measurements, coordinating with project teams, and keeping the reuse team focused on their goals. The primary difference between reuse managers and project managers is one of scope: reuse managers are responsible for the long-term enterprise reuse program, and therefore their primary stakeholders are project teams, whereas project managers are often responsible for short-term projects, so their primary stakeholders are typically from the business side.

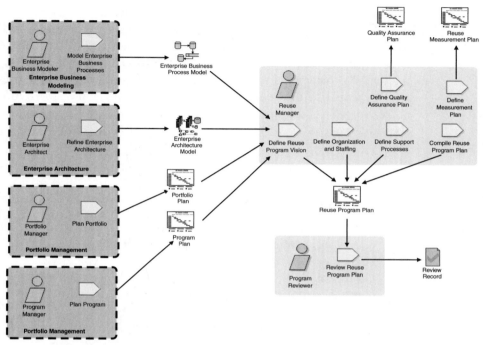

FIGURE 10-3 *Plan Reuse Program workflow details.*

It can be very difficult to organize several project teams to successfully implement a reuse program among them; the level of cooperation required is just too great when compared to the different schedules and needs of the individual teams. This is why the Strategic Reuse discipline is one of the seven enterprise management disciplines outside the scope of the system lifecycle. It shouldn't be dependent on projects; instead, it should exist to help project teams succeed at reusing existing assets.

Your reuse program must reflect both the goals of your organization, which are reflected in your enterprise architecture and your portfolio specification, and your willingness to fund—and follow—a reuse program. We can't overstate how difficult it is to succeed at strategic reuse. Most organizations fail because they make their programs too complicated, because they assign the wrong people to the reuse team, or because they starve the team of resources. Here are some important issues that your plan should encompass:

- **Goals:** What are you trying to accomplish with reuse? Getting rid of stovepipe applications (or organizations), saving money, reducing development time, or improving quality? A combination?

- **Staffing:** Your reuse team should be staffed with senior developers, ideally generalizing specialists (Chapter 3), called reuse engineers. A reuse engineer is typically a highly skilled, well respected, and experienced developer who is responsible for encouraging and supporting reuse within projects. He or she is also actively involved in harvesting and/or generalizing assets to make them reusable.

- **Initial startup strategy:** Our experience is that it is best if you start simple with a small team of reuse engineers. Many organizations start with a team of one, whose initial goal is to prove that it is possible to benefit from reuse by helping one or more teams do so.

- **Tool strategy:** Although a reuse repository, a tool that provides people access to robust assets that are meant to be reused, will not guarantee the success of your reuse program, it will significantly improve your chances. People can't reuse things if they can't find them, so they need to know where they are. Tools are discussed in detail in the "Tools" section later in this chapter.

- **Reuse potential:** Your plan should indicate the potential areas of reuse within your organization. Can you benefit from common security or persistence frameworks? From common web services? From common documentation templates? Domain components? By identifying your potential reuse needs, you will effectively define a "shopping list" of assets that you will want to harvest, obtain, or develop at some point in the future.

- **Communication strategy:** How will you inform reuse consumers (anyone who reuses existing assets in the creation of new assets (Fay 2004b)) of your reuse program? We've found that the most effective approach to communicating reuse is word of mouth. When you successfully help one developer, she will tell her coworkers, and word will get around that your reuse team is doing something valuable.

- **Team organization:** There are two basic approaches to organizing your reuse team. The first is a federated model, where people submit artifacts to the reuse team for review, generalization, and publishing. With a federated model, the reuse team can search for potential assets or can start an internal open-source effort in addition to waiting for suggestions. The second method is a "designed for reuse approach," where potentially reusable assets are built by reuse engineers. With this approach, the reuse engineers could be assigned to the first project team that needs the asset, or they could act as a separate group that builds the asset and then makes it available to the team.

- **Defined support limits:** A common problem that most reuse programs experience is that they become too popular too quickly—after a few initial successes, the reuse team often discovers that the demand for their services outstrips their ability to fulfill that demand. You will doom your efforts if you stretch yourself too thin; your plan should define the number of teams you can support, and when you reach that limit, you either need to grow your reuse team or start turning project teams away.

- **Asset evolution strategy:** Reusable assets must evolve over time to meet changing requirements, or your project teams will abandon the asset and redevelop it from scratch. An important part of your asset evolution strategy will be the configuration management of the assets themselves, a strategy that greatly reflects your organization's approach to the Configuration and Change Management (C&CM) discipline.

- **Measurement strategy:** It's crucial to measure your return on investment (ROI) so that you can concentrate on those reusable assets that are giving you the most value. The assets that you think will realize the most savings often prove not to, and instead another asset to which you paid little attention will save you the most money in the long run.

- **Growth strategy:** Assuming that your reuse program is successful, you will need to plan to grow your reuse team over time. A good rule of thumb is that with your IT department, you will want 1–2% of your development staff on your reuse team and 4–5% with a "design for reuse" approach (Lim 1998). You should build to these levels of involvement over time as your reuse efforts prove successful. Always remember that your goal is to support the reuse efforts of your organization; it is not to build a "reuse empire" within your IT department.

TIP	**Beware of Chargeback Schemes**

We've seen too many reuse programs fail because of ineffective accounting practices. In one company, the reuse team was charging more to reuse some assets than what it cost to build them from scratch. Not surprisingly, many teams created their own assets instead. We've also seen people build assets from scratch that they chose not to obtain from the reuse team because it was too difficult to work with them. We can't say this enough—make it as easy as you can to reuse things.

Our advice is simple—decide how much you want to spend as an IT department on reuse and then make that investment by setting up a reuse group of that size. Your measurement program should track how much benefit you're gaining from the reuse program within your IT department and, if possible, identify project teams that are doing the right thing by reducing overall costs through reuse—those teams should be publicly rewarded for doing so. Many organizations institute chargeback schemes so that a portion of the cost of the reuse effort is charged back to project teams that take advantage of the reuse program. Although chargeback schemes sound like a good idea to the bean counters who suggest them, they inadvertently punish people for doing what you want them to do.

The primary artifact created by this activity is the reuse program plan, which effectively encompasses all the information required to manage your reuse program, including staffing requirements, the vision and projected milestones, and a description of how your team intends to support project teams. Secondary artifacts include a quality assurance plan that describes how your reuse efforts will be reviewed and audited and a reuse measurement plan that defines the measurement goals and related metrics to be collected regarding your reuse program.

Harvest Existing Assets

Development teams build new things every day, and some of these things can be generalized into robust assets for reuse by other teams. This is particularly true for teams that are working with new technologies and techniques. For example, your first few C# teams are likely to develop useful utility classes, or the first few project teams to write use cases will develop use-case templates. The downside is that the first people to work with a technique or technology are most likely to make "beginner mistakes," so their work may not be something you want to share with others. The implication is that you either need to wait to harvest a higher-quality asset later or be willing to invest more effort into generalizing the asset. We've found that it's usually best to wait, giving you more time to gain experience with the technology and discover if there is actually a need for the asset on other teams. It takes much more effort to generalize an asset to make it reusable than it does to develop it for single-purpose usage. For example, Lim (1998) summarizes studies showing that development of reusable code costs 111% to 480% of the development cost of single-purpose code.

Figure 10-4 depicts the workflow diagram for harvesting existing assets. This activity usually begins when an existing asset is identified for potential harvesting. Perhaps a developer has suggested that the asset is potentially reusable (he may have even started generalizing it himself, often a point of pride with developers), perhaps a reuse engineer spotted the asset while working with a team or simply by talking with a team member, or perhaps one team is looking for a specific type of asset and you suspect that another team has a good start on it already. The existing asset must be assessed against the need for that asset. Your organizational needs should be captured in your reuse program plan, and relevant project-level needs should be communicated by the appropriate teams so that you can determine whether it makes sense to generalize the asset (often it doesn't). If you do decide to generalize the asset, you'll want to develop an asset rework plan to guide your efforts—this could be something as simple as a task list or something as complex as a full software development plan. Our advice is to keep it as simple as possible—define how other teams would use it, what you need to do to generalize it, and the strategy for evolving it in the future. You will need input from the project teams to accomplish this; otherwise, your assumptions may be incorrect, and you risk wasting resources.

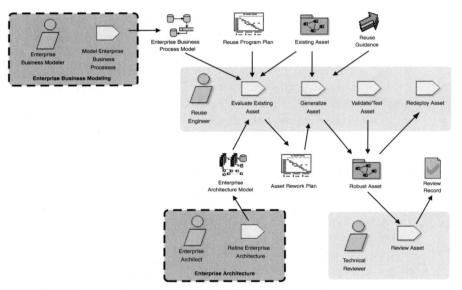

FIGURE 10-4   *Harvest Existing Asset workflow diagram.*

Generalizing an asset requires great skill. The reuse engineer needs to be familiar with not only the technology or technique behind the asset but also with how it will potentially be used in practice. Part of generalization is ensuring that it conforms to appropriate guidance (see "Support Project Teams" later in this chapter) and making it easy to understand by its intended audience. You also want to validate the asset. You'll need to unit-test code-based assets and review templates and non-code artifacts with their target audiences. Concise overview documentation is important, but far more important are one or two good examples showing how to use the robust artifact properly. In the case of code, your unit tests may be sufficient. For templates, you should capture an actual example of the document for which it is a template (for example, to support a use case template, you should harvest one or two well-written use-cases from a project team).

There are four basic harvesting strategies you can follow:

- **Harvest in progress:** You generalize an asset developed by a team before it has been released by working closely with the team; a common strategy is for the reuse engineers to take temporary ownership of the asset, generalize it, and then do the work required to redeploy it within the project. Make it as easy as possible for the project team— you may even decide to implement a few of the requirements they haven't gotten to yet to make generalization of their work more palatable. The advantage with this approach is that you know that there is at least one customer (the original team). The primary disadvantages are that it takes longer to develop a reusable asset than it does a single-use asset and that you risk slowing the project team down (the reuse engineers need to be actively involved to counteract this challenge).

- **Harvest at project end:** You wait until the team has finished building the asset, and then you generalize and perhaps even redeploy it afterwards. With this approach, you don't risk getting in the way of the team. However, you risk generalizing an asset that nobody else can take advantage of, thereby wasting valuable resources. In this situation, the original team has already deployed their system, so you're not doing much for them, and therefore you might be creating a "reuseless" artifact that simply sits on the shelf gathering dust.

- **Harvest a legacy asset:** Ulrich (2002) describes a range of techniques for transforming legacy assets into robust and potentially reusable assets. In addition to reworking/generalizing the asset, you can also wrap access to it using several technologies: application programming interfaces (APIs) written in Java or C, Common Object Request Broker Architecture (CORBA) interface definition language (IDL), or even something as mundane as screen-scraping software, which simulates keystrokes that are submitted to the user interface (UI) of the legacy asset. APIs perform well, but they are language-dependent. CORBA IDL is language-independent, but there is additional overhead with CORBA, which degrades performance when compared to APIs. Screen scraping is usually the last option you consider because it's very fragile—any change to the UI will potentially break your wrapper.

- **Harvest for a new project:** You wait until a project team needs an asset previously developed by another team and then decide to either reuse it as-is or to generalize the asset. The advantage of this approach is that you now have two clear customers for the asset, the original team and the new team. The primary disadvantages are that the original developers may not be available to work with the reuse engineers to generalize the asset and that the original team likely won't retrofit the new version of the asset into their system.

It is obviously easier to harvest high-quality assets than poor-quality ones. We suggest that all development teams follow good development practices such as building high-quality assets, refactoring assets as needed to keep them of high quality (Fowler 1999; Ambler 2003b), and following the appropriate development standards.

Obtain External Asset

A significant number of assets developed outside of your organization may be available to you. Years ago, our advice would have been to "buy before you build," but with the rise of open-source software (OSS) and other forms of free software, our advice is now "download and evaluate before you buy, and buy before you build." Figure 10-5 depicts the workflow details for obtaining external assets. As you can see, much of the effort is similar to harvesting an existing asset because you're likely to find that you need to tailor the external asset to meet your exact needs.

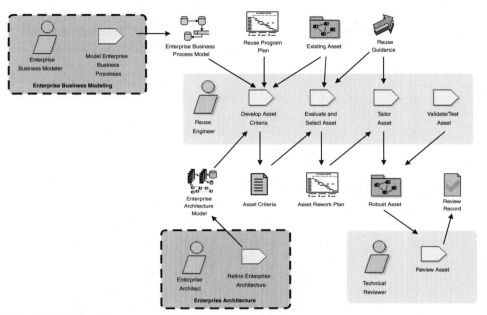

FIGURE 10-5 *Obtain External Asset workflow diagram.*

You need a "shopping list" of requirements against which to assess candidate assets. For example, if you're searching for a persistence framework, you'll discover that you have many options to choose from (visit `www.ambysoft.com/persistenceLayer.html` for a list), some of which will meet your needs and some of which won't. Without these requirements, you run the risk of being unable to determine which candidate assets meet your needs. We've seen searches that should have taken hours or days last for months because the people evaluating the candidates kept getting distracted by "really cool" features that they didn't even need.

You should consider several sources of external assets:

- **Open-source software (OSS):** Open-source projects are a significant source of reusable assets because people collaborate to improve the original software, to adapt it for different environments, to fix bugs in it, and then to share their modifications with the rest of the world. A great place to start is OpenSource.org (`www.opensource.org`), a nonprofit organization dedicated to supporting and evolving the open-source movement. CollabNet (`www.collab.net`) is an organization that provides tools and services based on open-source tools and principles, and SourceForge (`www.sourceforge.net`) is a free open-source hosting service. Organizations that do decide to reuse existing open-source software should be prepared to share any changes they make by submitting them back to the project—open-source is a give-and-take proposition, not just take. It's important to check with your legal department to verify your corporate policy regarding OSS.

- **Other freeware:** With a quick web search, you may find a wide variety of software, templates, and even development standards available for free use.

- **Commercial off-the-shelf (COTS) products:** A wide selection of products is available for purchase, ranging from class libraries such as Rogue Wave's LEIF (`www.roguewave.com`) to development frameworks such as DeKlarit (`www.deklarit.com`) or even full-fledged applications such as Oracle Financials (`www.oracle.com`).

When you adopt an external asset for use within your organization, you need to tailor it for use within your environment. Some of that effort may be reworking the source of the asset—be it code or documentation—although if you do that, you will have potential versioning issues when the vendor releases an update. You will want to create installation scripts that work within your environment, examples of how to work with the asset, and relevant overview documentation. This is in addition to a full regression test suite—if developers don't trust an asset, they won't reuse it (McClure 1997). An important goal of the tailoring effort is to make it as easy as possible to reuse an asset.

Versioning is one challenge of reusing external assets. This is seldom a problem at first, but over time, you will need a strategy for adopting new versions of external assets (this is part of your asset evolution strategy; see the section "Plan Reuse Program" in this chapter). More important is what you do when the vendor no longer supports the asset (or, in the case of OSS, if the project team dissipates). You could decide to purchase the product from the vendor (or restart the OSS project) and thereby incur the costs of maintaining the asset, accept the fact that the asset has stabilized, wrap the asset in your own specific implementation and evolve your wrapper accordingly, or redevelop the asset from scratch.

TIP	**Build a Reuse-Friendly Culture**

An organization that recognizes that it is honorable to reuse the work of others when appropriate, disgraceful to develop something that could have been found elsewhere, and virtuous to consider the needs of others by generalizing appropriately exhibits a reuse-friendly culture. Organizations with a reuse-friendly culture recognize that reuse is a cross-system, enterprise-wide effort based on cooperation and teamwork.

Develop Asset

Figure 10-6 depicts the workflow details for developing a robust asset for reuse. Our advice is rarely, if ever, to start building an asset specifically to be reusable because you run the risk of building something you don't need. How many projects have you seen where the team spent the first six months building the infrastructure that they "required" for the rest of the project, only to see the project get canceled before delivery? How many times have you seen a potentially reusable asset be built but never actually be used in practice? How many times have you seen an asset be built and then be reused, only to discover that the reuse consumers needed only a small portion of that asset? The bottom line is that when you build something to be reused before you have clear evidence of actual need, you run the risk of wasting resources by overbuilding. In the vast majority of cases, you are better advised to build something for specific use and then generalize it for reuse when you actually need it (Beck 2000).

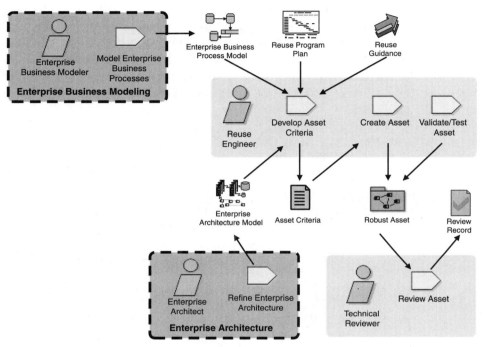

FIGURE 10-6   *Develop Asset workflow diagram.*

When it comes to building something to be reusable, several options are available to you (Basset 1997; McClure 1997):

- **Architected reuse:** You develop assets called out by your enterprise architecture (Chapter 9). As indicated in Figure 10-1, this is the most complicated strategy to accomplish, but it offers the biggest payback because it will support reuse across multiple systems. Only architecturally mature organizations should take this approach.

- **Single-use build:** You highly suspect that a specific asset will be needed by other teams, so you build it with reuse in mind. We suggest that you wait until at least two or more teams want the asset at the same time. If this is not the case, wait until it's appropriate to harvest the asset.

- **Public open source:** You start a normal OSS project hoping that others will do some "free work" for you. Public open source (Weber 2004) should be considered when you believe you have an idea for an asset that others may want, a similar project doesn't already exist (if so, simply reuse the existing OSS asset), and you're willing and legally able to share your work publicly.

- **Internal open source:** You host an OSS project within your private intranet where only members of your organization are involved with the project. The reusable asset would be available to others within your organization, who would evolve it and then share their changes as they see fit. This is a good idea when it is likely that teams will contribute to the project but you're unable to share your work externally. Developers are motivated to contribute to internal OSS projects for similar reasons that they contribute to public OSS projects—the desire to work on a project that interests them, the internal recognition of contributing to the project, and the potential to make contacts that in turn lead to a new job (in this case a position on a new team).

Evolve Asset

An often-overlooked issue in reuse programs is how you'll evolve your robust assets over time. When an asset is available for reuse, you will discover that you need to evolve it to meet new requirements, to fix bugs, or simply to port it to new platform versions. You need to consider three fundamental issues (Jacobson, Griss, and Jonsson 1997; McClure 1997):

- **Ownership:** Who owns a reused asset? The original team that built/bought it? The reuse team? The reuse consumer(s)? Ownership will help determine who is responsible for evolving the asset. We suggest a single owner, either the reuse team or the original team, to keep things simple. Whoever owns the asset requires the resources, including both funding and time, to evolve and redeploy the asset.

- **Configuration management:** Two basic strategies are available to you: insist that a single version of an asset be deployed into production, or allow multiple versions to be deployed. The first strategy requires that all systems be retested, potentially updated, and then redeployed whenever a new version of an asset is created. Allowing multiple copies in production increases both your support and maintenance costs; however, it also motivates you to develop a strategy for removing older versions of an asset from production. One way to do so is to simply give an older version a "shelf date" just as grocers put shelf dates on perishable food items, the implication being that after an asset's shelf date has expired, the reuse team will no longer support it. Ideally systems should be updated to use newer versions, but realistically this won't happen until the team is motivated to do so, likely when they need to deploy a new release of the application that fulfills new requirements.

- **Change management:** The owners of an asset must put a change management process in place to accept defect reports and new-feature requests that are applicable to the asset. We suggest that you simply extend your existing Configuration and Change Management discipline practices (IBM 2004) to do so.

TIP   **Reduce Coupling to Improve Evolution**

Assets that are loosely coupled to whatever is reusing them are easier to evolve because there is less likelihood that you'll break something. For example, if a system reuses an existing web service in a "black box" manner, you should be able to change the internals of the service without affecting the system as long as the service's interface remains the same. If a system reuses a component in a "white box" manner, which takes advantage of the internal workings of the component, a change to that component is much more likely to require changes to the system reusing it.

Publish Asset

After you have obtained a robust asset, you need to make it available to reuse consumers. If your robust assets are hard to find, they likely won't be reused. As Figure 10-7 shows, the Reuse Registrar is responsible for maintaining and supporting your reuse repository and registers the robust asset into your repository. The role of the Reuse Registrar is typically filled by a senior staff member such as the reuse manager, reuse engineer, enterprise architect, or project architect. Your reuse repository could take several forms, such as a shared directory, a version-control tool, or a full-fledged reuse repository tool. Tools are discussed in greater detail later in this chapter. Your registration procedure will vary depending on the tool; our advice is to keep it as simple as possible.

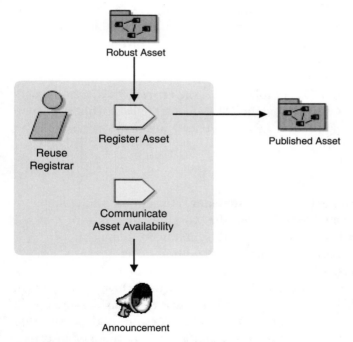

FIGURE 10-7   *Publish Asset workflow diagram.*

After the robust asset is registered, the next step is to communicate, and even actively market, its availability—it isn't enough to simply be able to search for assets. This can be done via mailing lists or web pages, although our experience is that word of mouth from successful project teams using the asset is often the key to your success. Just as some things get done through "official channels" and some get done through your informal network of contacts, sometimes you find reusable assets by looking in the repository and sometimes you get them from your friends. Your reuse engineers should become the people everyone trusts.

Retire Asset

One of the activities of a reuse registrar is to retire older versions of assets. As newer versions of assets are published into your reuse repository, you must decide whether older versions should be removed, because you can't support everything. The retirement of a reusable asset can be as simple as assigning it a "shelf date," after which your team will no longer support it. Anyone who continues working with the older version after this date is on their own because the reuse team can only do so much. The retirement of an asset can also be as complicated as the retirement of a full-fledged system (see Chapter 5, "The Retirement Phase"). This is particularly true of large-scale assets such as frameworks or common application architectures.

Support Project Teams

The primary goal of your reuse team is to support and enhance reuse within your organization, the workflow diagram for which is depicted in Figure 10-8. To do this, you want to make it as easy as possible to reuse the robust assets within your reuse repository. A critical success factor is to be flexible; remember that each reuse consumer has his or her own unique needs. A Java developer will be interested in Java code and frameworks, a business analyst in documentation templates and existing domain models, an architect in candidate architectures, and a project manager in project plan templates.

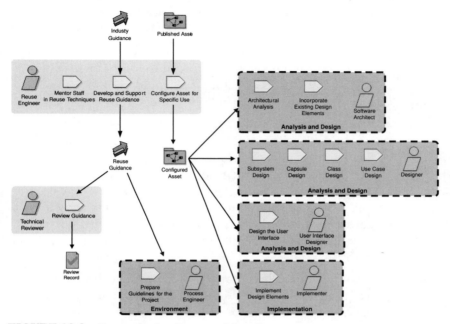

FIGURE 10-8 *Support Project Teams workflow diagram.*

An important part of a reuse engineer's job is to work with project teams to modify an asset so that they can reuse it effectively (Krueger 1992). Ideally this modification is nothing more than configuring the asset properly, as shown in Figure 10-8. However, sometimes the asset needs to be evolved to meet the needs of the team, which is the goal of the Evolve Asset activity (see the section "Evolve Asset" earlier in this chapter).

There are several techniques for effectively supporting reuse within your organization:

- **Foster communities:** Reuse happens within communities of people who trust each other. If you don't trust the people who created an asset, you're less likely to reuse it. Your reuse team can foster various communities within your organization by helping people with similar needs find each other, by helping people find relevant assets and then putting them in touch with the creators in the hope that they will collaborate to use and even evolve the asset, or simply by looking for opportunities to share success.

- **Adopt simple tools:** The easier it is to access and work with your reuse repository, the greater the chance that people will do so.

- **Adopt simple procedures:** We've seen reuse efforts fail miserably because people were forced to follow an overly bureaucratic process before they could even look at an asset, let alone reuse it in their project.

- **Provide effective guidance:** As with the other enterprise management disciplines, there is a need to develop and then support effective standards and guidelines (guidance). In this case, your reuse group should provide guidance that describes how to access your reuse repository, how to find assets, how to submit ideas/requests for assets, how to get support, and the qualities that an asset must possess to be considered suitable for submission into the reuse repository.

- **Communicate:** Whenever a project team visibly benefits from reuse, such as by reducing their schedule and/or development costs, trumpet this success. It will encourage other teams to consider reuse and make the successful team proud of reusing assets, increasing the chance that they'll do so again.

- **Reward a reuse mindset:** To get your reuse program started, you should consider publicly rewarding effective reuse practices, in particular rewarding people who have adopted a "reuse mind-set." The best reward programs that we've seen have been very simple, such as giving someone a bag of candy or a "reuse expert" stuffed animal. Rewards that are fun, equitable, and public are far more effective than private monetary rewards. IT professionals are often more motivated by the recognition of their peers (hence the need for a public and equitable reward) than by cash bonuses (DeMarco and Lister 1999). You should remove the reward program after you've instilled a reuse mind-set within your IT department—your goal has been achieved, and you likely have other issues that you want to address via rewards.

- **Get actively involved:** Reuse engineers need to be active members of project teams, acting as internal consultants to help people reuse existing assets, mentoring people to create high-quality assets, or helping people generalize their existing assets for potential reuse. Avoid the "ivory tower" approach of handing down orders from above.

- **Support the reuse repository:** You'll need to demonstrate your reuse repository to project teams, hold short training courses (which can be as simple as a brown bag lunch session) for the tool if it's very sophisticated, and even write a user guide if necessary.

Measure Reuse Program

When you put your reuse program in place, you define your goals for it, such as improving quality, reducing cost, and/or reducing time to market. It's very easy to set these grandiose goals, but it's not so easy to prove that you've achieved them in practice—and any good senior management team will certainly want evidence that their investment in your reuse program is effective. Your team will also want to collect metrics to determine how effective their efforts are so that they can redirect their energies accordingly.

To measure your reuse program accurately, you will need to either gather or estimate fundamental values such as the time it takes to build something. You'll also need to know the fully loaded charge-out rates for project developers and reuse engineers (some organizations use different rates; many use the same one). A fully loaded charge-out rate for a role includes the average cost of salaries, benefits, and appropriate overhead such as the cost of office space. For the following examples, we'll assume charge-out rates of $85 per work hour for developers and $110 per hour for reuse engineers (reuse engineers are often paid more because of their greater experience and productivity). We suggest that you consider collecting the following metrics:

- **Net hours saved (asset metric):** The net hours saved is the estimated time to build the asset for single usage minus the time it takes to reuse the robust asset (you need to find it, learn about it, deploy it, and so on). For example, it would take 20 hours to develop database access code for an application but 7 hours to install and learn your corporate standard persistence framework. Therefore, the net hours saved is 13 (20 − 7) for this project team.

- **Base asset cost (asset metric):** This is the cost to obtain a robust asset and make it available within your repository. It is calculated by multiplying the time required by the full charge-out rate for reuse engineers. For example, an OSS persistence framework was selected (12 hours), tailored for your environment (30 hours), and published (1 hour), for a total of 43 hours. Therefore, the base asset cost is $4,730 (43 * $110).

- **Net asset benefit (asset metric):** This is the summary of the net hours saved across all instances of reuse minus the base asset cost. For example, the persistence framework is reused by four project teams for a total savings of 147 hours (62 + 24 + 32 + 29). It's important to remember that the net benefit will be different each time an asset is reused because each time the asset is applied differently. If your base asset cost is $4,730, your net asset benefit is $7,765 (147 * $85 − $4,730). This is a critical metric because it enables you to identify which robust assets provide value for your organization.

- **Total benefit (program metric):** This is the total benefit of your reuse program. It is calculated by summarizing the net asset benefits for all robust assets obtained for potential reuse. For example, 7 project teams reused a total of 16 assets between them (some assets were reused by several teams) for a total of 13,500 net hours saved. Twenty-four robust assets were developed, and not all of the assets have been reused yet, for a total of 7,200 hours. Therefore, the total benefit is $355,500 ((13,500 * $85) − (7,200 * $110)). This metric is clearly important to your success because it is one that senior management should be interested in (McClure 1997).

The challenge with the metrics listed here, particularly if you insist on exact measurements, is that it is very difficult to gather the base information. For example, it is quite easy to measure how many times an asset is downloaded (your reuse repository should automatically gather that), but it is very difficult to determine how many times the asset is actually reused in practice. A persistence framework could have been downloaded 45 times but have been reused only 7 times—the only way you know this is to hope that people will tell you they're reusing the asset (good luck), wait for a support call (but some people will not require support), or ask your reuse engineers to report the assets they see being reused by the teams they support. You could even combine these figures, assuming you could account for overlaps, to estimate how much an asset is being reused. This figure is important because, all things being equal, you will want to invest more resources in supporting and evolving popular assets.

It is crucial that you do not make metric collection onerous for the people involved with collecting them. Otherwise, you run the risk that invalid information will be reported or, worse yet, that people will give up on your reuse program because you've made it too annoying—and counterproductive—to reuse things. If the cost of measuring the metric is greater than the value of the metric, why measure it?

TIP **Under-Promise, Over-Deliver**
The easiest way to fail is to tell senior management that your reuse program will result in an X% overall cost reduction in software development and then deliver only a portion of that. A 7% cost reduction is a great success when you promised only 5% but a failure if you promised 10%.

CASE STUDIES

This section summarizes three case studies, one where the reuse program was touted as a success but in practice was a relative failure, one that was very successful because it was driven by the desire for a common architecture, and one that was a grassroots success in spite of questionable decisions by senior management.

Quantity Over Quality

Telecom Co. invested heavily in a reuse program by harvesting and sometimes building a large number of potentially reusable assets, which they made available to developers in their home-built reuse repository. They even won an industry award for their reuse program; the primary reason for the reward was the fact that they had over 100 assets available to developers. This looked great on the surface, but in reality, developers were actually reusing less than 10% of the assets; the other 90%+ proved reuseless in practice. Presented with these metrics, Telecom Co. purged many assets from their repository and put an asset evaluation process in place to ensure that they supported high-quality items that people actually wanted to reuse. We cannot say this enough—it is very difficult to succeed at reuse.

Architected Reuse via Service Domains

One of our clients, Finance Co., decided to take an architected approach to reuse with web service-based technologies. Their enterprise architecture model was high-level, identifying reusable service domains (packages of related web services), which made it easy for potential reuse consumers to locate web services. When a development team needed a service, they would first look to see if it was available, and, if so, they would reuse it. When the service wasn't yet available, they would either develop it for their specific needs, or if it was potentially reusable, they would develop it to be more generic and add it into the appropriate service domain. This approach allowed Finance Co. to build a large base of assets over time on an as-needed basis, assets that were clearly needed by development teams. The only additional cost was the extra coordination overhead of assessing whether a newly developed service belonged in a service domain and then the minor update to the enterprise architecture model (a collection of web pages).

Grassroots Success

Several years ago, two of the authors worked on a reuse team whose goal was to develop and support Java frameworks throughout an IT department with 120 to 140 Java developers. The team started with three senior Java developers who developed a Java architectural vision to help identify where we needed to invest our time. Unfortunately we clashed with the enterprise architecture group, which was composed of mainframe experts with little knowledge of object-oriented development, let alone Java. Their architectural vision at the time didn't include Java (although they reversed direction six months later), and in the end they convinced senior management to cut the funding for our fledgling reuse team.

We were then asked to become the senior developers and mentors on a 20-person team developing a mission-critical application in Java, the largest project within the company. As we built the application, we invested the time to develop the portions of the reusable frameworks that we had identified previously that our application needed. In parallel we made these frameworks available to other Java teams by placing them in a shared folder on the network. These other Java teams, usually with fewer than five people, in turn either suggested or made improvements to our code. We also made the Java coding guidelines and documentation templates that we used on the project available to anyone who wanted them, and acted on any feedback we received. Our team quickly became the "go-to guys" for reusable Java stuff, and a little over a year later, senior management reinstated official funding for our team and publicly recognized the valuable work we had been doing.

TIMING

Your planning efforts will occur in parallel with or slightly after your initial enterprise architecture (see Chapter 9) and portfolio management (see Chapter 8) efforts. The remaining activities will occur on an ongoing basis throughout the lifetime of your organization (assuming that your strategic reuse efforts are a success).

From the viewpoint of a development project, during the Inception phase you will support the project team by helping them find templates for the artifacts they are creating as well as existing models or other relevant artifacts they can leverage. During the Elaboration phase, reuse engineers will work with the team to identify potential frameworks, components, or services they can reuse in their project architecture. In the Construction phase, the reuse engineers will help the team reuse existing assets or harvest project-specific assets. During the Transition phase, the team may work with reuse engineers to harvest assets they built earlier in the project.

ANTI-PATTERNS

Over the years we've seen the reuse efforts of several organizations run into trouble because they inadvertently adopted one or more of the following anti-patterns (Ambler 1998c):

- **Reuseless Artifact:** An artifact that is believed to be reusable, often because it is Declared Reusable, but in practice it is not reused by anyone. The solution is to have someone other than the original developer review reuseless artifacts to determine whether they are potentially reusable and then make any required changes.

- **Declared Reusable (a.k.a. Build It and They Will Come):** This reflects the belief that something is reusable simply because you state that it is. Although this approach does engender some reuse, the typical result is a collection of low-grade Reuseless Artifacts that nobody is actually interested in. Reuse is about quality, not quantity. The reality is that you know that something is reusable only after it's been reused.

- **NIH Syndrome Excuse:** Developers of a Reuseless Artifact often claim that others don't reuse it because those developers didn't create it themselves, which is the "not invented here" (NIH) syndrome. Professional developers constantly seek to reuse the work of others because it enables them to work on the domain-specific portions of their own applications (Meyer 1997). Our experience is that professional developers will readily reuse the work of others as long as it meets their needs, is of high quality, works, is well documented, and is easy to understand.

- **Unique Organization:** Many people like to think that their situation is radically different from everyone else's—that somehow they're unique and therefore need to build everything from scratch. The result is that these organizations do not benefit from reuse and lose productivity. The solution is to recognize that you're not unique and that you're working on the same collection of technologies as thousands of other organizations. Furthermore, you're addressing the same fundamental business needs as every other organization (accounting, human resources, marketing, and other departments really don't change between organizations). As you saw in Table 10-1, there is a wide range of opportunities for reuse.

■ **Reuse Comes Free:** The belief that you don't need to work hard to achieve significant levels of reuse. As you've seen in this chapter, the fact is that you need to invest heavily to make reuse a reality. You need to dedicate resources to develop reusable assets.

■ **Only-Code Reuse:** The idea that you can reuse only code. As you saw in Figure 10-1, you can reuse a wide variety of artifacts throughout the entire software lifecycle, not just source code during programming.

■ **Technology-Driven Reuse:** The idea that the adoption of a particular technology, such as objects or components, will drive reuse within your organization. Yes, some technologies, when used properly, can engender higher levels of reuse; for example, the object paradigm offers more potential mechanisms for reuse than the component paradigm, which in turn offers more than the structured paradigm. However, an item will be reused because it is of high quality, not simply because it is written in Java or because it implements a component interface.

■ **Repository-Driven Reuse:** The belief that the installation of a reuse repository, a mechanism that stores and automates management of potentially reusable items, will drive reuse within your organization. Many organizations achieve significant reuse simply by maintaining a directory structure of reusable artifacts, but people often find these artifacts through word of mouth, not through a fancy search mechanism. Yes, a reuse repository does provide many useful features such as a search facility and configuration management, but these features only support reuse; they don't guarantee it.

■ **Production Before Consumption:** Developers who try to build reusable artifacts without significant experience reusing the work of others typically develop Reuseless Artifacts. Developers who have extensively reused the work of others have seen a wide range of items, and as a result, they know what separates the robust assets from the reuseless ones.

- **Project-Driven Reuse:** The limiting of generalization decisions to the scope of a single project. A single project may be able to obtain some level of reuse on its own, but the reality is that reuse is actually a multi-project effort. Generalizing a date routine, a use-case template, or a user-interface design standards document offers little value to the project that created the source item being generalized. The benefits of generalization efforts are often realized by the projects that come later.

TOOLS

The main tool needed to support strategic reuse is a reuse repository. You have three basic options for implementing a reuse repository:

- **Shared directory:** Robust assets are stored in the shared directory accessible to everyone within your IT organization. This works well for very small companies with fewer than 10 IT people, although it suffers from a lack of version control and tracking features. You need excellent communication skills to ensure its success.

- **Version control tool:** A better option is to set up a reuse project within your version control tool, such as CVS (www.cvshome.org) or IBM Rational's ClearCase (www.ibm.com). The advantage of this approach is that programmers should already have access to and know how to use the version control tool. There are several disadvantages. First, non-programmers may not have access to the tool, and they might not know how to use it. Remember, non-developers can still reuse templates and artifacts. Second, the tool offers little in the way of metrics tracking or search capabilities.

- **Reuse repository tool:** A few reuse repository tools are available within the marketplace; the leader is Flashline (www.flashline.com), although Logidex (www.logiclibrary.com) is also a contender. The primary advantages of reuse repository tools are that they make it easy for reuse consumers to find assets, they make it easy for people to submit assets into the repository (there should be some sort of validation effort to ensure quality), and they provide mechanisms to collect selected metrics. The primary disadvantage of reuse repositories is that you have an extra tool to purchase, maintain, and support within your organization.

RELATION TO OTHER DISCIPLINES

All disciplines can benefit from reuse, as you see in the wide range of opportunities depicted in Figure 10-1 (for example, you can always reuse a documentation template). Specifically, the strategic reuse discipline is directly related to other disciplines in the following manner:

- **Enterprise Architecture:** The enterprise architecture helps identify whether potential assets fit into your architectural vision.

- **Enterprise Business Modeling:** The enterprise business process model provides insight into whether and how a robust asset will be potentially reused by other applications.

- **Analysis and Design:** The modeling efforts of your project teams will help identify potential opportunities for reuse within an individual project. Robust assets should similarly be considered for reuse during the modeling efforts of individual project teams. The reuse engineers will mentor software architects and designers in reuse techniques.

- **Implementation:** Implementers will reuse existing assets and work with reuse engineers to make their own assets reusable. The reuse engineers will mentor implementers in reuse techniques. Developers should actively strive to reuse technology-based assets such as source code, framework, services, components, and so on.

- **Configuration and Change Management:** As your robust assets evolve, they must be put under configuration management control. Ideally your reuse repository will integrate seamlessly with your configuration management tool(s).

- **Portfolio Management:** The list of upcoming projects can be used both to determine the likelihood that an asset will be needed and to identify the teams that reuse engineers may want to focus on supporting.

SUMMARY

It is possible to reuse a wide range of assets—from source code to templates to frameworks to entire architectures—but to succeed, you need to look beyond the scope of a single project. The Strategic Reuse discipline describes how to increase the levels of reuse with EUP projects by taking a cross-system approach. To succeed, you need to plan for, operate, and monitor a reuse program within your organization. There are several ways to obtain robust assets for potential reuse, including harvesting internal assets, downloading or purchasing external assets, and developing assets from scratch. Your reuse efforts must be supported; the easier you make it to reuse things, the greater the chance that people will do so. You should also measure the success of your efforts to ensure continual funding and management support for your project.

Suggested Reading

Several good books are pertinent to strategic reuse:

Software Reuse (Jacobson, Griss, and Jonsson 1997) describes an architecture-based approach to reuse.

Confessions of a Used Program Salesman (Tracz 1995) provides significant insights into the realities of setting up a reuse program within an organization.

Software Reuse Techniques (McClure 1997) is a great resource for anyone wanting to implement an effective approach to reuse within their organization.

Legacy Systems: Transformation Strategies (Ulrich 2002) describes real-world approaches to transforming legacy assets into reusable assets.

Chapter 11

The People Management Discipline

Reader ROI

- Planning for staffing requires a partnership—and flexibility—between your IT and human resources (HR) organizations.

- Create a balance of full-time employees and contractors on different projects according to your current specific needs.

- Career guidance depends on the IT organization, HR, and individuals working together to make it happen.

- Plan for the succession of employees—or get stuck with a leaderless organization and/or systems that cannot be maintained in the future.

The goals of the People Management discipline are to manage and improve the effectiveness of individuals within your information technology (IT) organization. Today organizations are competing on two different fronts—one for their products or services and to hire and retrain talented personnel (Hefley, Curtis, and Miller 2001). There is far more to managing software development efforts than the technical tasks of creating and evolving project plans and schedules. You need to manage your staff, help them grow, and mediate their interactions with others. This discipline describes the process of organizing, monitoring, educating, coaching, and motivating people to ensure that they work together well and successfully contribute to projects within your organization.

Your organization will apply the activities contained within this discipline in different ways, but the purpose of this discipline is to stress how people within the IT industry should be managed effectively.

WORKFLOW

People management is critical to the success of all aspects of your enterprise. In this chapter, our focus is on the issues pertaining to your IT staff. Our experience is that you need HR strategies that reflect the unique nature of the IT community. We recommend that the HR and IT teams work closely together on implementing concepts presented in the People Management discipline. The workflow for the People Management discipline is shown in Figure 11-1.

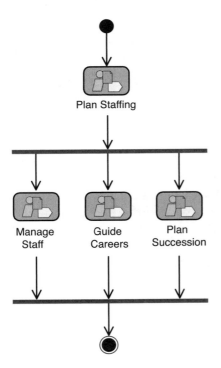

FIGURE 11-1 *People Management discipline workflow.*

Plan Staffing

It is important to assess the needs of the business from an enterprise standpoint when planning the staffing for your IT department. During the planning process, remember that staffing comes down to three points: Get the right people, make them happy so they do not want to leave, and turn them loose (DeMarco and Lister 1999). Figure 11-2 depicts the planning process for staffing in the People Management discipline. While not directly involved in the staffing of individual projects within the portfolio, the portfolio manager can help recommend aligning required resources across the various programs and projects in order to help maximize returns for the enterprise.

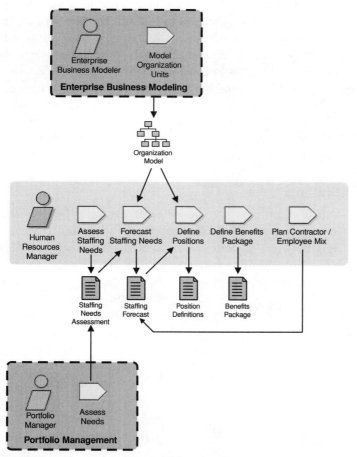

FIGURE 11-2 *Plan Staffing workflow detail.*

You need to recognize that IT people are different from other employees—they tend to be highly specialized (although the best ones are actually generalizing specialists; see Chapter 3) and relatively mobile (they can easily leave your organization for better opportunities). Because many IT professionals are focused on technical work and aren't interested in becoming managers, you need a technical career track in addition to a management career track. The result is that you may have senior developers who have been with you for a few years; they may have benefits equivalent to a vice president who has been with you for decades.

If your organization is considering outsourcing, do the planning up front and weigh the benefits against the risks. Many organizations adopt prescriptive processes such as the RUP or the EUP because they intend to outsource portions of their development efforts at a later date. Their first step is to put an effective process in place that involves well-defined hand-offs, because at some point, someone other than your internal staff may be performing the various tasks. The second step is to outsource portions of the development effort, typically the Elaboration and Construction phases, although the Transition phase can easily be outsourced if Production is too. Because the people you intend to replace via outsourcing will likely be upset by this decision, you may need to keep your intention to outsource confidential.

Diversify Staffing

When it comes to staffing, you need a wide range of people. For example, when recruiting IT professionals, two different skill sets are often sought—both IT and business skills. Recent graduates are likely to be more familiar with modern technologies and more willing to work longer hours. However, new employees often leave after a few years, looking for better opportunities (smart organizations provide those opportunities and benefit from a higher retention rate). Experienced employees are probably more knowledgeable within your particular domain and are probably willing to stay with your organization; however, their skills may be outdated, and they tend to be in an industry with rapid changes that may render existing skills obsolete (Agarwal and Ferratt 2002). Technically educated people often have the hard-core programming skills but have little appreciation for the softer skills required to be successful analysts or managers, whereas someone with a bachelor of arts may have the requisite people skills but may struggle with technical tasks.

A mix that we've seen that works well is to have one or possibly two senior people on each team and a mix of inexperienced and mid-experienced people. The senior people provide the technical leadership as well as guidance on the business aspects of the position.

Manage Staff

Your HR department must assist in managing the staff much like any other department within your organization. Some IT organizations try to form self-contained units, where they basically ignore any formal HR input. This is not a good idea; remember that the HR specialists bring many areas of expertise to the process, including HR legal risks, skills tracking (and assessment), and other trends—such as the use of contractors or consultants—that can help reduce IT uncertainty (Schwarzkopf et al. 2004). However, many HR departments struggle with dealing with IT staff, so you need to be prepared to work with them. Figure 11-3 depicts the fundamental activities required to manage your IT staff.

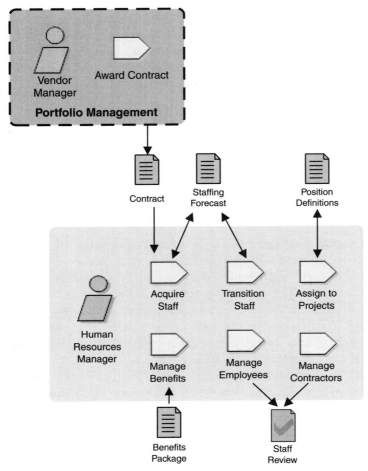

FIGURE 11-3 *Manage Staff workflow detail.*

The staff can include a mix of both contractors and full-time employees. Why do organizations need to utilize contractors? There are several possible reasons. The most obvious is staff augmentation—sometimes you simply cannot hire people fast enough to fulfill your needs. Contractors become a short-term solution to staffing problems. You may also not have a consistent enough need to justify hiring full-time people. If you have only an occasional need for people, hiring contractors may be more economical for you. Using external contractors and consultants to smooth the fluctuations in staffing needs is one way that organizations deal with this issue (Schwarzkopf et. al. 2004). Another reason is to acquire a particular skill set. One of the best ways to get the most for your money from a contractor is to assign him or her to transfer skills to employees by means of mentoring (see Chapter 3). By doing this, you can grow the skills of the full-time employees, which helps them—and your organization—grow professionally.

The downside of contracting is that you can become dependent on contractors. How do you break this dependence? One approach is to engage contractors only when absolutely necessary and where one (or more) contractor can help transfer the specialized skills to a full-time employee. Set specific goals for contractors—for example, to transfer knowledge instead of just plugging them into the organization. Manage them on these goals and ensure that you are not becoming dependent on them.

The EUP is evolutionary (iterative and incremental) in nature, a far cry from the serial processes of the past. If you decide to implement parts of the EUP, it would be helpful for people to have a new set of skills; a generalizing specialist (Ambler 2003b) is useful in this situation. A generalizing specialist is someone who is very good in one or two IT specialties, such as domain modeling or project management, and who also has a good understanding of the entire IT lifecycle and hopefully of your business domain as well. Here are some advantages of using generalizing specialists:

- **Less documentation:** A generalizing specialist will write less documentation than a specialist because she has a greater range of options available—she can record information in the best place possible, which is often the source code.

- **Good overall view:** A generalizing specialist is someone with a good grasp of how everything fits together. As a result, she will typically have a greater understanding and appreciation of what her teammates are working on. She is willing to listen to and work with her teammates because she knows that she probably will learn something new. Specialists, on the other hand, often don't have the background to appreciate what other specialists are doing, often look down on other work, and often aren't as willing to cooperate. Specialists, by their very nature, can become a barrier to communication within your team.

- **Not a "jack-of-all-trades":** A generalizing specialist is more than just a generalist. A generalist is a jack-of-all-trades but master of none, whereas a generalizing specialist is a jack-of-all-trades and master of a few. Big difference. A team of generalists can easily flounder because none of them has the skills to get things done.

As you adopt the EUP, you need to acquire staff with modern skills such as object-oriented programming, Agile Model-Driven Development (AMDD) (Ambler 2002), Test-Driven Development (TDD) (Astels 2003; Beck 2003), and evolutionary database development (Ambler 2003b). Many of your existing staff will be able to learn these modern development skills, but they might require help doing so via training, education, and mentoring (see the next section). However, not everyone will be able to make this transition, nor do they need to—these people can be transitioned into maintenance or operations/support positions.

How do you hire IT professionals effectively? You need to spend enough time planning your interviews (including auditions) so that you can differentiate between the people who talk the great talk and the people who can do the great work. By using behavior-description questions ("Tell me about a time when...") and creating an audition, you can get a glimpse of people at work. These are the two most valuable techniques that seem to work best in practice (Rothman 2004).

TIP	**Don't Track Time Without a Reason**

Don't Track Time Without a Reason
You need to develop an effective time-tracking strategy so you can compare actual costs versus budgeted costs. Time tracking is useful for many reasons—to double-check contractor hours, to track actual expenditures for projects, to see how close estimates turn out to be, and so on. However, it doesn't come without a cost. If people take a half hour out of their workweek to track and report hours, you are asking your people to spend 1.25% of their time on time tracking. In an IT organization of 400 people this is the equivalent of wasting the time of five full-time people.

Part of the process of transitioning people includes the use of project retrospectives at the end of each project (Chapter 13)— whether the project was a success or a complete failure. Feedback can also be obtained during iteration and milestone reviews. Although some organizations tend to use these sessions as an opportunity for negative criticism, we have found it best to stress that they are about improvement opportunities for both the individual and your entire organization.

Guide Careers

The goal of this activity, depicted in Figure 11-4, is to have both the IT and HR departments working together to ensure people on the various teams are being guided along their careers. Although everyone should realize that their own professional career is in their own hands, it is beneficial to your organization to foster growth in its employees.

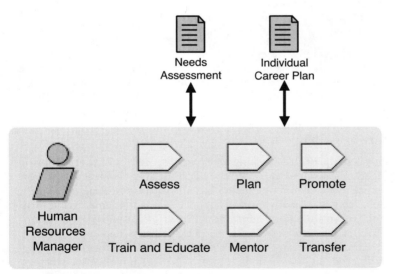

FIGURE 11-4   *Guide Careers workflow detail.*

Table 11-1 summarizes the options to help grow the skill sets of your staff.

TABLE 11-1   *Techniques for Training, Education, and Mentoring*

Technique	Advantages	Disadvantages
Hands-on experience	The employee learns by doing, which is often the best way to learn a new skill, and produces work at the same time.	Inexperienced people learning a new skill are often not very productive when they first apply it.
Training	This focuses on teaching people specific, narrowly focused skills that are often immediately applicable to their current position. Examples of training courses include courses focusing on a particular vendor's implementation of an Enterprise Java Bean (EJB) application server, on Microsoft Windows user interface design, and on working with the new version of a particular vendor's Java integrated development environment (IDE).	Can be costly. This is usually a one-time event that cannot be applied immediately at an expert level within your organization.
Education	This imparts longer-term skills and knowledge that are typically applicable over someone's entire career. Examples include attending conferences, talking with or working with experts, using new tools and techniques, and applying concepts in real life.	Can take a longer time to see any ROI if someone looks only at the numbers and not the other benefits to the enterprise.
Mentoring	This is the process of having an experienced professional impart his or her expertise to others on a hands-on basis. Mentoring is typically used to support both your training and education efforts. Effective mentors must understand the fundamentals of their jobs as well as the skills needed to perform their jobs on a day-to-day basis and be able to transfer those skills to the people they are mentoring. Mentoring can take place at all levels of your organization—from the novice to a C-level executive. The goal is to help people within your organization grow both personally and professionally.	Requires that you bring people on board to perform the mentoring. If it is implemented improperly, your organization may become dependent on mentors if knowledge is not effectively transferred to your staff.

In order to effectively plan for the training, education, and mentoring of your IT staff, you should speak with your IT people to find out what they want to do. Techies usually like to learn new things. You might not be working with the newest technologies, but there's nothing stopping you from trying new techniques such as pair programming (Williams and Kessler 2002) or TDD (Astels 2003; Beck 2003). It's good for the organization, and it builds individual resumes. We know that some organizations worry about investing in their staff because they're afraid that other companies will steal their employees. Do you really want staff that nobody else wants?

As part of promoting career growth for both team members and their leaders, personal goals should be set and reviewed at least annually. This can be as formal as using a tool from a Human Resources Management System (HRMS) to something as simple as a piece of paper to be filed for future review. The goals should include specific target areas such as gaining new experience on the job, receiving training and education, and mentoring goals for the coming year (either acting as a mentor to others or receiving mentorship from another person). If you are thinking about promoting anyone within your IT organization into management, remember that studies have shown that as a manager rises through the ranks, more soft skills (for instance, leadership) are required for that manager to be successful (Bunker, Kram, and Ting 2002).

When people gain new skills, they also need to be rewarded to reflect their greater value to the organization. This does not always need to be monetary. Make books, magazines, and online subscriptions to various reports available. The worst thing you can do is cut your training/conference budget, because this part of the budget is important for the long-term viability of your organization; however, this is often the first thing that gets cut when times are tough.

Motivate people to stretch themselves. This may appear counterintuitive; however, in practice this helps people grow. For example, don't send a Java programmer to JavaOne (`java.sun.com/javaone`), where he will only learn more of the same skills he has. Instead, send him to Software Development Best Practices (`www.sdexpo.com`), where he'll learn a wider range of skills such as domain modeling or interviewing. Similarly, send your business analysts to JavaOne to gain a better understanding of what your developers are doing. In the end, both roles will have a better understanding of what the other has to do on a daily basis, thus improving overall communication within the organization.

> **TIP**   **Utilize Existing Frameworks to Develop Existing Employees**
> For those organizations familiar with the Capability Maturity Model (CMM) (CMM 2004), the People Capability Maturity Model (P-CMM) (SEI 2004c) is now available (version 2) as a framework for assessing the people issues within an organization. Much like the CMM, the P-CMM rates organizations on maturity levels—up to Level 5 (optimization).

Succession Planning

Succession planning is a serious challenge for most of today's organizations. The goal of succession planning is to make sure that your organization is ready for future generations of your IT staff to take over when your current staff is no longer with your organization. This includes both management and key technical staff. Figure 11-5 depicts the activities associated with succession planning.

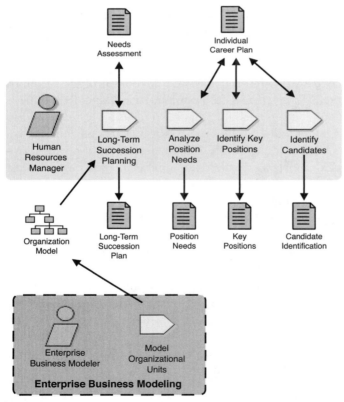

FIGURE 11-5   *Succession Planning workflow detail.*

Your organization needs to do this for key technical and management people. It is probably more important for the technical folks, but this is often ignored. If you are in a position of maintaining and developing COBOL systems on mainframes (and many organizations are), you must recognize that many of the people with these skills will retire within the next decade. This makes room for new thinking. You need to either transition away from those technologies or start transitioning new staff into the appropriate positions. In doing this for either the technical or management positions, one of the key areas that successful organizations focus on during succession planning is the need to keep it flexible. This may be possible only at organizations that have executive-level support for candor and risk-taking (Conger and Fulmer 2003).

TIP   Cover Your Assets (CYA)
Organizations with one or two key personnel often take out what is called "Key Person Life Insurance." This is life insurance taken out by the organization on a key member of your team that will protect the organization in the event that something unfortunate happens to that person. It is not intended as a windfall should someone meet with an accident; instead, it recognizes that someone is a valuable member of the team who would cause harm to the organization in the event of his or her absence.

CASE STUDY

The case study presented here discusses the implications of hiring a contractor to help with a process rollout—and utilizing the contractor as a true mentor in order for the project to succeed.

At a recent HR outsourcing company, one of us was brought in to help with the initial rollout of the RUP and EUP. He was the only one with extensive RUP and EUP expertise on the process team. In order to ensure transfer of knowledge, he worked with the program manager to make sure that he wasn't the only one with specific knowledge about the process. Whenever possible, he engaged the client's employees and worked on specific deliverables and activities on the process rollout with them. This included process tailoring and developing and delivering training.

By the time the contract expired, the client's employees were able to carry on because we planned for it in advance.

TOOLS

There are several excellent sources of tools for managing people. The first thing to remember is to keep it simple—it comes down to people dealing with people. This process may be as simple as utilizing a spreadsheet to track hours (if that is required) or matching training needs to skill sets for the people on your team. However, in larger enterprises, it is valuable to utilize some commercial off-the-shelf (COTS) systems. Some of these include time tracking and training tools such as the following:

- **Intelex Technologies, Inc.:** Intelex, (`www.intelex.com/training`) is a web-based training tracking and management system.

- **PeopleSoft:** The Enterprise Human Capital Management (`www.peoplesoft.nl/corp/en/products/ent/hcm/index.jsp`) suite provides various HR solutions, including assess-design-develop, optimize-track-monitor, plan-attract-onboard, plan-incentive-reward, and workforce performance solutions.

- **Open-source options:** In addition to COTS systems, several viable time-tracking systems are available via open source. Visit `dmoz.org/Computers/Software/Accounting/Time_Tracking` for a list.

ANTI-PATTERNS

Several process anti-patterns pertain to people management:

- **One Strategy to Rule Them All:** Many organizations think that IT people can be managed the same way as non-IT people. Practice shows that this is not the case, generally speaking. The solution is to recognize that you may need a different approach.

- **Management-Only Promotions:** The perception in many organization is that sometimes the only way to earn a lot of money is to become a manager. Unfortunately many technical people are uninterested in management positions and thus are forced to leave the organization if they want to earn more, draining valuable resources from your organization. The solution is to introduce a technical career track.

- **Petered Out:** The Peter Principle (Peter 1993) states that people will be promoted to their level of incompetence. When someone does a good job in a position, he is promoted and eventually reaches a position that he is not good at and becomes stuck there. The end result is that your IT department can promote itself into oblivion. The solution is to recognize that a promotion is not the only way to reward achievement. Do not force a promotion on people who do not want one or who cannot perform in the new position.

TIMING

The timing for the People Management discipline should be continual—annual career management is insufficient. At beginning of each new project, find out what people's goals are and help them achieve them by getting them the required training, education, and mentoring.

Toward the end of the project, find out if they want to do something else within the company, and start helping them transition to a new team—you don't want to lose someone because he thinks he's stuck in one spot. Open and honest communication can yield returns beyond any preset expectations.

RELATION TO OTHER DISCIPLINES

We think an argument can be made that people management hits every discipline because, in reality, it is people who work through all of the disciplines. Specifically, this discipline is related to others as follows:

- **Portfolio Management:** This involves the higher-level planning for using resources effectively throughout the organization.

- **Project Management:** This focuses more on the specific day-to-day project-management–related issues for contractors and employees.

- **Enterprise Business Modeling:** This provides the organizational model used in the plan staffing process.

SUMMARY

The People Management discipline examines how to manage people on IT teams to complete projects successfully. This discipline includes planning for staffing needs, managing the staff, guiding careers, and planning for succession. Although many different approaches to people management exist, this chapter has focused on specific needs within the IT industry. The implication is that IT people are different than others within your organization and should be looked on as such.

Suggested Reading

Here are some excellent resources on people management:

PeopleWare, Second Edition (DeMarco and Lister 1999). This book is considered by many to be the premier book on building productive projects and teams.

Death March, Second Edition (Yourdon 1997). This is a must-read book. Unfortunately, if you are in this situation, you probably do not have time to read it. Make the time. Today.

The Mythical Man-Month: Essays on Software Engineering, Anniversary Edition, Second Edition (Brooks 1995). We consider this to be the source of project-management techniques. It's timeless—it is worth the read even 30 years after the original publication.

Object-Oriented Training, Education, and Mentoring: Retraining Your Staff for Modern-Age Development (Ambler 2001). This white paper examines in greater detail the things an organization should consider when creating a training and education program for its IT staff.

Chapter 12

The Enterprise Administration Discipline

| **Reader ROI** |

- Enterprise administration includes the management of physical assets, information assets, and security for the enterprise.

- Enterprise administrators should work with project teams on a daily basis both to aid their efforts and to ensure compliance with organizational policies.

- Enterprise administrators are responsible for overseeing the build-out of infrastructure assets in accordance with your enterprise architecture.

- Your organizational security management includes physical elements, IT, or a combination of both through convergent technologies.

The goal of the Enterprise Administration discipline is to define how an organization creates, maintains, manages, and deploys physical and informational assets in a secure manner. The goal is not to simply add a new level of bureaucracy, but rather to streamline these activities.

It is easy to see how a bureaucracy could be formed within your organization as you read this chapter. Some people look at enterprise administration as an extension of the Operations and Support discipline (see Chapter 6), but we separate it because its activities cross almost every discipline within the EUP. In particular, this is a fundamental aspect of the advice provided by the Information Technology Infrastructure Library (ITIL) (ITIL 2003). Like any phase or discipline within the EUP, different organizations will apply the activities contained within this discipline in different ways. Do what makes sense in your environment.

There are five roles in this discipline, one abstract and four concrete:

- **Enterprise administrator:** This abstract role is actively involved in managing physical and informational assets along with security and working with project teams. The other four roles in this discipline all inherit from this one.

- **Network administrator:** This person is responsible for managing and supporting the hardware and network for the organization.

- **Facilities administrator:** This person manages facilities for the organization such as buildings, new construction, and undeveloped land.

- **Information administrator:** This person is responsible for managing the information assets of your organization, including data, intellectual property (IP), and licenses.

- **Security administrator:** This person is accountable for physical and informational technology (IT) security.

In many ways, the people filling the various roles of enterprise administrators are the "keepers of the enterprise gates," supporting project teams while at the same time guiding them to ensure that the long-term vision of the enterprise is fulfilled. Successful enterprise administrators do the following:

- **Work closely with enterprise architects:** Enterprise administrators will communicate the constraints imposed by the current environment to the architects. More importantly, the enterprise administrators need to understand the enterprise architecture to ensure that their efforts reflect the long-term direction of the organization.

- **Become generalizing specialists who take an enterprise view:** A generalizing specialist (see Chapter 3) is someone who has one or more specialties (such as data administration) and who understands a wide range of issues pertinent to the enterprise.

- **Are flexible in their approach:** Effective enterprise administrators work in a manner that reflects the project teams they're supporting. If a team works in an agile manner, the enterprise administrator will work that way; if the team is following a traditional serial process, the enterprise administrator will work that way.

- **Recognize that budgeting is a fact of life:** Budgeting takes place at regular intervals for most organizations, so get involved early and do not fight that process.

- **Support project teams:** Successful enterprise administrators focus on things that will make members of the project teams more effective in their jobs—few people refuse a helping hand.

WORKFLOW

The workflow for the Enterprise Administration discipline, depicted in Figure 12-1, includes the management of physical assets, information assets, and security for the enterprise. One of the most important activities within this discipline is working effectively with the project teams to support their efforts while ensuring that the long-term needs of your organization are still met.

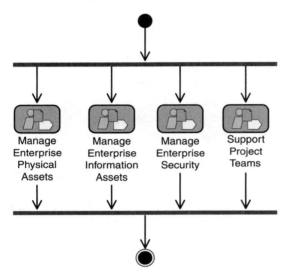

FIGURE 12-1 *Enterprise Administration discipline workflow.*

Manage Enterprise Physical Assets

Figure 12-2 presents the workflow diagram for managing enterprise physical assets within your organization, including hardware, networks, and the computing facilities. In the Zachman Framework (ZF) (see Chapter 3), this effort maps to the Where (Locations) column of the framework.

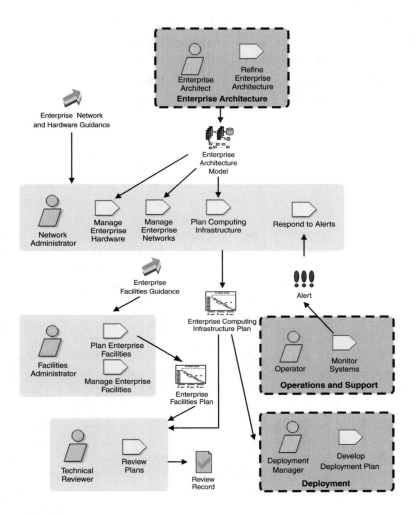

FIGURE 12-2   *Manage Enterprise Physical Assets workflow detail.*

The network administrator is responsible for managing both hardware and networking infrastructures within your organization. This person, if he or she is not someone from the operations and support staff, works closely with these people at all times. The network administrator must keep both the hardware and network plans up-to-date and ensure that information is available and communicated to the various project teams. Network administrators follow the relevant network and hardware guidance (see the "Support Project Teams" section later in this chapter) to ensure that their work reflects the long-term vision captured within your enterprise architecture model (refer to Chapter 9). Here are some critical issues that must be addressed:

- **Defining a standard configuration for hardware within the organization:** Your organization should define standard computer configurations to make purchasing and support easier. These standard configurations get outdated quickly, and our experience is that you need to rethink them once a quarter to take advantage of improved options. It's okay to have different machine configurations. Is it really that difficult to support a desktop machine with a bigger hard drive or more memory than what you were supporting last month? You will also need configurations specific to various roles. For example, developers may need two monitors and high-powered Linux workstations, while your graphic art department needs an Apple Macintosh machine, a single large monitor, and top-of-the-line desktop printers.

- **Financial depreciation of computing hardware:** Your financial department may want you to get more time out of hardware than you can realistically obtain. You might be able to get two years out of a desktop for an IT person, yet in Canada you have to depreciate its useful life over four years for tax purposes. Work with the different teams to come up with creative solutions (such as passing down hardware to other people within your organization) or simply write off the equipment when it's no longer useful (then donate it to worthy charities if appropriate). It is critical that people have adequate computing power—it makes no sense to have a highly paid employee (or contractor) waiting on a comparatively inexpensive computer. Finally, the network administrator needs to work with the enterprise architects to ensure that the long-term computing planning reflects the future architecture for the organization.

- **Computing infrastructure build-out:** It takes time to install or upgrade hardware or your network. In order to meet the future demands of upcoming projects, your network and hardware administrators will plan for and then implement changes to your computing infrastructure in advance of these projects.

- **Hardware and software sourcing:** Your goal is to ensure that your planned infrastructure needs are met with adequate purchasing. Most IT organizations work closely with the purchasing department to ensure that the proper equipment is procured.

Network administrators are involved during the initial stages of a project to help get the team set up with the appropriate hardware, software, and network infrastructure. They will be called on throughout the Construction phase to help the project team with issues such as networking and infrastructure support and establishing a test environment in parallel with a production environment. At the end of the Transition phase, network administrators are involved to ensure smooth deployment into your production environment. During the Production phase (see Chapter 4), they help the operations and support staff with any monitoring situations that arise. Finally, when a system is retired, network administrators are heavily involved in sunsetting aspects of the system that affect the network.

Facilities administrators are responsible for the computing facilities of the organization, including telecom and network infrastructure creation and maintenance (outside the IT world, this can also include buildings or undeveloped land). Much like the network administrator, this person is tertiary, working with the project teams throughout all phases, and helping with any operations and support-monitoring situations. Facilities administrators face the following issues:

- **Timelines and growth:** Facilities take a long time to build, so you need to do long-term capacity planning. If your capacity forecast is wrong, renting or leasing facilities temporarily is an option.

- **Increasing the perception of value:** When working with the project teams, frequent communication and the adoption of a "customer-friendly" orientation is a key to success (IFMA 2004).

- **Workspace planning and build-out:** When a team or department is spread across several locations, even if it's different floors, their effectiveness is greatly reduced. Requiring people to move their workspaces on a regular basis also disrupts the flow of their work. Facilities managers need to balance these two forces when they are performing workspace planning.

Manage Enterprise Information Assets

The information administrator is responsible for managing the information assets—data, intellectual property, and licenses—of your organization. Figure 12-3 depicts the management activities for information assets.

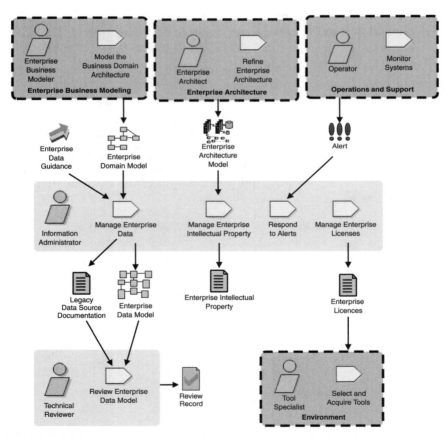

FIGURE 12-3   *Manage Enterprise Information Assets workflow detail.*

The information administrator must deal with the following goals:

- **Data stewardship:** The goal of data stewardship is to ensure that responsibility, accountability, and authority are associated with auditing and reviewing the quality of data (Loshin 2004a). Three basic roles are applicable to data stewardship (Seiner 2000): data definers, who are responsible for the definition, communication, and quality of the data; data creators, who are responsible for the accuracy, quality, and timeliness of data that is captured; and data readers, who are responsible for the integrity of the data usage, confidentiality, and data quality.

- **Effective metadata management:** Process solutions should be considered in information-rich industries, which are especially prone to experiencing metadata-related pain. Metadata repositories generally support both technical and business aspects. Technical metadata is generally for the IT staff and users; business metadata is used by business users within an organization (Borenstein 2004). Enterprise administrators can then use this knowledge to communicate needs to the project teams and get an accurate view of where the organization may need to move in the future. Only maintain the metadata that you need. Many metadata efforts fail because they collect too much data. You should apply the Agile Modeling (AM) principles and practices such as *Model with a Purpose* to ensure that you gather metadata that people can actually use, *Maximize Stakeholder Investment* to ensure that you maintain metadata that provides value to the enterprise, and *Travel Light* to ensure that you maintain just enough metadata and no more (Ambler 2002).

- **Data storage build-out:** Your enterprise architecture model defines, among other things, the data architecture within your organization, including your forecasted data storage needs. Information administrators must ensure that the data storage infrastructure is upgraded in a timely manner to meet these needs.

■ **Support both online transaction processing (OLTP) and business intelligence (BI)/data warehousing:** Information administrators should work with the specific project teams to support both approaches, overviewed in Table 12-1 (Rittman 2004).

■ **Information quality:** Quality of information is a subjective term, and measuring quality is even more onerous. Information valuation is at best misunderstood and at worst an extremely flawed academic exercise (Loshin 2004b). The different types of data stewards (definers, creators, and readers) are responsible for maintaining quality of the information, and because they have different goals, they will provide checks and balances within your environment. The information administrator should work with the project teams to educate them about data quality concepts; these can include concepts such as data types and complexities, data integrity, the usage of keys, how to avoid duplicate rows, normalization, data hierarchies, redundancy, and metadata (Pascal 2000). One way to do this is by describing the transformation of data to knowledge for the enterprise—that is, by specifying how each different steward type can impact this change.

TABLE 12-1   *Differences Between OLTP and Warehousing Data*

Type	Usage	Real-Time Data	Users
Online Transaction Processing (OLTP)	Data that is required to run the organization on a daily basis. This includes business transactions (activities) such as order entry, invoicing, or a record from an online security system.	Yes, because the data is transactional.	Usually created by multiple users (such as help desk users or order entry clerks).
Data Warehousing	Often referred to as business intelligence (BI)—it includes subjects such as reporting (nightly, weekly, quarterly, or other predetermined time periods) and the consolidation of data for research purposes.	No, because this data is used for reporting purposes.	Used by management for short- and long-term planning.

The information administrator is responsible for managing the data within the enterprise. This person is normally involved during all phases. The need for flexibility with project teams here is paramount—the team will need leeway to try different things. The information administrator must ensure that before a system goes into production, all of the information assets are correctly defined and in place, including ensuring that licensing is completed. Effective information administrators recognize that

- **Data is one of many enterprise assets:** Although some people within your organization may claim to "own" all of the data, in reality many people have input into this vital enterprise asset. You must work with the project teams to make this point clear. In the ZF (see Chapter 3), enterprise data maps into the What (Structure) column of the framework.

- **Data is only one of many important aspects of an application:** Too many organizations allow the data tail to wag the application development dog. The reality is that data is one of many important issues (this is the first philosophy of the Agile Data method (Ambler 2003b)), and it often isn't the primary one (regardless of what data professionals may think).

- **Some data will be inconsistent:** Ideally data should be consistent and should be stored in one place only. Realistically, that's not going to happen; however, this should be one of your primary goals.

- **You need to make trade-offs:** Sometimes you need to sacrifice long-term investment in your data for the sake of the short-term need of development teams. Ineffective information administrators will focus solely on the data, insisting that data issues are completely thought through early in a project. This serial approach ignores the fact that Unified Process development teams work in an evolutionary manner. Information administrators should work closely with project teams to learn the team's specific needs, to communicate enterprise realities to the teams, and to develop a plan that works for both.

■ **You must be flexible:** Bureaucracy breeds inflexibility. If the information administrator is handing down orders and ideas in a one-way fashion, he or she should not be surprised to see project teams avoiding or working around them. Open, two-way communication and teamwork are critical to your success.

■ **You need to maintain legacy documentation:** The information administrator needs to develop and maintain documentation and models about legacy data sources. Ideally the owners of the legacy systems are responsible for the models, and the information administrators will just need to have access to them.

■ **You may need to maintain an enterprise data model:** You (optionally) need to develop an enterprise data model based on your enterprise domain model (refer to Chapter 7). A domain model is typically high-level (see Figure 12-4), whereas your enterprise data model will typically have more detail. Figure 12-5 depicts a portion of Figure 12-4 as it would appear in your enterprise data model. Although enterprise data modeling is often viewed as an enterprise business modeling endeavor, the reality is that the information administrators are the people who develop, own, and support this model.

■ **You must comply with external regulations:** External regulating bodies and legislation require organizations to comply with their specific regulations. From a legal and ethical standpoint, remember that ignorance is not an excuse for noncompliance. For example, in the U.S., the Sarbanes-Oxley (Sarbox) Compliance Act of 2002 (U.S. Government 2002) requires public companies to document their financial processes and show how the data was calculated, including traceability back to the source. The Health Insurance Portability and Accountability Act (HIPAA) of 1996 (U.S. Government 2004) provides federal protection for U.S. workers. Ensuring that you comply with relevant guidance is a small part of IT governance (refer to Chapter 3) that information administrators cannot ignore.

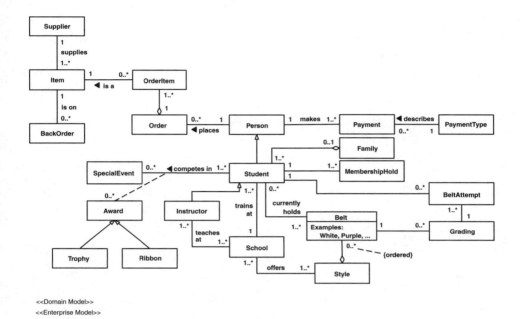

<<Domain Model>>
<<Enterprise Model>>

FIGURE 12-4   *The enterprise domain model for a karate school.*

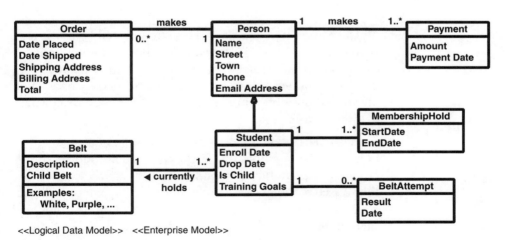

<<Logical Data Model>>   <<Enterprise Model>>

FIGURE 12-5   *A portion of an enterprise data model for a karate school.*

The next activity for the information administrator is the management of Intellectual Property (IP); this is critical within organizations because it is a valuable resource. Consider the SCO Group, which on March 3, 2003 filed a billion-dollar civil lawsuit for IP infringement against IBM, claiming things such as "misappropriations of trade secrets, torturous interference, unfair competition, and breach of contract" (SCO 2004). Do you want to risk this happening to your organization? Yes, this is an extreme case; however, it shows how important this topic really is to your organization. Your license compliance and adherence to standards are often the last things on the minds of developers, so enterprise administrators will need to mentor and guide teams regarding these issues.

TIP   Intellectual Property (IP)

The United States Patent and Trademark Office (USPTO) (www.uspto.gov) defines IP as creations of the mind—creative works or ideas embodied in a form that can be shared or can enable others to re-create, emulate, or manufacture them. Definitions vary by countries.

In the United States, there are four ways to protect IP within your organization:

- A *patent* is defined as a property right granted by the Government to an inventor "to exclude others from making, using, offering for sale, or selling the invention throughout the United States or importing the invention into the United States" for a limited time in exchange for public disclosure of the invention when the patent is granted.

- A *trademark* is defined as protecting words, names, symbols, sounds, or colors that distinguish goods and services from those manufactured or sold by others and to indicate the source of the goods. Trademarks, unlike patents, can be renewed forever as long as they are being used in commerce. An example of this is the abbreviation RUP® from IBM Corporation. A *service mark* is a word, name, symbol, or device whose purpose is to indicate the source of the services and to distinguish them from the services of others; this is the same as a trademark, except that it identifies and distinguishes the source of a service rather than a product. The terms "trademark" and "mark" are often used to refer to both trademarks and service marks.

■ A *copyright* protects works of authorship, such as writings, music, and works of art that have been tangibly expressed. The U.S. Library of Congress registers copyrights, which last for the life of the author plus 70 years.

■ A *trade secret* contains information that companies keep secret to give them an advantage over their competitors. An example of this is the recipe for a cola drink sold almost everywhere on Earth.

An additional activity performed by an information administrator is license management. License management is important from both a cost and legal standpoint. From the cost standpoint, you do not want to overspend on licenses for unnecessary software. From a legal standpoint, the last thing you need is someone from the Business Software Alliance (BSA)(www.bsa.org) showing up at your organization with claims of piracy of commercial software; besides receiving negative publicity, the imposed fines are steep and can have an impact on your financials. Software licenses typically allow end users to use the software but not actually own it. Software licensing refers to allowing an individual or group to use a piece of software. Enterprise licenses are utilized in the Environment discipline for selecting and acquiring new tools; our recommendation is to try any software prior to purchasing licenses. There are many possible models for licensing software; their descriptions, advantages, and disadvantages are described in Table 12-2.

TABLE 12-2 *Approaches to Software Licensing*

Approach	Advantages	Disadvantages
Single license	Used for software installed on a single device utilizing a unique related activation or registration code for legal usage. An example of this is Microsoft Windows for a home user.	This is a costly way to license software for an organization when more than one or two copies are required.

continues

TABLE 12-2   *Approaches to Software Licensing (Continued)*

Approach	Advantages	Disadvantages
Site/networked/ Concurrent licenses	Utilized normally for one physical location and allows for a certain number of authorized users. Software can be installed on any device at the location, but only the licensed number of software packages can be active at one time. It is common for companies to purchase a site license for Microsoft Office.	Administration and license compliance can be more difficult than using a single license.
Subscription/ evaluation/demo licenses	Much like the single or site license models, this model utilizes a key or subscription code to enable a user to use the system for a certain period of time. Most software development tools can be downloaded for a 30-day evaluation period.	Extra security and enforcement are required to keep users from overextending their usage time.
Keyed access control	For software installed on multiple devices for a single user. Usually a dongle-type device is used via a USB or other type of connection to validate that a user is authorized to use the system. The dongles let extra licensed users use the system. An example is a patient monitoring system used in a hospital setting, where a practitioner must log on to multiple systems throughout his daily rounds and may need to use the same system on multiple computers.	While increasing security, the maintenance and upkeep of the system can be expensive. Also, some applications for the enterprise may not work well if they are not coded for this type of access.

Manage Enterprise Security

Figure 12-6 depicts the workflow for managing security within the EUP. There are two different types of security that a security administrator needs to address—physical security and information technology (IT) security. Physical security includes the measures an organization takes to control access to restricted locations; this type of security helps prevent terrorism or some less-intrusive security breaches. Information security includes actions taken to prevent unauthorized access to organizational data and is performed at the IT level; this type of security helps prevent cyber-terrorism, hacking, or types of industrial espionage. Examples of technologies used in physical security are described in Table 12-3; IT security technologies are described in Table 12-4.

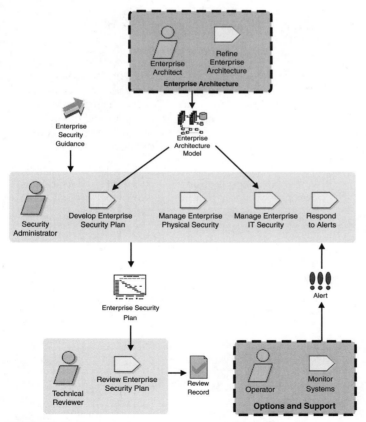

FIGURE 12-6 *Manage Enterprise Security workflow detail.*

TABLE 12-3   *Physical Security Technologies*

Technology	Description	Usage
ID cards	Electronic or manual ID checks. Can also include Radio Frequency Identification (RFID), magnetic, or other types of bar-coding requiring verification before entry.	At entry points to secure locations.
Biometrics	Biometrics is the use of someone's physical or biological properties of a person. Usual approaches include retinal scanning, fingerprint scanning, or voice recognition.	Usually used in conjunction with security doors and control panels.
Secure doors	A "secure door" is a door that protects restricted areas and is usually protected by a control panel or other locking mechanism.	Often used with a key card entry, ID card, or biometric system.
Control panels	A key-coded alarm entry system that activates or deactivates a security alarm system or allows entry into a physical location.	Used in situations where key codes can be easily entered. (Delivery areas are not good candidates because people may have their hands full.)
Surveillance cameras	Cameras that record either live 24/7 or when motion occurs in a specific location.	Used to secure an environment such as a Network Operations Center (NOC).

TABLE 12-4   *IT Security Technologies*

Technology	Description	Usage
Intrusion detection systems	This is used to protect a system from unauthorized entry.	Approaches include some type of hardware or software (such as a firewall) to protect the organization from external threats such as hacking or cyber-terrorism.
Password policies	An organizational policy that defines the protocol for managing individual passwords.	The policy may require frequent changes of passwords, unique passwords to individual systems, a combination of letters and numbers for a password, or a means to automatically check that this is being utilized.
Anti-virus software	Can be a commercial off-the-shelf (COTS) system from vendors such as Symantec (www.symantec.com), McAfee (www.mcafee.com), or Kaspersky (www.kaspersky.com). Updates of both virus definition files (the files that contain virus information) and program files should be scheduled on a regular basis.	They are used to protect against viruses, worms, and spam e-mail from both external and internal threats.

The blending of both physical and IT security is heavily pursued and supported by both types of security vendors today. Here is an example of a convergent security solution: A person leaves the building at 6:00 p.m., and later an attempt is made to log on to the network—internally—at 12:00 p.m. Two different types of security, biometrics and password policies, work together to automatically disable any network entries until the exception is dealt with the next day.

A security administrator should be involved during all phases of the EUP, from setting up new security aspects at project inception to ensuring that after a system is retired, everything from a security standpoint is in line with the organizational guidance. Security administrators must address the following issues:

- **Enterprise IT protection:** This protection is for your information assets within the organization. A combination of both physical and IT security works best in an enterprise environment.

- **IT budgets for security:** Options to consider when budgeting include providing additional training to employees, increasing IT staff dedicated to security management, hiring a third party to conduct a security audit, purchasing an event security management system, purchasing new point solutions, switching operating system vendors, or fully outsourcing the security operations (Roberts 2004).

- **Security infrastructure build-out:** Your enterprise architecture model should indicate the infrastructure required for your IT infrastructure. Your security administrators will need to implement this infrastructure in advance of the project teams to ensure that it is available in time and sufficient for their needs.

- **Look internally for threats:** Various security consulting firms such as the National Security Institute (NSI) estimate that as many as 70% of security problems come from inside your own company (NSI 2004)—whether they are mischievous or unintentional (such as opening an e-mail attachment that spreads a new worm behind an enterprise firewall).

- **Security education:** Because most security threats come from within your own organization, employee education is clearly critical to your success. This is discussed in detail in the next section.

- **Operating system flaws:** Your perimeter defenses don't always work. Forty percent of respondents said they had been attacked through an exploit utilizing a flaw in an operating system (Roberts 2004).

Support Project Teams

Figure 12-7 depicts the workflow details for supporting project teams. The primary danger of the Enterprise Administration discipline is that you will create a huge bureaucracy to implement it. Instead, your goal should be to streamline the activities of this discipline so that application teams will want to work with enterprise administrators instead of work around them. You need to communicate with the project teams and gain their respect and trust while educating and supporting them.

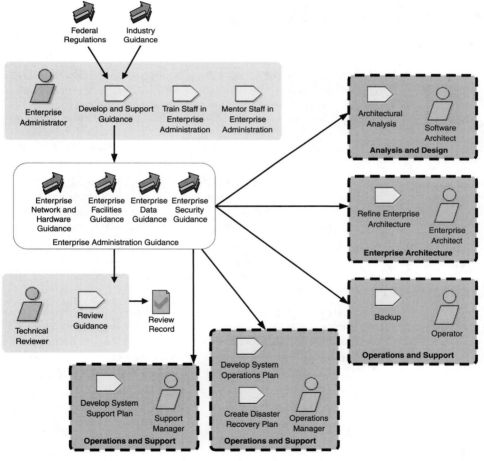

FIGURE 12-7 *Support Project Teams workflow diagram.*

It is critical that each type of enterprise administrator develop the relevant guidance for his or her specialty and then support project teams in its application. In the ZF (refer to Chapter 3), this effort maps to the How (Functions) column. If the guidance reflects common best practices, if it's written well, if it's easy to conform to, and if it's supported effectively, project teams should be willing to follow them; you should expect project teams to resist following your guidance otherwise. Table 12-5 summarizes the various types of enterprise administration guidance that may be contained within a single document.

TABLE 12-5   *Enterprise Guidance and Issues Addressed*

Type of Guidance	Contents
Network and hardware guidance	Describes the types of network devices and protocols supported, how network outages will be handled, and how to help prevent system downtime outside of the normal maintenance windows (see Chapter 6, "The Operations and Support Discipline"). This also includes the standards for hardware usage within your organization, financial depreciation recommendations for computing systems, and recommended sources for required purchases.
Facilities guidance	Describes the organizational standards and guidelines for procuring hardware and other infrastructure items (such as cubicles and conference room sizes and layouts). Also describes the timelines and projections for physical growth within the organization.
Data guidance	Describes the data quality management directive or activity, the concepts that support it, any associated roles and responsibilities, and any technical, operational, or administrative implementation details (Loshin 2004a).
Security guidance	Describes password policies (and enforcement), specific hardware and software vendors to work with on security issues, and how to keep security software (such as anti-virus or anti-spam definition files) updated. It describes the differences between physical and IT security along with ways that they are converging within the organization.

Mentoring and training people in the fundamental skills of working with the enterprise administrators effectively is needed because, although most IT staff know about the issues facing their daily work routine, the enterprise concerns must be taught to and understood by the various project teams. Mentoring and training is discussed in detail in the People Management discipline (see Chapter 11). People in any of the four concrete enterprise administration roles can specifically mentor or train project team members about their specific needs in the following ways:

- **Network administrator:** This role works with project teams to let them know about future infrastructure changes and planned outages, mentoring the team on various networking topics.

- **Facilities administrator:** This role works with project teams to plan any physical moves.

- **Information administrator:** This role mentors teams in data quality, data modeling, data architecture, enterprise data modeling, and legacy data sources. Along with the data stewardship responsibilities for the enterprise, this role communicates the need for consistency among the different databases within the organization.

- **Security administrator:** This role is actively involved in the mentoring and training of IT staff in the various types of, and approaches to, security.

The following is general advice for enterprise administrators working with project teams:

- **Focus on collaboration:** This is often overlooked and must be two-way. Jim Highsmith (2004) reflects that communication is basically one-way (even if you respond to it). He prefers the term collaboration, in which the team works to achieve a common result. One way to do this is to work with the various project teams—even though it may garner looks of disbelief from some project teams.

- **Avoid ivory-tower administration:** Get involved with the teams and keep any attitudes out of the mix. Tom DeMarco and Tim Lister (1999) state that "the purpose of a team is not goal attainment but goal alignment." They argue that sometimes little teamwork is actually required; however, teams serve as a device for getting everyone moving in the same direction.

- **Respect people:** Everyone brings value to the team. Any of the enterprise administrators can learn from even novice developers of the project team if they keep an open mind. DeMarco and Lister (1999) also talk about a concept of chemistry, which some people overlook as luck. What they want you to understand is that without trust and mutual respect, a team will not gell, and the organizations will continue to be unhealthy.

CASE STUDIES

The two case studies presented here discuss data management. They show right and wrong things that various teams are doing with respect to data management. They also show how being flexible is important when implementing a convergent security policy.

Data Management

At one large client, we discovered a data management team that was making an attempt at being more agile in their approach. All of the data management staff were experienced and flexible and understood the long-term vision of the organization. However, the developers were located at one physical location, while the data people were at the other location, with almost 1,200 miles and a time zone between them. Partly because of the location problem, the developers were not up to speed on the data issues (and vice versa).

Although it was clear that both teams wanted to move toward a more effective environment, the different physical locations erected a huge barrier to communication. The organization knew this was a problem; however, they said they were a family-oriented business and did not want to relocate people in order to have them all in one place.

On the positive side, the teams have worked well together, have gelled, and understand where they are going with regards to the business goals and objectives. On the negative side, we reported the following issues: communication barriers prevent the IT organization from working together effectively, from taking advantage of shared resources, and from working consistently based on a common set of guidance, and the developers are still making fundamental data-oriented mistakes due to their lack of skills and experience.

Security

While working at Software Co. as contractors, we were called in late at night to work on a high-priority problem. Unbeknownst to any of us, our badges did not allow us to enter the building after normal business hours. So when the badges did not work at the main entrance, a call was made to someone in the building from the project team so we could get in. After that, we badged into the high-security room (more physical access) without even thinking about it—as we did every time we entered the room.

About 12 minutes into our work, three large security guards came and drilled us about how we were able to enter the building and our reason for being there. At that point, we were informed that our badges did not allow 24-hour access because we were contractors. They contacted the manager at home, and then we had to leave the building. Reprimands followed, but the client manager was thankful that we got the job done before we were kicked out of the building.

This case teaches three important lessons. First, it shows that no matter what, there are still ways (even innocent, like ours) for people to get around any of the established—and tested—physical security measures. In addition, this showed the need to be flexible with your organizational rules and to work with the individual project teams to apply the correct security measures; clearly access was required but not communicated to the security personnel. Finally, it showed the convergence of physical security (badge readers) and IT-related security (flagged in an IT security system) and how they can work with predictable outcomes.

ANTI-PATTERNS

Over the years working with clients, we have found anti-patterns, which describe common approaches that prove to not work well in practice. Here are some enterprise administration anti-patterns:

- **Enterprise Nazi:** Project teams are ignoring your enterprise guidance. The solution is to adopt the rule of thumb that if you need to act as "standards police," you have lost the battle. Effective enterprise administrators strive to support guidance, not enforce it.

- **Administration Hammer:** Nobody in the organization is following your great-looking process or management edicts. The solution is for the enterprise administrator to work with the project teams to support them in their endeavors.

- **Single Hardware Configuration:** Project teams are not following your standard hardware configuration, and they keep requesting hardware that you do not support. The solution is to be flexible when needed and work with the project teams to ensure that they have the tools to do their jobs effectively. Different roles within IT—and the rest of your organization—require different solutions to effectively perform their jobs.

- **Interior Decorator:** People are trying to work outside of their assigned cubicles. Trying to create a facility that is pleasing to the eye may not always be effective for IT teams to work together. For example, a team implementing the Scrum project management technique requires a collaborative team workspace and a place for their daily Scrum meetings (Schwaber 2004). Or perhaps a project team is taking an Agile Model-Driven Development (AMDD) approach but can't get whiteboards installed because their workroom has nice paintings on the wall. The solution is to work with the project teams as needed to create workplaces that will enable them to get their job done effectively.

TIMING

Enterprise administration efforts occur on a continual basis. From the point of view of a project team, the various roles increase during the middle of both the Inception and Elaboration phases, when the need for tools and administration for development environments is identified and implemented. For example, development teams may need additional or nonstandard hardware and software for evaluation licensing purposes. Similar activities occur in the Construction phase and at the end of the Transition phase. Administration also occurs during the Production phase as the infrastructure is maintained and updated to support systems in production, and similar efforts occur as systems are pulled from production during the Retirement phase.

TOOLS

Several excellent sources of tools are available to enterprise administrators:

- **IBM Tivoli** (`www.tivoli.com`): A suite of application, database, network, middleware, security, and operating system monitoring tools.
- **360Facility** (`www.360facility.com`): This tool is used by facilities administrators to produce work order and procurement management information.
- **ManageSoft** (`www.managesoft.com`): License management for all of the different desktop platforms. This includes help with tasks like asset tracking and deployment assistance and tracking.

RELATION TO OTHER DISCIPLINES

The Enterprise Administration discipline is related to other disciplines as follows:

- **Analysis and Design:** Support the definition of architecture by working with the project team if they have specific questions and concerns about the requirements during analysis.

- **Deployment:** Support the development, operations, and support teams by increasing the network capacity if a new system requires this.

- **Environment:** Support the team with the necessary infrastructure requirements such as database and licensing infrastructure issues.

- **Operations and Support:** Respond to alert requests as needed.

- **Enterprise Business Modeling:** Supply the enterprise domain model for use by the information administrator in managing the enterprise data.

SUMMARY

The Enterprise Administration discipline within the EUP extends the RUP to cover the administration needs from an enterprise level. This discipline includes managing both physical and information assets and the security for the enterprise; it also includes information on how to support project teams with the various initiatives and activities within this discipline.

Suggested Reading

Peopleware, Second Edition (DeMarco and Lister 1999). This is considered by many to be the premier book on building productive projects and teams. Effective enterprise administrators recognize that they must be customer-focused and must have good people skills.

Practical Issues in Database Management: A Reference for the Thinking Practitioner (Pascal 2000). A guide to understanding the core issues of database management.

ITIL Fact Sheet: Security (ITIL 2003). An introduction to the way security is managed within the ITIL; it provides a solid foundation for this discipline.

Enterprise Unified Process

Chapter 13

The Software Process
Improvement Discipline

- Software process improvement is an ongoing effort; your process will evolve over time.

- The goal of SPI is to ensure that your organization can define, implement, and evolve one or more appropriate processes to help you meet your IT goals.

- There are many proven software processes; one or more of them will likely meet your needs.

- Your software process must be tailored to reflect your organization's strengths, weaknesses, culture, and business needs.

Even the smallest IT department needs a software process that project teams can follow and tailor; larger IT departments may need several different processes, typically one base process for each category of project that they work on. In the Rational Unified Process (RUP), these base processes can be described by organization-level development cases; the effort of creating and supporting them is encompassed by the Software Process Improvement (SPI) discipline.

When you think about it, the term "software process improvement" is a misnomer when it comes to the Enterprise Unified Process (EUP). Considering the scope of the EUP, we should really be talking about "information technology process improvement," but unfortunately the term SPI is far more common, so that's what we've chosen to use.

Process definition is not a "silver bullet." Defining and implementing a system development process does not guarantee results. It can, however, go a long way toward helping you reach your business goals.

TIP   **Process Certification Isn't an End Unto Itself**

An organization can use various levels of certification to measure its software process, such as the Capability Maturity Model / Capability Maturity Model Integration (CMM/CMMI) (CMMI 2004) and International Organization for Standardization (ISO) 9003 (ISO 2004). They have similar goals: to assess how an organization develops software. Some organizations require certification to bid on or win contracts; others use it as a marketing device. It also can be an important tool for assessing how well your company's software process improvement effort is working.

However, you need to keep in mind that certification is a measurement. Your true goal should be to have an efficient process that works for your organization. Achieving CMMI Level 3 is meaningless if it actually hampers your ability to achieve your business objectives.

WORKFLOW

The SPI discipline extends the RUP Environment discipline. As with many other enterprise management disciplines, the difference is one of scope. The Environment discipline is concerned with the process configuration for a specific project, while the SPI discipline addresses process configuration for the entire organization.

The workflow for the SPI discipline is shown in Figure 13-1.

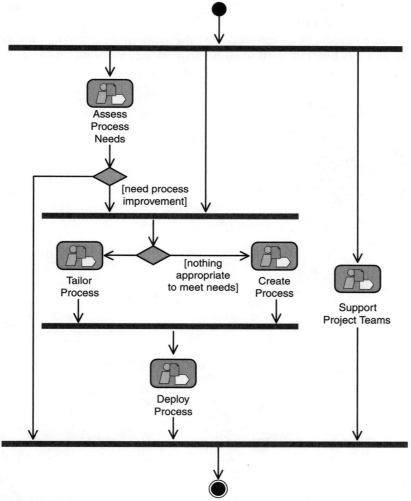

FIGURE 13-1 *Software Process Improvement discipline workflow.*

Assess Process Needs

It's crucial to recognize that the primary drivers for process improvement are business-oriented—implementing a process for its own sake is a bad idea. Process improvement is an enabler, not an end in itself. You must understand the business goals of your organization in order to implement an effective IT process. For example, the goal of always being first to market with new functionality will require a process with a different emphasis than that of minimizing defects in a highly regulated industry. The point is that you must start by determining your business needs. The workflow detail diagram for doing so is presented in Figure 13-2.

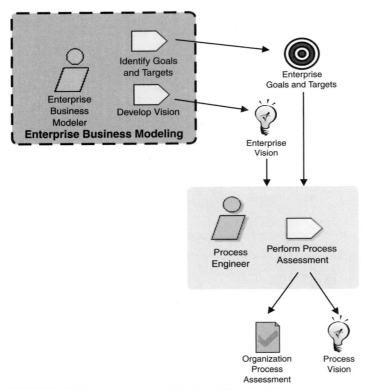

FIGURE 13-2   *Assess Process Needs workflow detail.*

You may find that your process-related needs are complicated and subtle. Different business units typically have different priorities, particularly in mid-to-large-size organizations. You must identify and prioritize these needs and then choose to address them accordingly. How you approach this will depend on many factors: Do you have global issues that need to be addressed—for

example, improved quality, faster time to market, or consistency—
or are individual business units' needs paramount, such as the Research and Development area's need for quick feedback? If the latter is the case, you may need a tailored process for R&D that emphasizes quick feedback rather than low defects.

The nature of your organization will shape your process needs. What are your strengths and weaknesses? Understanding your culture will allow you to maximize your strengths and compensate for your deficiencies. Here are some issues to consider during a process assessment:

- **Process culture:** Is your organization accustomed to a rigorous or prescriptive approach? An agile approach? No formal process at all? Rigorous folks will like the EUP but may make it overly bureaucratic; agile folks will demand that it be instantiated simply; anti-process folks will fight you all the way. All three groups may exist within your organization.

- **Existing RUP expertise:** Have you successfully delivered projects using the RUP? Do your people understand the difference between architecture and design? Do they truly understand what it means to be use-case-driven? The EUP is an extension to the RUP; you cannot succeed with the EUP without a good grasp of the underlying concepts in the RUP.

- **Coordination across groups:** How well do the groups work together? How well do the groups representing users work with the technical staff? Stakeholder participation is crucial to an iterative process such as the EUP; if you do not currently practice this, you will have to take steps to get the stakeholders more involved.

- **Acceptance of change:** How well does your organization respond to change? Will resource shuffling be necessary to put people in place who can handle the new approach? Does the organization even recognize a need to change its IT process? Is it willing and able to retrain its people in a new process? Cultural acceptance of change is crucial to SPI efforts. You will need a champion to lead the effort as well as senior management support to let people know that they are expected to learn and apply the new approach.

■ **Acceptance of an evolutionary (iterative and incremental) approach:** This may be your biggest challenge because there is a large difference from the waterfall approach. No longer will analysts detail all requirements and give them to designers, who fully design a system and then hand it off to coders, who implement it and then give it to testers, who give their final approval. Instead, teams will work on a small slice of the system together, detailing the requirements for it and designing, coding, and testing it before moving on to the next slice. If this is a new concept, you can facilitate the transition by using mentors who are familiar with this approach. As team members are mentored and learn the evolutionary approach, they become mentors to others.

■ **Technology expertise:** It takes time to adopt new technologies or techniques. Switching to the object-oriented (OO) paradigm is not simply a matter of sending people to UML and/or Java training. Moving to an Internet-based or service-oriented architecture (SOA) imposes similar issues. If you are shifting technologies as part of your SPI effort, recognize that training and mentoring will probably be necessary.

■ **Testing expertise:** Testing plays a large part in evolutionary approaches. Testers must work as part of a team to validate the portion of a system developed during an iteration and regression test earlier functionality. Automated testing is crucial to evolutionary development. Testers who are not familiar with testing in an evolutionary environment will need time to adjust. Expect to invest in new tools, training, and mentoring.

Keep in mind that different business units within your company have different people and will likely have different strengths and weaknesses. Some business units may be successful only through the heroic effort of a few individuals, while others may be suffering from heavyweight, burdensome processes. Make sure you get a broad view and, when necessary, note differences between areas. You may end up doing things slightly differently for different groups. This may not be reflected in your process definition, but it may need to be addressed during process rollout. You may, for example, schedule more training and mentoring for a specific group to learn a particular skill.

Also remember that an assessment is essentially a snapshot, measuring strengths and weaknesses at a point in time; your IT department may (and probably will) change quite a bit over time. Be wary of using an assessment that was done 18 or even 12 months ago, because a lot can change; out-of-date assessments could indicate issues that are no longer there and miss issues that are.

Tip	**Keep It Open and Honest**
	It's vital that you be honest with any assessment—brutally honest. Sugar-coating or ignoring weaknesses at this juncture will undermine the entire effort. It's also critical that you share the assessment and your process improvement plans openly with everyone involved. Process improvement can be very scary for everyone involved. They want to know how they'll be affected and what they need to do to succeed in the new environment; otherwise, rumors will run rampant. Consider bringing in someone from the outside who is not tied to your internal politics if you feel that you cannot perform an honest assessment by yourself.

Create Process

It is possible that no existing process that meets your needs is available; this is very unlikely, given the wide array of processes available today (see Table 13-1). However, it is possible that you will discover that you need to create specific, detailed procedures and guidance that reflect your exact needs. Figure 13-3 shows the activities, inputs, and outputs of the Create Process workflow detail.

TABLE 13-1   *Modern Software Processes*

Process/Method	Description	When to Use It
Agile Modeling (AM) www.agilemodeling.com	A practices-base method that focuses on effective modeling and documentation of software-based systems.	Tailor AM's practices into the EUP to streamline your modeling and documentation efforts.
Agile Data (AD) www.agiledata.org	A method that defines strategies pertaining to the data-oriented development aspects of software systems.	Tailor AD's philosophies and supporting techniques, such as agile data modeling and database refactoring, into EUP development projects.
Crystal Methodologies alistair.cockburn.us/ crystal/ crystal.html	This family of methods recognizes that every project needs its own unique tailoring, that people issues are critical to your success, and that better communication and frequent deliveries reduce the need for intermediate work products.	For project teams working in flexible, high-collaboration environments.
Dynamic System Development Method (DSDM) www.dsdm.org	An agile software development methodology that has received ISO 9001 certification. In many ways it is a formalization of the Rapid Application Development (RAD) methodologies of the 1980s.	To develop a user interface-intensive system and/or complex business application.
Enterprise Unified Process (EUP) www.enterpriseunified process.com	A rigorous, full-lifecycle methodology that includes development, operation, and retirement of software-based systems. The EUP extends the RUP to incorporate a multi-system view that includes enterprise architecture, reuse management, portfolio management, and people management activities.	When you have been successful at several RUP projects and want to take the full system lifecycle into account as well as cross-project issues such as portfolio management, strategic reuse, and enterprise architecture.

continues

TABLE 13-1 *Modern Software Processes (Continued)*

Process/Method	Description	When to Use It
Extreme Programming (XP) www.xprogramming.com	An agile software development methodology that focuses on the critical activities required to build software.	Small, co-located project teams (4–10 people). Requirements are uncertain. Good relationship (potentially) exists with project stakeholders.
Feature-Driven Development (FDD) www.featuredriven development.com	An agile software development methodology based on short iterations, which includes explicit modeling activities.	Small project team (4–20 people). Requirements are uncertain. Team is willing to follow a modeling-driven approach.
ISO 12207 www.iso.org	A rigorous full-lifecycle methodology process that includes development, operation, and retirement of software-based systems.	Medium to large project teams (20+ people). Mandated (such as by government) to follow this approach. Outsourcing.
Rational Unified Process (RUP) www-306.ibm.com/ software/awdtools/rup	A rigorous software development process that is iterative and incremental. Can potentially be instantiated in an agile manner (Evans 2001).	Medium to large project teams (10+ people). Phased approach to development supports outsourcing of large portions of the lifecycle.
Scrum www.controlchaos.com	An agile methodology that describes effective project and requirements management techniques.	Tailor Scrum into agile or near-agile development methods.

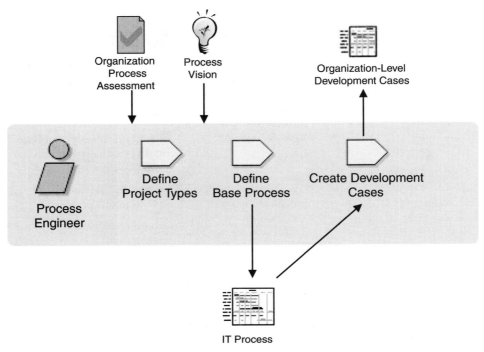

FIGURE 13-3   *Create Process workflow detail*

Be cautious in this approach. We suggest that if groups are unsure about some aspect of a standard process, such as iterative development, they should try it out. We often get so set in our ways that it becomes difficult to contemplate other ways of doing our work. If you try a standard process, you may be pleased with the results of the test and decide that you can use it after all. If this fails and you need to create your own process, we suggest the following:

- **Identify the issue(s) you need to address:** If you don't understand the issue, you cannot develop an effective process for it.

- **Look for existing process material similar to what you need:** You'll often discover that your "unique need" is not so unique after all.

- **Engage the appropriate people:** Identify people within your organization who are currently fulfilling this need and work with them to identify what they actually do. This will result in processes that people accept and that reflect your environment.

- **Write less process documentation than you think you need:** The hard truth is that very few people will actually read the process in its entirety. People usually read relevant portions of your process when they join your organization or when they're performing an activity for the first time. After that, they may only read the appropriate guidance documentation and use your standard artifact templates, ignoring the rest of your documentation altogether.

- **Take a just-in-time (JIT) approach:** Writing the process(es) when you need them will help you reduce your overall effort because you'll discover that you don't need as much as you think.

Tailor Process

It is very likely that you can tailor an existing process, such as the RUP or EUP, to meet your needs. If you examine the wide array of processes in the industry, you will most likely determine that you can tailor one (or more) to meet your assessed needs (see Figure 13-4).

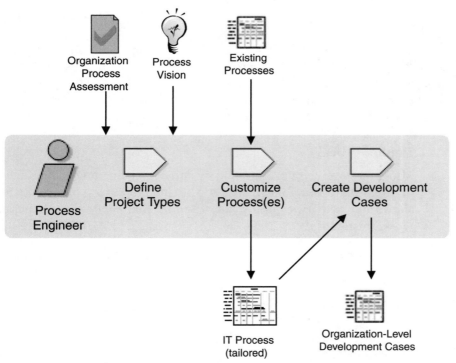

FIGURE 13-4 *Tailor Process workflow detail.*

Boehm and Turner (2003) present a risk-based approach for choosing a methodological strategy, which describes how to combine agile with rigorous/prescriptive approaches. They advise that uncertain requirements, complex technologies, and low employee turnover favor agile techniques, whereas larger teams and a diverse group of stakeholders favor more prescriptive methods.

There are many processes in the industry today, as depicted in Table 13-1, and they are at varying degrees of maturity and acceptance. Pick one (or more) that will help you achieve your goals. Remember that you will still need to tailor your adopted process. Rarely will a process, even a widely accepted one like the RUP, be a perfect fit for an organization. Choose what works for you, take out what doesn't, and tweak the rest. Do you really think that you need all 3,000+ pages of the RUP product (IBM 2004)?

Process tailoring is best done in an iterative manner: tailor some, implement some, and then repeat. You can spend months or even years defining and tailoring the perfect process for your organization, but you won't know how it will work until you try it. You'll save time and effort (and therefore money) in the long run by taking an iterative approach. Chapter 14, "Adopting the EUP," provides an in-depth discussion.

TIP   Adopt Processes Because They Make Sense
If a process makes sense to you, and you believe it will add value to your organization, adopt it. Otherwise, do not. Do not implement processes just because someone else does.

Deploy Process

After you have defined a process by either tailoring an existing one or creating a new one, you need to implement it. Figure 13-5 shows the activities, inputs, and outputs for the Deploy Process workflow detail.

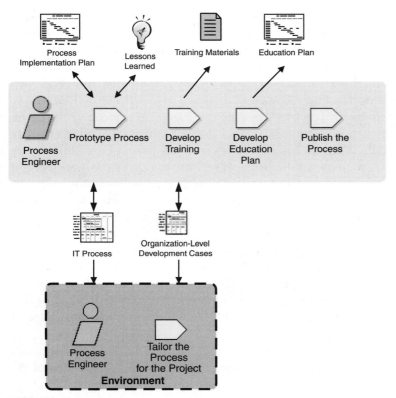

FIGURE 13-5 *Deploy Process workflow detail.*

In the cycle of defining/tailoring and implementing, you may identify the need to have slightly different variations of the process. For instance, you may find it beneficial to define different tailorings of the process for green-field (new development) and commercial off-the-shelf (COTS) implementations. With the EUP, these tailorings can be accomplished with organization-level development cases.

A development case is typically defined for each project using the RUP. It defines the particular process tailoring that will be used on that specific project. This allows teams to create process definitions to meet their particular needs. An organization-level development case is a development case with a wider scope; it is applicable to many projects. For example, you may have organization-level development cases for both new development and minor enhancement projects. New development projects may stress business modeling and architecture efforts because new development projects are riskier, whereas enhancement projects often have less business and technical risk and are more concerned with backward compatibility (hence their emphasis on regression testing).

You have two fundamental strategies to choose from when documenting organization-level development cases. One strategy is to define an organizational-level development case that covers 80% of the material the projects will use and have each project use this case as a starting point and modify it as needed. Alternatively, you can develop a fully detailed organizational-level development case and just have each project note deviations from it, usually in their software development plans.

Survey projects after a process has been rolled out to attempt to generalize project types. If you find that development cases for certain types of projects are very similar, you may want to develop a new organization-level development case for this category of project. Projects of that type can utilize them in the future to speed their efforts.

Before you deploy the process, you should define how you will train and mentor people on the process. Training and mentoring are a crucial part of deploying the process to a wide audience. Chapters 10 and 14 discuss these issues in detail, as well as the steps involved in deploying the process.

One deployment option is to not tailor the RUP material at all, except perhaps to install plug-ins. As show in Figure 13-6, you can develop a collection of HTML pages that overview the procedures you want developers to follow. These pages will reference the RUP material and other process-related materials including the EUP (www.enterpriseunifiedprocess.com), IEEE (www.ieee.org) standards, and your own detailed procedures, as well as agile methodologies such as Agile Modeling (www.agilemodeling.com) and agile database techniques (www.agiledata.org).

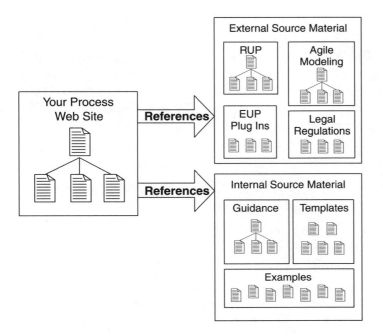

FIGURE 13-6 *Deploying process documentation as a wrapper.*

There are several advantages to this approach:

- You don't need to purchase, learn, or work with complex process authoring tools.

- There are fewer maintenance headaches when a new version of RUP comes out, which is at least an annual occurrence. The RUP pages are just like externally developed source code—if you modify them, you need to merge the changes from new releases of the source into your modifications.

- You can still take advantage of plug-ins for Extreme Programming (XP), J2EE, Real Time, and others. IBM Rational maintains an exchange site for RUP plug-ins on the IBM developerWorks site (`www-136.ibm.com/developerworks`).

- You can easily reference other process material, not just the RUP. This allows you to truly take advantage of all industry best practices, not just the ones included within the RUP.

- You can tailor your own process very quickly because you've kept it simple.

- You can have several sets of process pages, perhaps one for each major type of project within your organization. For example, you could have a set of pages for large projects, a set for small projects, a set for projects taking an agile approach, and a set for outsourcing efforts.

- Project teams can easily tailor their own version of the process, such as by building development cases and by reworking their own copies of these pages.

The main disadvantages are as follows:

- Someone needs to initially learn and understand the RUP so that he or she can develop the initial pages. This is also true of an RPW-driven approach, however.

- Your version may be in contradiction with the RUP, or other process materials, at certain points. Having the source material available "as is" may cause confusion unless people understand that you have overridden portions of it. An effective approach is to set a specific design scheme for your pages and then make sure that everyone is aware that your pages are official and that all other pages are simply reference. Your staff members are adults—they can follow this simple rule.

- Providing a process where people must understand the base description and then understand the changes to it at another location may be confusing for some people.

- Your organization needs to maintain your specific process pages. When new process materials, such as a new version of the RUP, are released, you will want to evaluate the material and determine what changes (if any) should be made to your tailored pages. All you can hope to achieve is a significant reduction of the maintenance burden, not a complete removal of it.

Support Project Teams

After a software process has been defined and implemented, it must be maintained, and teams must be assisted in order to apply it. Figure 13-7 shows the workflow detail for Support Project Teams.

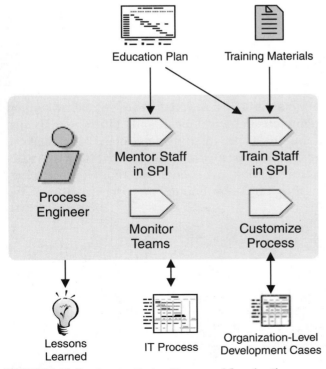

FIGURE 13-7 *Support Project Teams workflow detail.*

Immediately after deploying a new process, you should spend considerable time adjusting it, as you adapt based on lessons learned. Running a pilot project or two will definitely help you identify major issues, but there will always be a need for improvement. This is normal; expect it.

One way to identify "lessons learned" is to hold retrospectives (Kerth 2001). How often you hold them will depend on your comfort level with your process. During the pilot projects, you need feedback early and often to ascertain how the process is working, and you should hold retrospectives at the end of each iteration. As your process is deployed to a wider audience, you will find that the project teams need to hold retrospectives less often, perhaps at the end of each phase, or perhaps they can simply hold them less formally. After the process has been rolled out and assimilated into your culture, retrospectives can be held at the end of the project. Kerth recommends that retrospectives focus on four simple questions:

1. What did we do well that, if we don't discuss it, we might forget?
2. What did we learn?
3. What should we do differently next time?
4. What still puzzles us?

A mature IT process should be continually evolving, allowing you to adapt to changing business, technical, and cultural conditions. If you don't find that teams are offering suggestions to change the process, you may want to take a closer look at what they are really doing. The teams might not know enough yet to provide meaningful feedback—or they might be finding ways to circumvent the process.

TIP	**"Lessons Indicated" Aren't Enough**

"Lessons Indicated" Aren't Enough

A common problem with holding retrospectives is that they produce a list of "lessons learned," which are never assimilated by your organization. When you think about it, these are really "lessons indicated," not lessons learned. If you have no intention of acting on the results of a retrospective, there is no value in holding it. Successful organizations actually learn their lessons.

After the initial deployment period, emphasis shifts to fine-tuning the process. You can use metrics to help you do this. Continuous improvement is your goal, and metrics help immensely in achieving it. They can give you definitive measures on how things are proceeding. See Chapter 14 for a list of metrics that we have found useful.

CASE STUDIES

This section describes two organizations' SPI experiences—one taking an all-at-once "big bang" approach and another taking an incremental approach.

The Big-Bang Approach to SPI

Retail Co. made the mistake of trying to roll out their tailored version of the EUP following a "big-bang" approach. They did not have a pilot project; they simply decreed that all future projects would use the new process. The project teams and the organization as a whole struggled to adapt to the new process.

The process they deployed was the RUP "out of the box" with some additions from the EUP. It was not modified to reflect their culture or organizational structure. They quickly learned that the RUP is not a panacea that can be applied "as is"—it is a process framework that must be adapted to local conditions.

The organization had many projects running concurrently, and when there was a problem (whether it was a process definition issue, a cultural issue, or some other issue), all the projects struggled with it concurrently. The organization employed mentors to assist teams, but the large number of teams using the new process made it difficult for the mentors to devote sufficient time to each project.

Productivity dropped significantly while the process was being rolled out. It was over 18 months before the organization really understood the new process and was able to apply it correctly. By that time, many people had a negative impression of the new process, including many senior managers.

An Incremental Approach to SPI

Service Co. succeeded using an incremental approach to process adoption. Their first process definition covered just the essentials. They started with the RUP and pared it down to the essential artifacts and activities. They used subject matter experts (SMEs) from throughout the company who had a solid grasp on the company culture and its people.

The first version of the process was rolled out to a limited number of pilot projects. Those projects experienced growing pains, but the pain was limited to this manageable number of projects. They provided valuable feedback to the process team, who modified the process before rolling it out to a wider audience. The process team brought in mentors (a combination of employees and a small number of outside experts) who were able to mentor project teams effectively due to the small number of teams. The members on the pilot projects were able to carry their experience with the new process to other teams.

After the pilot projects, the process was rolled out company-wide. A training curriculum was developed that included multiple courses aimed at different groups. The process team delivered training to each site in the company and offered tailored training when requested. This was followed by mentoring from the mentors and members of the pilot teams as needed.

Only after they became proficient at the RUP did they move on to the EUP. The second iteration of the process added the Production phase and associated activities. At the time of this writing, they are adopting other portions of the EUP in an incremental fashion.

Their process adoption went much more smoothly, even though they were more geographically distributed than the previous company. The incremental approach worked quite well for their organization.

Publishing and Supporting Corporate Guidance

When implementing an IT lifecycle such as the EUP, everyone must understand and adhere to common and accepted practices. This often takes the form of guidance (standards and guidelines) and suggested patterns, reference implementations, and "how-to" guides.

Publishing and maintaining such resources is crucial to the success of various EUP disciplines and is described in previous chapters.

These resources will evolve over time. Instead of developing them from scratch, you can save time and effort by adopting existing material and then modifying it for your particular needs. Resources that include obsolete or nonsensical provisions are often ignored in their entirety.

TIP   Hold Everyone Responsible for Process Improvement

Senior management must be willing to actively support and sustain process improvement, project managers must be held responsible for ensuring that their teams follow the defined processes, and developers must be held responsible for learning and then following the processes. This can be a difficult task because senior management often demands immediate results, whereas process improvement often takes years. Project managers resent diverting scarce resources from their projects, and developers often resent being told how to do their jobs.

Corporate Governance

Governance is the act of specifying the decision rights and accountability framework to encourage desirable behavior in using IT (Weill and Ross 2004). This is an important concept during SPI efforts. Implementing a new IT process such as the EUP within an organization is a significant cultural change that requires adequate governance to succeed.

Corporate governance has become much more visible recently with the corporate scandals that have occurred and the legislative response to them in the U.S. For example, the U.S.'s Sarbanes-Oxley Act of 2002 (U.S. Government 2002) requires not only that corporate officers verify that their financial reports are correct but also that they vouch for the processes used to arrive at the figures. Unless your company is using calculators and stacks and stacks of paper, this means that the IT department is under heavy scrutiny. Failure to properly oversee systems, especially financial systems, can lead to large fines or can even land Chief Financial Officers (CFOs) in jail.

IT governance can take different forms. We've found that a middle-of-the-road approach works fairly well. Various groups publish and maintain IT guidance, including enterprise architecture (architecture guidance, including reference architectures and enterprise patterns, and coding standards), the process improvement team (process definitions, templates, modeling guidelines), data administration (data naming conventions, metadata conventions), and others. Formal reviews are conducted for "major" artifacts or milestones, such as application architecture and EUP milestones, by the appropriate reviewers, who are often part of a corporate governance body, whereas teams self-govern for smaller items. For example, coding standards can be governed by code reviews or satisfied by pair programming. At the beginning of each project or major effort, the team defines the approach that its members will take. If they are undertaking a course of self-governance for compliance, the approach is often reviewed by a person or group representing the corporate governance board to ensure that it meets the overall corporate needs.

ANTI-PATTERNS

You should try to avoid several SPI anti-patterns:

- **The Big Bang:** A new process is developed, tailored, or adopted and deployed everywhere at once. Multiple teams struggle with the same issues at the same time. The solution is to develop and deploy processes iteratively. Do not assume that you will get it right the first time, and be prepared to update the process based on the input of the initial teams to follow it.

- **Silver Bullet:** An industry software process is adopted "as-is." Proponents expect that it will work off the shelf, but your organization soon discovers that the cultural and technical aspects of your particular company present challenges. The solution is to recognize that your company has a unique culture and strengths and weakness that require you to tailor a process to meet your particular needs.

- **One Size Fits All:** This is the belief that every project team within an organization will follow the same process. The motivation is often to make project management easier by having project teams create the same artifacts, but the end result is that most project teams are hobbled by the process—a short project built by three people needs a significantly different process than a two-year, 50-person project team. The solution is to recognize that you will need several versions of your process, one for each major category of project, which you in turn will tailor to meet the exact needs of each team.

- **Process for Process' Sake:** The objective of implementing a software process is to help the company meet its business goals. Sometimes organizations forget this and concentrate on the process instead of the business that it is intended to support. The solution is to define business goals before you begin your process effort and make sure that you are meeting them with your process.

- **Overzealous Process Police:** Occasionally an SPI effort will lose sight of the true goal of software development and focus too much on process compliance. This is often characterized by frequent process reviews and noncompliance defects against teams that aren't following the process to the nth degree. The solution is to keep in mind that the goal of a software process is to develop software, not to earn a merit badge in process compliance. Your specific needs may vary (a low number of defects, time to market), but it's still about the software.

- **Going It Alone:** This involves implementing a software process based solely on something read in a book or after attending a training class. The solution is to acknowledge that process adoption is not something you can do only with book knowledge. Bring in someone who has practical experience in the process and in mentoring people in the process to lead the process effort. Hire someone if possible; if you can't, bring in someone temporarily. Complement that person with someone who has extensive knowledge of the company and its culture.

TIMING

Introducing a new software process is not an activity that will happen often. Depending on your current culture and how dynamic your business is, you may adopt a process once every several years. On the other hand, if your company is expanding into new areas and growing by hiring or mergers and acquisitions, you may find that your process needs change every six months. Process improvement, however, is a continuous effort. You should constantly monitor and fine-tune your processes, no matter what type of business you are in.

TOOLS

Several tools can assist you in your SPI efforts:

- **IBM Rational process authoring tools:** The most obvious tools that can be used for SPI with the EUP are the IBM Rational tools to modify and extend the RUP: RUP Modeler, RUP Process Workbench, RUP Builder, and of course the RUP product itself. These are all available through IBM (`www.ibm.com`). RUP plug-ins are also freely available on the Internet, including forthcoming EUP plug-ins at `www.enterpriseunifiedprocess.com/downloads`.

- **Other process authoring tools:** Other tools can assist you in documenting your process; the EUP (or RUP) does not have to be configured with the IBM Rational toolset. The RUP can be deployed "as is," and you can denote your tailoring in other fashions. One approach is to use IRIS Process Author (`www.osellus.com`) with its RUP bridge. Another mechanism, discussed previously, is to "wrap" the RUP with your changes. Any HTML authoring tool like Microsoft FrontPage (`www.microsoft.com`) or Macromedia Dreamweaver (`www.macromedia.com`) can be used for this.

- **Automated process mentors:** Jaczone, one of Ivar Jacobson's companies, offers a tool called Waypointer (`www.jaczone.com`) which mentors people who are taking a RUP-based approach to software development. Waypointer is the electronic equivalent of someone watching you over your shoulder as you work, providing tips and suggestions for improving your approach.

- **Feedback and discussion:** Promoting feedback from teams to institute continuous process improvement is a long-term goal of SPI efforts. To that end, implementing a mechanism for discussions is vital. We suggest something simple, such as an internal mailing list or a wiki (`www.wiki.org`). Your goal is to provide people with an easy mechanism to pose questions to process engineers (and each other) and eventually provide a knowledge base for people to search for answers to process questions.

- **Groupware and collaboration:** You may also opt to deploy a collaboration tool like eRoom (`www.documentum.com`) or Groove Virtual Office (`www.groove.net`) for project teams to use. Such tools allow project teams to share and control artifacts and offer features like announcements, discussion groups, and instant messaging to facilitate project communication. They can also serve as project repositories that can be reviewed by process engineers when performing project retrospectives.

RELATION TO OTHER DISCIPLINES

The SPI discipline interacts with the following other disciplines:

- **Enterprise Business Modeling:** The enterprise vision, goals, and targets that are developed during Enterprise Business Modeling are used during the process assessment to develop the vision for the process improvement effort.

- **Environment:** The SPI discipline expands on the Environment discipline to address a larger scope—namely, all of IT (or a particular subset of IT). It forms the basis for the development cases used to tailor the process for individual projects.

SUMMARY

Successful SPI is a cross-project endeavor that must be managed at the enterprise level. The Software Process Improvement discipline defines the activities necessary to define and support the software process(es) for your organization. It describes how to determine your process needs, how to craft a new process or tailor an existing process, and how to deploy and manage the process. SPI is an iterative process that will entail adjustment based on feedback and actual results.

Suggested Reading

Chapter 14, which provides guidance on how to adopt the EUP, also discusses how to treat an SPI initiative as a project.

CMM Implementation Guide: Choreographing Software Process Improvement (Caputo 1998). Although you may want to take some of the CMM-based advice with a grain of salt, this book provides critical insights into SPI within large organizations.

Fearless Change: Patterns for Introducing New Ideas (Manns and Rising 2005). This book describes a multitude of techniques for changing your organization.

Project Retrospectives (Kerth 2001). This is the fundamental book on project retrospectives, a critical technique for identifying what went right and wrong during a project. Kerth also maintains the site www.retrospectives.com, posting new insights into this technique.

The IDEAL (SM) Model (Software Engineering Institute 2004b). The Initiating, Diagnosing, Establishing, Acting, and Learning (IDEAL) model defines one approach to adopting processes into an organization.

Strategies for Information Technology Governance (Van Grembergen 2003). This book explores the process, organizational structures, and other mechanisms that help an organization meet its IT strategies and objectives.

Part IV

Putting It All Together

Chapter 14

Adopting the Enterprise Unified Process

Reader ROI

- Manage your EUP process adoption effort like a project.
- Adopt the RUP before you adopt the EUP extensions.
- Take a staged approach to avoid overwhelming people.
- Prepare and execute training and mentoring plans.
- Be prepared to adjust the process over time.

It's one thing to identify the need for a system development process (or, more importantly, a full-fledged information technology process); it's another to actually adopt one within your organization. This chapter discusses our suggested approach to adopting the Enterprise Unified Process (EUP).

As we pointed out in Chapter 13, "The Software Process Improvement Discipline," the primary drivers for process improvement are business ones. Implementing a process for its own sake is a bad idea. Process improvement is an enabler, not an end unto itself. Furthermore, defining and implementing a software process does not guarantee results, but it can go a long way toward helping you reach your business goals.

SOFTWARE PROCESS IMPROVEMENT IMPLEMENTATION

Chapter 3 described how the EUP is a wrapper around, and an extension to, the Rational Unified Process (RUP). Although the Production phase, Retirement phase, and Operations and Support discipline are fairly straightforward to adopt, the enterprise management disciplines typically are not.

TIP   **Succeed with the RUP First**

Organizations that are struggling at succeeding with single projects don't have much of a chance at succeeding with the cross-project issues that the enterprise management disciplines address. Our advice is simple—take a "first things first" approach and adopt the enterprise management disciplines only after you can honestly claim that you can apply the RUP successfully.

We've found that the best way to introduce the EUP into an organization is to follow the EUP, forcing you to practice what you preach; others also advocate a similar approach (Pollice, Curtis, Barnard, and Kruchten 2002) by following the RUP phases as an implementation strategy. We prefer the EUP because software processes must be maintained after they have been deployed, which fits well with the EUP's Production phase.

TIP   **Start Slowly**

You cannot make all the changes you want to immediately; it is simply too great a change for most organizations to absorb at once. Prioritize the process improvements that your organization needs to make, expect that it will take several years and that you will experience difficulties while doing so.

As in everything else, be practical and do what works best in your particular environment. Too many organizations issue a decree such as "We're going to use RUP/EUP/XP/FDD/DSDM/..." and then expect to immediately reap untold benefits, only to be disappointed when these benefits are not immediately forthcoming. Like any other complex effort, process improvement must be managed properly. This means planning, communicating, managing people and resources, and so on—all the things you do on any other project.

> **TIP** **Bring in an Expert to Help You**
>
> Process improvement is a complex and difficult endeavor, one you are likely to need help with. You can increase your chance of success by bringing in someone, either as an employee or a consultant, who has a process background—someone who has been actively involved in process improvement programs in the past. In addition, you will benefit from having experienced RUP and EUP mentors on hand when adopting these techniques.

Proceed Incrementally

We can't stress this enough: proceed incrementally. Deploy a new process as you would eat the proverbial elephant—one bite at a time. We've seen too many organizations fail because they think they can do it all at once. That approach is a recipe for disaster and frankly is a classic anti-pattern for SPI. IT is a complex endeavor, and asking people to accept a large change such as adopting a new process all at once is asking too much.

Start with a tailored RUP process. Get that working first to demonstrate that you can handle development projects iteratively following the RUP. This is not as easy as it sounds. If your organization has a waterfall background, this alone could take you several years.

Next, select the portions of the EUP you will deploy first. This will typically be the Production phase, the Operations and Support discipline, and the Retirement phase, in that order. The enterprise management disciplines are harder and usually are done last for two reasons. First, they may be similar to RUP activities but taken to a higher, more complex level. For example, the Enterprise Architecture discipline is similar in many ways to activities in the RUP Analysis and Design discipline. However, architecting solutions across the enterprise is much more difficult than architecting solutions for a single system. It's a simple matter of scope—the enterprise management disciplines have a much larger scope than project activities. Second, the enterprise management disciplines have a broad impact. For example, your strategic reuse program will impact just about all your projects, as will your enterprise architecture effort. This makes it difficult to do a lot of the EUP at once.

Our suggested approach is this: After you have deployed the RUP process, begin another release of the EUP adoption project. Define a vision of what you are doing, prove that you can do it, construct it iteratively, and then roll it out and support it using the approach outlined in this chapter. Proceed from there, prioritizing and implementing portions of the EUP. You may even decide to run two or more adoption efforts in parallel, although this can be difficult, as they will overlap to some extent.

Let's examine the EUP adoption process one phase at a time.

The Inception Phase of an EUP Adoption Project

During the Inception phase, your primary goal is to "achieve consensus among all stakeholders on the objectives of the project" (IBM 2004). EUP adoption stakeholders include but are not limited to senior management, project managers, business representatives, architects, developers, testers, quality assurance, operations staff, support staff, and end users. During this phase, you will do the following:

- **Identify the vision:** Work with the stakeholders to create a vision, which will document your stakeholders' needs and their success criteria. The vision should describe why you're adopting the EUP, showing how it addresses the organizational needs of your stakeholders. You should use the vision document to keep your adoption team focused and on track.

- **Develop a business case:** The business case describes the economic plan, including the return on investment (ROI) and payback period, for adopting the EUP. This is crucial information for determining whether to go forward at the Lifecycle Objectives (LCO) milestone. Potential benefits include decreasing time to market, lowering defect rates, and improving responsiveness to customers.

- **Assess the organization:** You should honestly assess your organization's process to identify your capability gaps. You should consider bringing in an outsider to provide a more objective viewpoint. Chapter 13 provides advice on how to conduct an assessment.

- **Create a communication plan:** It is essential that you let others know what are you doing, why are you doing it, the business case for it, success stories, and the defined methods for feedback. Keeping people informed about how things are going, even if you are encountering difficulties, will help get them (and keep them) on board. Trumpet your successes and share your lessons learned with everyone. There are various options for this: a newsletter, a web site, periodic e-mails to key personnel, and so on; do what makes sense in your culture.

- **Identify risks:** There are inherent risks in changing an organization's software process. Some can be anticipated, and some cannot. Start planning to address those risks now, with a workable and prioritized risk list, and keep it updated throughout the project.

- **Develop a plan:** Based on the vision that was laid out and the risks you have detailed, you should develop a high-level plan for the rest of the effort. Analogous to the Software Development Plan in RUP, the Process Implementation Plan will lay out the high-level plan for the effort, the resources required, and the high-level timeline.

TIP   Align the EUP with Business Goals and Objectives
The best process in the world is meaningless if it doesn't meet your organization's goals. Keep the business goals first and foremost as you craft and implement your software processes.

At the end of the Inception phase of the EUP adoption project, you should assess whether you should continue with the effort—the focus of the LCO milestone. You must demonstrate that you have a vision of what you are trying to accomplish, define the scope of your project, have a list of risks you are facing and a plan for dealing with them, and have developed a high-level plan for the rest of the effort. Your stakeholders must agree that you have done all this and that it is acceptable in order for you to proceed.

The Elaboration Phase of an EUP Adoption Project

During the Elaboration phase of an RUP project, the primary goal is to baseline the architecture to provide a stable basis for future work. During an EUP adoption project, you will identify organizational changes that will need to be made and then identify and acquire tools you will need. This work will provide the stable base for the rest of the project.

It is difficult to make software process changes without impacting your organization. Depending on your current structure, your stated needs, and success criteria, you may need to make significant changes such as the introduction of an Enterprise Architecture Group, a Program Management Office, and so on.

> **TIP** **Expect Changes to Your Organization Structure**
> Process, organizational structure, and corporate culture all go hand-in-hand—change one, and you will impact the others.

> **TIP** **Form a Software Engineering Process Group (SEPG)**
> You should consider forming an SEPG (Software Engineering Institute 1995) to own and shepherd the EUP. Your SEPG's sole responsibility is to support the improvement of your organization's software process. The change agent responsible for defining and implementing your organization's software process is usually a member of the SEPG and is often the leader. The SEPG should be kept small—as a rule of thumb, we suggest one SEPG member for every 100 developers in your organization—and should be a full-time job. The SEPG will assist in the efforts of the assessment (SEPG members often take on the role of Auditor) and will shepherd the development, deployment, and maintenance of the EUP.

The tools you choose to define and disseminate the process at your organization will vary. In addition to process authoring tools, you will most likely need additional tools for project teams to use when they implement the EUP. A typical list is shown in Table 14-1. Some you will purchase and put in place immediately; for others, you will wait until project teams need them.

TABLE 14-1   *Potentials Tools for Process Adoption*

Tool Type	Usage	Examples
Process definition	Tailor/define the process	Rational Process Workbench (www.ibm.com), Microsoft Frontpage (www.microsoft.com/frontpage), Macromedia Dreamweaver (www.macromedia.com/software/dreamweaver), Iris Process Author (www.osellus.com)
Documentation tools	Document the requirements, vision, architecture, and others for your adoption efforts	Microsoft Visio (www.microsoft.com/office/visio), Microsoft Word (office.microsoft.com)
Version control	Track changes to artifacts as they are developed	Rational ClearCase (www.ibm.com), CVS (www.cvshome.org), eRoom (www.eroom.net)
Change management	Track reported defects and change requests, to prioritize and assign them to developers, and to track progress	Rational ClearQuest (www.ibm.com), BugZilla (www.bugzilla.com), CVS (www.cvshome.org)
Planning	Plan, schedule, and track tasks, resources, and their interdependencies	Microsoft Project (www.office.microsoft.com/project), WBS Chart Pro (www.criticaltools.com/wbsmain.htm), Mr. Project (mrproject.codefactory.se)
Groupware	Share models, documents, and so on with others	eRoom (www.eroom.net), Apache (www.apache.org), Groove (www.groove.net)

Just as you develop a working technical prototype on a RUP project to prove your system architecture, you also need to prove your EUP process deployment architecture. Your first step is to set up your process development environment by installing your chosen tools. The next step is to use those tools to deploy an initial version of the EUP; perhaps you'll edit a few pages to put your corporate logo onto them and post it to your intranet. Although this effort sounds trivial, the end result is that you've proven your process architecture, thereby ensuring that you're ready to begin actual construction.

At the end of the Elaboration phase, you should have identified the technological tools and techniques that you will use to deploy the process. You also have identified the organizational changes that need to be implemented to support the process. Finally, you will have detailed the plan for the Construction phase, typically by updating your process implementation plan. At the Lifecycle Architecture (LCA) milestone, you must demonstrate that you have a stable vision and architecture, that your cost and time estimates are acceptable, and that you have a realistic plan to succeed.

The Construction Phase of an EUP Adoption Project

During this phase of the EUP adoption project, you will "construct" the process and implement it on a pilot project or two before you deploying it to a wide audience. You will review the EUP process content and modify it based on your organizational, business, technical, and cultural needs. Your goal is not to make it perfect but rather to make it good enough for pilot projects to use. To do this, you will

- Tailor the EUP content
- Create development cases
- Tailor guidance and templates
- Run pilot projects

Tailor the EUP Content
Your goal is to tailor the EUP process content based on your vision for what your process needs to do to support your business. Our advice is to take a minimalist approach and not attempt to change every minute detail so that your process definition is perfect; instead, concentrate on the high-priority issues and get it "good enough." If your organization adopts pair programming, for example, you need to note that. If you have implemented the Enterprise Architecture discipline, your Analysis and Design discipline must reflect this so that people understand what is expected of them.

You also need to take into consideration your particular culture. You should involve subject matter experts (SMEs) from various disciplines with your company. Leveraging their knowledge, along with the outcome of your assessment, will enable you to tailor the process based on what is known to work in your organization and what you struggle with. The EUP is a process framework; you need to use it to create a process that is tailored specifically for you.

TIP	**Tailoring the EUP is the Easy Part**
	Many organizations are very successful at defining a software process, often producing binders of documentation or web pages, but if you visit them a few months later the process will be all but forgotten. Getting people to accept your new process and making the organizational and cultural changes that go along with it will take significant time and effort. Writing a process is the easy part; integrating it into your corporate culture is the hard part.

Create Development Cases

Development cases define the process tailoring that is followed on a particular project. Organizational-level development cases, described in greater detail in Chapter 13, are optional. We recommend them because they help provide consistency across project teams and can speed project efforts. If you decide to utilize them, you should have several types of organizational-level development cases, depending on project types, such as one for small projects, one for large projects, one for maintenance upgrades, and so on.

If you choose not to implement organizational-level development cases, you should detail your strategy for how projects will document development cases. You can use the development case template that comes with RUP; that works fine for many organizations. We've found that including your process deviations in a section in the software development plan works well, too, and is easier to develop and maintain. Whatever approach you decide to take for development cases, you should lay the foundation for it during your EUP adoption efforts.

Tailor Guidance and Templates

As discussed in Chapter 13, you'll also need guidance (standards and guidelines) and templates, which will evolve over time. You'll probably start with the RUP and EUP templates as an initial set. Keep in mind that you're not trying to get everything 100% perfect. For example, you want a use case specification template that is sufficient to get you started on your first project; the one that comes with RUP will most likely be good enough to start with. You should identify the sections that you feel are important to your organization, but you don't need to try to anticipate everything that you might need in a use case specification. Process adoption is an iterative and incremental effort. You will learn and adapt as you go; do not try to do it all at once in the beginning.

Run Pilot Projects
You should demonstrate your tailoring(s) of the EUP before releasing them into your organization. The best approach is to run a pilot project to see how well the EUP works within a controlled environment. The primary objective of the pilot project is to prove that your process works, enabling you to develop and deploy applications effectively. You should pick a pilot project that meets the following criteria:

- **Important but not mission-critical:** You want a project that people will perceive as being a fair test of the process, yet at the same time you don't want to put your organization at risk because you've chosen an inappropriate process.

- **Low visibility:** You don't want senior management asking about your pilot project during the CTO staff meeting, except of course in the context of your process adoption effort.

- **Non-time-critical:** Not only will you work slower than usual, you'll learn new ways of working. Therefore, you'll also make some mistakes. The point is that you'll need ample slack time in the project schedule to recover from these challenges.

- **Manageable scope:** You don't need to solve a large, complex problem on the initial run-through of the process. Similarly, if the project scope is trivial, people will not believe that your process will work for them.

- **Reasonable size:** Likewise, you don't need to prove that you can handle a project team of 35 people at first. On the other hand, showing that it works for a team of two people wouldn't be all that impressive.

- **Staffed with experienced people:** You want to concentrate on the process during the pilot project, not on getting people trained on new techniques (to them) such as use cases or Java. If possible, select senior people from many different groups so that they can share their experience with a wide audience.

During the pilot project, you will iteratively and incrementally define and implement the process. If you are working on the Requirements discipline and find that you must adjust the process to work within your organization, do not wait until the end of the pilot project to make changes to the your process definition. Adjust as you go so that you create a software process that actually works for your pilot project. For example, you may decide that it's important to recognize future potential changes that are architecturally significant, so you may add change cases (Bennett 1997; Ambler 2004) to the process, something that the RUP currently does not have. Use them on the project and add them to the process definition during the pilot project.

At the end of the pilot project, evaluate your results. Make adjustments to the process and organization as necessary. If you feel it's warranted, particularly if the previous pilot project identified significant challenges, run an additional pilot project. Otherwise, develop a detailed plan for the Transition phase. A strategy to assess how the adoption is proceeding should be part of your plan. See the later section "Measure Progress" for a discussion of measurements for an EUP adoption effort.

At the end of this phase, you will have a software process that you have proven actually works within your organization. At the Initial Operational Capability (IOC) milestone at the end of Construction, you must demonstrate a stable process, acceptable risks, cost and time estimates, and a plan for deploying the EUP to your IT organization.

The Transition Phase of an EUP Adoption Project

You deploy your tailored version of the EUP to your organization during the Transition phase. During the Construction phase, you tailored the EUP to meet your specific needs and proved it on one or more pilot projects under controlled circumstances. Now you must roll out the EUP to a much wider audience with varying skills and experience. Our advice is to

- **Seed projects with people from the pilot project(s):** These people have experience with your newly defined process and are therefore the best candidates to either lead or mentor the next round of project teams. Build up your organization's comfort level with the process as well as your people's expertise.

- **Trumpet your successes:** Let people know when things are working and that the process will work for them.

- **Learn from your mistakes:** Expect to make mistakes, and when you do, learn from them.

- **Leave well enough alone:** Do not try to adopt the process into existing projects, because you could easily put them at risk of failing. Allow them to proceed as they were, but let them leverage some parts of the process where appropriate.

- **Consider a staged release of the process:** If you have a large IT organization but a relatively small process team, you probably will be well suited to deploy the process incrementally to manageable groups one at a time, perhaps by location or department.

However you organize it, the Transition phase ends when the process has been deployed for the organization to use. The Product Release milestone at the end of Transition requires that you have user acceptance of the EUP, that stakeholders are satisfied, and that your SPI group is ready to support the EUP.

The Production Phase of an EUP Adoption Project

During the Production phase, you need to support and maintain the process. That means continuing the communications effort (perhaps via a newsletter or web site), continuing training and mentoring, and continuing to adjust of the process as you learn more and as your organization grows.

By this point you should have identified the metrics you will be gathering. You will gather them and learn from them during this phase. You should be holding retrospectives (Kerth 2001) when projects close so that you can improve your instantiation of the EUP.

You will need to evolve your instantiation of the EUP as your organization evolves. This is not unusual; change is a constant in software processes. Although you will probably reduce the number of people on your process team after it has been deployed and incorporated into the organization, the need for process support never truly goes away. It may ramp down to a part-time position for a while, but it will most likely require more resources on an occasional basis, such as when your business priorities shift or when new technologies or methodologies emerge.

The Retirement Phase of an EUP Adoption Project

Let's be honest—if there is one lesson that the IT industry has learned in its short lifetime, it is that something better always comes along. Although the EUP reflects the industry's current best practices and techniques, we have no doubt that it will eventually be superceded by an even better approach. This likely won't be anytime soon, but you should still be prepared to adopt a new IT lifecycle when the time is right. During the Retirement phase, you will still need to continue supporting teams following the EUP as your IT organization incrementally adopts its new process. You may want to archive your process definition; this is particularly true in regulated environments where you must be able to show that you followed a defined process so that you can roll back to the EUP if your new process isn't successful.

TRAINING

You will most likely have to offer process training for teams and individuals. It is highly unlikely that all your people have the skills required to follow the process. Your training curriculum will be driven by your organization's knowledge of the process being deployed and its strengths and weaknesses as determined by the assessment done at the beginning of the process adoption effort.

A sample curriculum for an EUP adoption effort is summarized in Table 14-2.

TABLE 14-2   *Training Curriculum Example*

Course	Description
EUP for Executives	A brief overview given to executive management explaining the EUP and stressing the goals of the process and how project status will be reported up the hierarchy. This will likely be half a day in length.
EUP for Project Teams	A course outlining the EUP in broad terms for project teams, usually lasting four to eight hours. Topics include phases and disciplines, the iterative nature of projects, and roles and responsibilities.
Iterative Project Management	A tutorial for project managers detailing how to manage iterative projects. It stresses the iterative nature of the EUP and how to plan, run, and report on iterative projects. This can take from a single day to as long a week, including hands-on exercises.
Discipline-Specific Workshops	A one- to two-day course concentrating on a specific discipline may be helpful in your efforts. It would concentrate on a single discipline such as requirements, analysis and design, strategic reuse, or enterprise architecture and provide in-depth coverage of how it is applied on projects.
Skill-Specific Workshops	Concentrates on a particular skill, such as how to write use cases, Agile Model-Driven Development (AMDD), fundamentals of the Unified Modeling Language (UML), test-driven development (TDD), or agile database techniques. This is targeted to a wider audience than a discipline-specific workshop.

TIP   Just-In-Time (JIT) Training Works Best
Training undertaken too early will be mostly forgotten before it can be applied, whereas late training may disrupt a project schedule. Try to hold training a week or two before it will be applied. Put training in project schedules; make it part of the project and budget the time and costs.

Your particular training curriculum will be driven by your specific needs as identified in your process assessment. Develop and/or adapt training materials during your pilot project. If you do it any earlier, you'll likely need to rework your training materials based on process changes made during the pilot. You can even wait until the end of the pilot project if appropriate. Regardless, be prepared to adjust the material as you update the process and as you learn more about what works well and what doesn't in your environment.

Training is a start, but it will take a while for people to develop fundamental skills. An analyst new to use cases can be taught the basics of capturing requirements using use cases, but it will take a while for him or her to develop the fundamental skills for doing it properly. Do not expect people to become experts after a round of training. Some skills take time to develop. One way to help reduce the learning curve is through mentoring.

MENTORING

Mentoring involves having an expert provide teams and individuals with hands-on assistance in applying new skills. Having a mentor or mentors work with teams will greatly assist the process adoption effort. Not only will this help ensure that the process is applied correctly, but it will also reduce stress on individuals and help increase productivity. Who you mentor and how much will depend on the strengths and weaknesses of teams and individuals. In our experience, you can get the most benefit by addressing project managers, architects, and requirements specifiers and analysts.

As described in Chapter 3, we recommend a four-step mentoring approach: step one, train and educate in the EUP; step two, show people how to apply it; step three, help people apply it; step four, support and review their work as they work on their own. The complexity of the subject being mentored is a large factor in how quickly mentoring can proceed. People also absorb new concepts at different rates. Some people are more amenable to being mentored, while others prefer to strike out on their own as soon as possible. The actual time spent on each step depends on these and other factors. Some companies express a preference for skipping the second step and moving directly to the third step, although in our opinion, this slows down the entire process.

Good mentors know the subject area and how to transfer those skills to others. It can cost a lot of money and yield little return if the mentor is skilled in the particular technique but cannot transfer skills effectively. A mentor's interpersonal skills are just as important as, if not more important than, his or her technical skills. This also applies to a "train the trainer" approach to mentoring, where a mentor is brought in to mentor people who then become mentors to others. Although the people initially mentored may become proficient in the particular skill set, they may not be good at mentoring others because they lack knowledge-transferring skills.

Training and mentoring both have the same goal: to increase expertise in a particular area. Thus, the training and mentoring efforts need to be coordinated closely. The ultimate solution is to have the mentors deliver the training. If that is not possible, have your mentors audit the training to ensure that your training and mentoring messages are consistent.

MEASURE PROGRESS

You'll want to start gathering metrics as soon as possible. Continuous improvement is your goal, and metrics help immensely in that regard because they provide a data-based indication of how the process is helping you meet your goals. Table 14-3 lists some possible metrics.

TABLE 14-3   *Potential Metrics for Process Adoption*

Metric	Category	Usage
Return on Investment (ROI)	Financial	The net benefits of a project divided by its total costs. Enables you to compare projects of different sizes.
Number of defects	Quality	A measurement of the number of errors in systems. A large number found by end users may indicate that you need to improve your testing efforts.
Time per project	Efficiency	A key metric if time to market is a key business driver. This will allow you to measure how rapidly you are building and deploying systems.

The metrics you implement should support the goals as defined in your vision for the EUP adoption effort. Metrics should not be viewed in isolation. There are trade-offs in software development; you can usually speed time to market if you are willing to live with more defects in your products or to ignore change requests, for example. A positive trend in time-to-market metrics should be viewed in the over-all context of all your metrics. Did you reduce time to market by becoming more efficient in your software development efforts, or did you just throw something together quickly that is of poor quality? You need to examine all pertinent metrics to get a true picture of what is happening.

TIP   **Trends Are More Important Than Absolutes**

Knowing that you have 27 defects in a product does not necessarily mean much; knowing that you had 56 defects six months ago, 42 defects three months ago, and 27 defects currently is much more meaningful.

You should define metrics that you want to capture, but you must use them with discretion early on. Metrics on the pilot project, for example, are meaningless until they can be compared to metrics (or estimates) from a "traditional" project approach in the organization or to later projects. Comparing them to earlier projects that used a different process may be misleading.

SUCCESS?

Have you truly succeeded? Review your original (or updated) vision document. Have you met your stakeholders' success criteria? Is everyone satisfied with the results? Are you realizing the ROI you defined in your business case? If not, why not? Have business conditions changed? Do your metrics indicate areas that need improvement? Do the metrics still make sense to you?

TIP   **Keep the Real Goal in Mind**

Our experience has been that the EUP, when applied intelligently, increases the productivity of developers. Our experience has also been that when processes are applied less than intelligently, as when the paper pushers have too much influence within an organization, processes can decrease your productivity. Organizations that keep the end goal in mind—developing, maintaining, and supporting software that fulfills the needs of their user community—will be successful in implementing software processes. Those that follow processes simply for the sake of doing so are likely to fail.

Process improvement is an ongoing effort. Even if you have satisfied your original goals, you still have work to do in the Production phase. Monitor your execution. Do not become complacent; look for ways to improve. Be prepared to respond to a changing business environment or changing priorities.

> **TIP** **Have Patience**
> Progress will be slow at first—slower than you hoped or expected. In fact, you will most likely see a decrease in productivity at first. Introducing the EUP into your organization will take time—it's a cultural shift.

SUMMARY

Adoption of the EUP is a complex endeavor. Start with the RUP and implement a tailored version of it first. Treat that effort as a process adoption project, following the EUP phases and milestones. Run a pilot project or two and test drive it before you roll it out. A good strategy is to add the EUP phases and disciplines after you have succeeded with RUP, rolling out your overall process a bit at a time. Keep the lines of communication open and learn and adjust the process as conditions change.

Suggested Reading

Adopting the Enterprise Unified Process (Nalbone, Vizdos, and Ambler 2003b) goes into greater detail about the adoption effort. It formed the basis for this chapter.

Adopting the Rational Unified Process (Bergstrom and Raberg 2004) takes an in-depth look at adopting RUP, which is the first step for successfully adopting EUP.

RUP Implementation Guide Part I: Recommended Strategy and Typical Issues and Risks (Pollice, Curtis, Barnard, and Kruchten 2002) overviews a strategy for implementing RUP in an organization.

Chapter 15

Parting Thoughts

Software development is very difficult, and the Rational Unified Process (RUP) does a very good job of describing how to succeed at it. Running an information technology (IT) department is even harder; not only do you have to be good at software development, you also have to be good at operating and supporting systems after they're in production and even retiring them from use after they've served their purpose. Because you probably have many systems either proposed, being developed, or in production, you need to consider a myriad of cross-system issues. The Enterprise Unified Process (EUP) starts where the RUP ends, describing how to turn the RUP into a full IT lifecycle.

It is crucial for an IT organization to follow one or more software processes. A system development process such as the RUP helps guide project teams in a consistent, affordable, and (relatively) predictable manner. This should result in high-quality systems that meet the needs of their stakeholders. An IT lifecycle such as the EUP, depicted in Figure 15-1, goes beyond system development to look at the entire picture. This book has described the EUP, focusing on the two phases and eight disciplines it adds to the RUP.

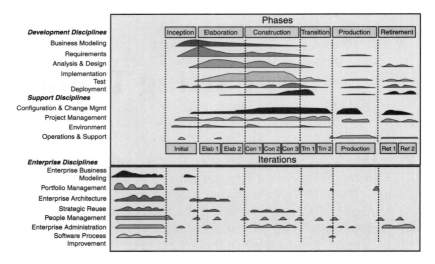

FIGURE 15-1   *The EUP IT lifecycle.*

There is a lot to the EUP. Luckily you don't need to adopt all of
it at once; you can choose the portions of it that address your most
immediate needs. All things being equal, we suggest the following
order of adoption:

1. **Software Process Improvement (SPI) discipline:** The SPI
   discipline is required to manage your successful adoption
   of the EUP and then improve it over time. Start with a simple and small process group that is focused on immediate,
   measurable results.

2. **Production phase and the Operations and Support discipline:** Our philosophy is that the best developers realize that
   the systems they are building today need to be maintained,
   operated, and supported tomorrow. We also recognize how
   difficult it is to do these things—you need a defined process
   if you are to be successful. Chances are very good that
   you're already doing these things within your organization
   and that you're reasonably good at them (although you
   could always improve). We've found that most organizations
   can easily adopt this phase and discipline and thereby have
   the majority of their IT department follow a common tailoring of the Unified Process.

3. **Enterprise Business Modeling, Enterprise Architecture, and Portfolio Management disciplines:** These disciplines provide the high-level business, technical, and management vision and direction for your IT department. Furthermore, because they're highly related and interconnected, you really want to adopt all three at once.

4. **People Management and Enterprise Administration disciplines:** These two disciplines describe critical support activities that your IT department needs to succeed. Many people want to leave these until last, often believing that they're already doing fine at these activities, but the reality is that these disciplines need to work in an evolutionary manner just like the other disciplines. We've seen too many IT departments hobbled by administration and human resources groups that are still following traditional techniques when everyone else has adopted the RUP. Don't let this happen to you.

5. **Strategic Reuse discipline:** Successful reuse requires you to have a common business and technical vision in place; hence, it needs to come after enterprise business modeling and enterprise architecture (or in parallel with them).

6. **Retirement phase:** Although retiring systems is a very difficult task, it is one that occurs very infrequently—instead, it is far more common to evolve a system over time. As a result, this is often the lowest-priority portion of the EUP to adopt.

We've provided a lot of good advice throughout this book for succeeding with the EUP. Here's the most important advice we can give you:

- **Keep it simple:** In general, people don't read detailed process documentation, and when they do, it's often as part of their initial training in a subject. The reality is that you don't need a lot of detail. What you do need is a good overview of what needs to be done, templates for critical artifacts, good examples of those artifacts, and realistic guidance (standards and guidelines) for creating the artifacts. Consider yourself lucky if your staff uses even that much of your process-related materials.

- **Focus on people:** Systems are developed, maintained, and supported by people. If you want to be successful, you need to ensure that the people involved have the skills and knowledge required to do their jobs. People, not process, roles, or extensive documentation, are the major component of your IT success. Get your people the right training and mentoring that they need in a timely and organized fashion.

- **Your process, architecture, and organizational culture must reflect one another:** You'll follow different development processes for COBOL mainframe applications than you will for Java server-based applications. You'll follow different processes within a formal, regulations-oriented culture than you will in an Internet startup. Remember that what is a best practice within one organization may be a worst practice for yours.

- **Get help:** It's very hard to succeed at IT, and if you're not very good at it now, you probably don't have the in-house expertise to become good at it. You'll need help, ideally from people who not only have solid RUP experience but more importantly who also understand that there is far more to the IT lifecycle than what the RUP covers—not to mention that there are alternative techniques to those that the RUP does include. These people are very difficult to find. You'll likely need to hire people from a boutique consulting firm that specializes in software process improvement and mentoring; most large firms don't seem able to attract senior people with the formidable skill set that is required to mentor people in the EUP.

- **Respect the anti-patterns:** At the end of each discipline chapter we shared several anti-patterns, common approaches that are proven to not work very well in practice, to help you to identify strategies that likely won't work for you. Chances are fairly good that your organization exhibits several of these anti-patterns already. Our advice is simple—stop doing stupid things and start doing smart things.

There no longer needs to be dark and stormy nights when your IT department fails to deliver once again. By adopting and tailoring the EUP to meet your needs and then executing on that vision effectively, your organization can succeed at the software game. It won't be easy, but without an effective IT process to help guide your efforts, you will continue to struggle at IT. If this continues, it will only be a matter of time until senior executives give up on you and choose to outsource parts or all of your IT department. It doesn't have to be that way if you choose to succeed.

Appendix A
Roles

This appendix describes the roles of the EUP.

Customer Support Representative (CSR): The initial and primary contact point with the user for providing technical support.

Enterprise Administrator: This abstract role is actively involved in managing physical and informational assets along with security and working with project teams. The four roles that inherit from this one are the network, facilities, information, and security administrators.

Enterprise Architect: Responsible for modeling, communicating, evolving, and supporting the business and technical architectures of your organization.

Enterprise Business Modeler: Works closely with enterprise stakeholders to define the goals, targets, and vision for your enterprise.

Enterprise Configuration Control Board (ECCB): Responsible for reviewing any incoming change requests, including both enhancements and defects.

Enterprise Stakeholder: Senior business executives, senior IT executives, suppliers, customers, and domain experts (often senior business analysts) who provide input into your enterprise modeling activities.

Facilities Administrator: Manages the facilities—such as buildings, new construction, and undeveloped land—for your organization.

Human Resources Manager: Responsible for assisting with staffing projects and supporting individuals with their career management efforts.

Information Administrator: Responsible for managing the information assets of your organization, including data, intellectual property (IP), and licenses.

Network Administrator: Responsible for managing and supporting the hardware and network for the organization.

Operations Manager: Responsible for managing operations efforts. This includes planning for operations and disaster recovery and executing the disaster recovery plan if required.

Operator: Responsible for keeping systems running, backing up and restoring data, managing any problems, performing periodic cleanup, fine-tuning and any system reconfigurations, monitoring systems, and re-deploying systems as necessary.

Portfolio Manager: Responsibilities include evaluating and prioritizing potential projects. This can be either a single person or a board composed of senior business and IT management.

Process Engineer: Responsible for determining process needs, creating or tailoring the process, ensuring that project teams have access to the process, and assisting project teams in the application of the process.

Program Manager: Responsible for ensuring that projects within the program meet the goals of the program, making sure that individual projects are on track according to the plan, and taking corrective action if necessary.

Program Reviewer: Responsible for planning and conducting the review of enterprise programs such as your strategic reuse or portfolio management efforts.

Reuse Consumer: Anyone who reuses existing assets in the creation of new assets.

Reuse Engineer: Responsible for encouraging and supporting reuse within projects as well as harvesting and/or generalizing assets to make them reusable.

Reuse Manager: Responsible for allocating resources, shaping priorities, establishing reuse quality practices and measurements, coordinating with project teams, and keeping the reuse team focused on its goals.

Reuse Registrar: Responsible for maintaining and supporting use of your reuse repository.

Security Administrator: This person is accountable for physical and information technology (IT) security.

Support Developer: Responsible for resolving and deploying high-priority defects to production systems.

Support Manager: Responsible for managing support efforts. This includes planning, prioritizing work, assigning work to people, and then managing work activities.

System Support Representative (SSR): Responsible for evaluating issues and creating change requests.

Vendor Manager: Responsible for identifying contractors and then awarding and monitoring contracts (often someone from the purchasing department).

Artifacts

This appendix describes the artifacts of the EUP.

Alert: A notion that something requires immediate attention while monitoring systems in a production environment.

Announcement: Communicates the availability of an asset.

Asset Criteria: Defines the requirements that an existing asset must conform to for you to consider generalizing it into a reusable asset.

Asset Rework Plan: Defines your approach to generalizing an existing asset to make it reusable.

Backups: The media where data is stored for restoration purposes.

Benefits Package: Supplementary advantages to people within your organization.

Candidate Architecture: A potential technology or concept you may want to integrate into your enterprise architecture.

Configured Asset: An asset created for a specific use.

Contract: A legally binding document between two entities.

Defect Report: A type of change request that defines a system-related problem; that is, the system is not working the way it is supposed to.

Development Case: Defines the particular process tailoring that will be used on a specific project.

Disaster Recovery Plan (DRP): Defines the steps you will follow to get your critical systems back up and running in case something catastrophic happens.

Education Plan: Defines the strategy to train and mentor an individual.

Enhancement Request: A type of change request describing an addition or modification to one or more systems.

Enterprise Architecture Model: Depicts the frameworks, networks, deployment configurations, supporting technical infrastructure, and domain infrastructure for an organization.

Enterprise Business Architecture Requirements: Non-technical requirements applicable to the enterprise architecture.

Enterprise Business Glossary: Defines a common vocabulary within your organization.

Enterprise Business Process Model: Captures the fundamental business processes, external entities (customers, suppliers, partners, or competitors), and the major workflows between them.

Enterprise Business Rules Specification: The definition of the constraints that influence or guide the everyday workings of an organization.

Enterprise Computing Infrastructure Plan: Documents the infrastructure plans, including both hardware and networks.

Enterprise Data Guidance: Describes standards and guidelines pertaining to data-oriented development issues. Includes, but is not limited to, logical naming conventions, standard logical data definitions, and physical naming conventions.

Enterprise Data Model: A detailed model depicting the major business entities, their attributes, and their relationships applicable across your organization.

Enterprise Development Guidance: Standards and guidelines applicable to all systems within your organization.

Enterprise Domain Model: A high-level representation of the business entities and their relationships within your organization.

Enterprise Facilities Guidance: Standards and guidelines for facilities, which address building design and usage issues.

Enterprise Facilities Plan: Describes the plans for the facilities within the organization.

Enterprise Goals and Targets: Used to develop organizational strategies and vision and to gauge the effectiveness of your organization.

Enterprise Intellectual Property (IP): This includes patents, trademarks, service marks, copyrights, and trade secrets that your organization owns and maintains.

Enterprise Licenses: Licenses to software products that your organization utilizes across departments.

Enterprise Mission Statement: A statement of the strategies to be followed to achieve the enterprise vision.

Enterprise Network and Hardware Guidance: Standards and guidelines for networks and hardware that address common configurations, common protocols, and so on.

Enterprise Risk List: Identifies and assesses the risks to the enterprise at both a program and portfolio level.

Enterprise Risk Management Plan: Defines the strategy for how risks are managed for the enterprise.

Enterprise Security Guidance: Standards and guidelines for security that address both IT and physical security protocols.

Enterprise Security Plan: Describes the plan for use of both physical and IT security.

Enterprise Technical Requirements: Requirements to which all IT assets within your organization must conform.

Enterprise Vision: A statement of the primary goal(s) of an organization.

Existing Processes: The existing processes within your organization.

Federal Regulations: Rules that your organization must comply with on a federal level.

Fix: A change to a deployed system to address one or more defects.

Hot Fix: A fix that is inserted into a production environment to address one or more high-priority defects. Often applied on an emergency basis to address defects that cannot wait until the next scheduled maintenance update.

Individual Career Plan: Describes the career plan, including goals and educational needs, for an individual IT professional.

Industry Guidance: Includes industry best practices and commonly used standards and guidelines.

IT Process: Addresses the full IT lifecycle, defining procedures, templates, and examples for software development, operations and support, and cross-system issues such as enterprise architecture and portfolio management.

Legacy Data Source Documentation: Includes information about your enterprise data model.

Long-Term Succession Plan: Defines how the organization will fill both technical and business positions within the organizations as people leave the team.

Modeling Guidance: Describes techniques such as naming conventions, layout style guidelines, and even notation style guidelines for how models should be organized and documented.

Needs Assessment: A document describing needs in an organization.

Organization Assessment: A description of the organization, including structure, culture, competencies, and skills.

Organization Model: Describes your organizational units (teams, groups, divisions, and so on), the primary positions, the senior people, the roles and responsibilities that the people and organizational units fulfill, and the relationships (potentially including both reporting and flow of control) between them all.

Organizational-Level Development Case: A development case with a wider scope than a project development case; it describes process tailorings that are applicable across many projects.

Portfolio: The collection of programs, projects, and systems that exist in an organization.

Portfolio Plan: Describes project and program priorities that are required to fulfill the overall business goals of your organization.

Position Definitions: Describe the roles and responsibilities for the different positions within your organization.

Process Implementation Plan: The plan to roll out a process within your organization.

Process Vision: Describes how you would like to see a process implemented within your organization.

Program: A collection of related projects or systems.

Program Plan: Prioritizes projects within the program.

Project Proposal: A proposal for a new software develpment project.

Published Asset: A robust asset that is made publicly available within your organization for potential reuse.

Reference Architecture: An architectural approach designed and proven for use in a particular domain, together with supporting artifacts to enable their use; it often provides the basis for creating an application architecture.

Request for Information (RFI): Issued to vendors to request interest and availability for a contract.

Request for Proposal (RFP): An announcement to solicit proposals from vendors in order to address a specific organizational need.

Reuse Guidance: Defines techniques and guidelines for succeeding at reuse.

Reuse Measurement Plan: Defines the measurement goals and related metrics to be collected regarding your reuse program.

Reuse Program Plan: Encompasses all of the information required to manage your reuse program, including staffing requirements, the vision and projected milestones, and a description of how your team intends to support project teams.

Robust Asset: A well-documented asset that is generalized beyond the needs of a single project; it is thoroughly tested and has several examples to show how to work with it.

Service Pack: A collection of fixes that are collectively applied to a production environment.

Staff Review: A document that reflects the current staffing levels within your organization.

Staffing Forecast: A plan to fulfill the human resources requirements of your organization; this can include a combination of full-time employees and contractors.

System: A working software-based product in a production environment.

System Operations Plan: Describes the approach for operating systems in a production environment. Includes contact personnel, the operations SLA, system operating procedures, and backup and restore procedures.

System Support Plan: Describes the approach for supporting systems in a production environment. Includes how support will be provided, system contact personnel, defect reporting and change request strategy, the support service level agreement (SLA), and how to deliver fixes outside a normal production release.

Trouble Ticket: An issue from an end user about the system that can become either an enhancement request or defect report.

Usage Reports: A summary of system logs produced during the normal monitoring of a production system.

Appendix C
Glossary

24/7: Pronounced "24 by 7," a term used to define support levels which includes operational coverage all day, every day. Also known as 24/7/365.

Accountability: Being held responsible for your actions within an organization.

Aggregated Risks: A collection of common small project-level risks that may add up to a large risk for the enterprise.

Agile Alliance (AA): A non-profit organization (`www.agilealliance.org`) that supports individuals and organizations that use agile approaches to develop software.

Agile Data (AD): A philosophy and role-based methodology that describes how to take an agile approach to the data-oriented aspects of systems.

Agile Model: A model that is just barely good enough.

Agile Model-Driven Development (AMDD): An iterative and incremental approach to development where you create agile models before you implement source code.

Agile Modeling (AM): A practices-based methodology whose focus is on effective modeling and documentation.

Agile Software Process: A software process that reflects the values and principles of the Agile Alliance (AA).

Analysis and Design Discipline: A collection of activities whose goal is to analyze the requirements for the system and to design a solution to be implemented, taking into consideration the requirements, constraints, and all applicable guidance.

Anti-Pattern: A common approach that people apply that is proven to not work very well in practice.

Application Programming Interface (API): Provides external access to an application, typically implemented as a collection of functions.

Archived System: Includes backups of the system software, its data, all system documentation associated with it, and any proprietary hardware.

Artifact: A document, model, file, diagram, or other item that is produced, modified, or used during the development, operation, or support of a system.

Asset: An artifact that is retained at the end of a project.

Backout Plan: A strategy for uninstalling a portion of a system or an entire system.

Backup Procedures: Procedures that define how critical information will be copied so that it may be restored if a problem occurs. See also **incremental backup, full backup**, and **data backup.**

Baseline: A defined collection of versioned artifacts. For example, this baseline is composed of version 1.5.3 of the requirements specification and version 3.4.0 of the software architecture document.

"Big Bang" Retirement: An approach to removing a system from production where you convert the data, install the system updates, and remove the old system in one fell swoop.

Branch and Merge: A method of taking all current system artifacts and then basing these artifacts on a new version of the system.

Business Intelligence (BI): See **data warehousing**.

Business Modeling Discipline: A collection of activities whose goal is to understand the business of the organization, usually confined to the scope of the business that is relevant to the system being developed.

Business Process Management Initiative (BPMI): An emerging standards group for business processes (`www.bpmi.org`) and creators of the Business Process Modeling Notation.

Business Process Modeling Notation (BPMN): A specification from the Business Process Management Initiative that defines a (potentially) standard graphical notation for expressing business processes.

Business Software Alliance (BSA): An enforcement agency responsible for showing up at your organization when claims of commercial software piracy are made.

Business Stakeholder: An end user or manager of end users who will work with or be affected by the deployment of a system and/or an IT strategy.

Capability Maturity Model (CMM) Integrated (CMMI): A framework for assessing an organization's ability to consistently develop systems.

Change Request: An artifact to track requests for modifications to a system, providing a record of decisions and potentially an indication of the impact of the change.

Charge-Out Rate: The fully burdened average rate at which time is accounted for. This rate typically includes the base salary of staff as well as operational expenses such as office costs, network costs, and so on. For example, a developer may be paid $50 an hour, but his charge-out rate may be $85 an hour to fully account for IT costs.

Chief Executive Officer (CEO): The top-level manager of the senior management team.

Chief Information Officer (CIO): A top-level manager responsible for the IT aspects of the enterprise.

C-Level Management: The senior-level—or "chief"—management roles within an organization.

Coaching: See **mentoring**.

COBOL: A legacy mainframe programming language, very popular even today for supporting systems for an organization.

Communication: The act of sharing information.

Computing Facilities: The physical location for the various resources to maintain the IT environment within an organization. See also **Network Operations Center (NOC).**

Configuration and Change Management Discipline: A collection of activities whose goal is to manage access to the project artifacts. This includes not only tracking artifact versions over time but also controlling and managing changes to them.

Construction Phase: A stage in the lifecycle of a system where the primary goal is to develop the system to the point where it is ready for deployment.

Consultant: A person brought onto a project team for a short period of time, often days or weeks, in order to fill an immediate gap or to mentor the existing project team.

Contingency Platform: A system setup for redundancy in the event of a disaster.

Contractor: A person brought onto a project team for a long period of time, often months or years, who is not an official employee of the company.

Convergent Security: A combination of both physical and information technology security.

Copyright: Intellectual property defined to protect works of authorship, such as writings, music, and works of art that have been tangibly expressed.

Customer Relationship Management (CRM) System: A back-office system to integrate sales and marketing efforts within an organization.

Data Backup: A backup of just the data within a data source (database, file, and so on). Data backups are faster to perform than full backups and are an effective approach in an environment where data is centralized and changes often but the executable code seldom changes.

Data Stewardship: The act of ensuring that responsibility, accountability, and authority are associated with auditing and reviewing the quality of data within the organization.

Data Warehousing: Often referred to as business intelligence (BI), it includes functionality such as reporting and the consolidation of data for research purposes.

Decommissioning: See **retirement phase**.

Deployment Discipline: A collection of activities whose goal is to plan for the delivery of the system and to execute the plan to make the system available to end users.

Development Case: Defines the particular process tailoring that will be used on a specific project.

Development Release: A system, and its supporting artifacts, deployed internally within your development and/or demo environments.

Discipline: A collection of related activities.

Earned Value Management (EVM): A metric used to communicate progress on a project, measuring project performance by comparing work completed against work planned.

Education: Imparts longer-term skills and knowledge that are typically applicable over someone's entire career.

Elaboration Phase: A stage in the lifecycle of a system where the primary goals are to specify requirements in greater detail and prove the architecture for the system.

End User: A stakeholder who is the recipient of a running system in a production environment.

Enterprise Administration Discipline: This discipline includes setting up and administering tools, processes, and facilities that are key infrastructure components of your IT organization.

Enterprise Architecture: The frameworks, networks, deployment configurations, and supporting infrastructure that form the IT foundation for an enterprise. It comprises the environment within which all applications of an enterprise are deployed.

Enterprise Architecture Discipline: This discipline addresses the overall architecture issues associated with your organization. A common enterprise architecture helps ensure consistency across systems and greatly facilitates application architecture efforts.

Enterprise Business Modeling Discipline: The goal of this discipline is to explore the business structure and processes of the enterprise. It provides a common understanding of the business activities, customers, and suppliers of the business. Enterprise business modeling helps identify problems and areas that are candidates for automation.

Enterprise Change Management: Extends the single system change management covered by Configuration and Change Management (C&CM) to manage change across a collection of systems.

Enterprise Java Bean (EJB): Reusable code that you can use to assemble enterprise applications utilizing the Java platform.

Enterprise Management disciplines: These disciplines address cross-system issues. See also **Enterprise Business Modeling discipline, Portfolio Management discipline, Enterprise Architecture discipline, Strategic Reuse discipline, People Management discipline, Enterprise Administration discipline,** and **Software Process Improvement discipline.**

Enterprise Resource Planning (ERP): A technique that integrates all facets of an organization, including planning, manufacturing, sales, and marketing,

Enterprise Unified Process (EUP): An information technology process that extends the RUP to include the operation and support of a system after it is in production, a system's eventual retirement, and cross-system enterprise issues.

Environment Discipline: A collection of activities whose goal is to support the rest of the effort in terms of ensuring that the proper processes, guidance, and tools are available for the team as needed.

Escalation Support Strategy: A support strategy based on the idea that most support requests are fairly basic and therefore can be handled quickly, whereas small minorities of requests are complicated and must be assigned or escalated to more knowledgeable staff members.

Evolutionary Development: An approach where development proceeds in an iterative and incremental manner.

Extract-Transform-Load (ETL): A phased approach for migrating data.

Five Nines Uptime: A stringent system uptime requirement that requires that a system be available 99.999% of the time; this allows for roughly five minutes of downtime per year. Availability requirements are usually a component of operational service-level agreements (SLAs).

Full Backup: This is the backup of an entire system, minimally all of the data and potentially all of the deployment elements of the system. The main advantage of this is that you are assured to have a complete image of your system.

Generalizing Specialist: Someone who is very good in one or two IT specialties, such as domain modeling or project management, who also has a good understanding of the entire IT lifecycle and hopefully of your business domain as well.

Go/No-Go Decision: The point at which you determine whether your project should continue.

Good-Enough Metric (GEM): A measurement that uses a combination of actual data captured within your organization and estimates based on industry information. You use the industry data to provide missing information until the point in time where you have your own data.

Governance: The act of specifying the decision rights and accountability framework to encourage desirable behavior.

Greenfield Project: A project started completely from scratch without any legacy system(s) to constrain it.

Guidance: Standards and guidelines.

Guidelines: A form of guidance that you should follow but are allowed to deviate from when the situation warrants it.

Health Insurance Portability and Accountability Act (HIPAA): Legislation passed by the U.S. government that provides federal protection for U.S. workers.

Human Resources Management System (HRMS): A tool used for tracking individual goals for training, mentoring, and education.

Hump Chart Diagram: A slang term for the RUP lifecycle diagram.

Implementation Discipline: A collection of activities whose goal is to transform the design into executable code and to perform a basic level of testing—in particular, unit testing.

Inception Phase: A stage in the lifecycle of a system where the primary goals are to achieve stakeholder consensus regarding the objectives for the system and to obtain funding for it.

Incremental Backup: This backup style copies/deletes only the items that have changed since the last backup.

Information Assets: The data, intellectual property, and licenses for the enterprise.

Information Technology Infrastructure Library (ITIL): A process resource that focuses on IT Service Management—in particular, operations and support. ITIL is developed and owned by the Office of Government Commerce (OGC) in the UK.

Information Technology (IT) Lifecycle: A process lifecycle that encompasses the activities of an IT department, adding the enterprise management disciplines required to effectively manage your organization's portfolio of systems.

Infrastructure Hardware: The computing hardware used throughout your organization.

Integrated Development Environment (IDE): A programming tool to develop applications on one or more platforms, which usually includes a graphical user interface and debugging tools.

Intellectual Property (IP): Creations of the mind—creative works or ideas embodied in a form that can be shared or that can enable others to re-create, emulate, or manufacture them. See also **patent**, **trademark**, **service mark**, **copyright**, and **trade secret**.

Intrusion Detection System: A type of physical security used to protect an organization from unauthorized entry.

ISO 12207: A standard that defines a high-level system lifecycle.

IT Security: An action taken to prevent unauthorized access to organizational data to help prevent cyber-terrorism, hacking, or types of industrial espionage.

Iteration: A period of time, often a few weeks in length, where you address only a portion of the entire system being developed. RUP phases are divided into one or more iterations. Iterations build on the work done by previous iterations and assemble the final system incrementally.

Iterative Development: An approach where you move back and forth quickly between development activities—you model a bit, you code a bit, you test a bit, you code some more, you model some more, you test some more, you plan a bit, and so on.

Java 2 Platform Enterprise Edition (J2EE): Often called "J2 Double E," this defines the standards for developing enterprise-level applications using the Java language.

Key Person Life Insurance: Life insurance taken out by the organization on a critical member of your company.

License Management: The act of keeping track of all licenses for software and other IT assets within your organization.

Management Career Track: A term used in organizations to define a path for individuals interested in progressing through the ranks of management.

Mentoring: A process where one person transfers his or her skills to another person.

Metadata: A type of data that describes the information in either a business or technical manner.

Metric: A measurable attribute of an entity or activity.

Milestone: At this point, the stakeholders assess the project, including what has been done and the plans for moving forward, and a go/no-go decision is made.

Milestone Review: See **milestone**.

Model: An abstraction describing a problem domain and/or a solution to a problem domain. Traditionally, models are thought of as diagrams plus their corresponding documentation, although non-diagrams, such as interview results and collections of CRC cards, are also considered to be models.

Model-Driven Architecture (MDA): A framework for software development, defined by the Object Management Group (OMG), where development efforts are driven by modeling.

Network Operations Center (NOC): A type of computing facility within an organization for operations staff to monitor systems running in a production environment.

Object Management Group (OMG): An industry standards body responsible for several standards, including the UML and MDA.

Objectory Process: A precursor to the Unified Process.

Office of Government Commerce (OGC): A standards group responsible for the development and upkeep of the ITIL.

Offshoring: The practice of outsourcing customer support to third-party organizations in another country.

Off-Site Storage: A physical location where backed-up items, particularly data, are stored for disaster recovery purposes.

Online Transaction Processing (OLTP): A collection of programs that allow for the input and processing of real-time information within a database application.

Operations: The primary focus of this effort is to ensure that software is running properly, that the network is available and monitored, and that the appropriate data is backed up and restored as needed within a production environment.

Operations and Support Discipline: The goal of this discipline is to operate and support your production systems. Operations activities include monitoring systems, tuning systems, upgrading hardware, archiving data, and disaster recovery. Support activities include responding to user requests, escalating serious problems, and recording suggested fixes and improvements to existing systems.

Organization Lifecycle: A process lifecycle that encompasses the activities of your entire organization, including both the IT and business aspects.

Organizational-Level Development Case: A development case with a wider scope; it describes process tailorings that are applicable across many projects.

Outsourcing: The practice of relying on external firms for some of your organization's work. See also **offshoring**.

Pair Programming: An approach where two developers work on a piece of code or a system together at one workstation.

Patch: See **hot fix**.

Patent: Intellectual property defined as a property right granted by a governing body to an inventor to exclude others from making, using, offering for sale, or selling the invention throughout a defined territory for a limited time in exchange for public disclosure of the invention when the patent is granted.

People Capability Maturity Model (P-CMM): A framework for assessing people issues within an organization.

People Management Discipline: This discipline describes the process of organizing, monitoring, coaching, and motivating people in a manner to ensure that they work together well and successfully contribute to projects within the organization.

Phase: A stage, or season, with a well-defined purpose that a system goes through over time. Each phase ends with a milestone. See **Inception phase, Elaboration phase, Construction phase, Transition phase, Production phase,** and **Retirement phase.**

Physical Assets: Hardware, networks, and facilities within your organization.

Physical Security: Includes the measures an organization takes to control access to restricted locations; this type of security is to help prevent terrorism or some less-intrusive security breaches.

Pilot Project: A software development project that is used to test or prove a concept or approach.

Portfolio Management Discipline: Organizations often have suites of applications, called programs, that can be better managed as a whole than as individual applications. This discipline enables you to track and plan your organization's entire software portfolio as well as individual programs within your overall portfolio. Doing so allows you to schedule and implement new requirements in a more strategic fashion. This also helps avoid implementing the same functionality within different applications.

Portfolio Risk: The aggregated risk across all projects and systems that make up your system portfolio.

Prescriptive Process: A process that includes detailed procedures, templates, and examples.

Process: The set of activities needed to produce a result of perceived and measurable value.

Process Lifecycle: Defines the scope of a process and the relationships between its activities. See **information technology (IT) lifecycle, system lifecycle, system development lifecycle,** and **organization lifecycle.**

Production Phase: This phase encompasses the period of the system lifecycle where you operate and support a system until it is either replaced with a new version or retired and removed from use.

Production Release: A baselined system, and its supporting baselined artifacts, deployed into your production environment.

Program: A group of related projects or systems. See also **software portfolio.**

Project Interdependencies: The relationships between various projects that may have an impact on the overall program or portfolio.

Project Management Book of Knowledge (PMBOK): A standards guideline published by the Project Management Institute.

Project Management Discipline: A collection of activities whose goal is to direct the activities that take place on the project. This includes managing risks, directing people (assigning tasks, tracking progress, and so on), and coordinating with people and systems outside the scope of the project to be sure that it is delivered on time and within budget.

Rational Unified Process (RUP): An industry-standard, prescriptive system development process that is defined and maintained by IBM Rational.

Reference Architecture: An architectural pattern designed and proven for use in a particular domain, together with supporting artifacts to enable their use; it often provides the basis for creating an application architecture.

Regression Testing: The validation that existing software still works after changes have been made.

Regulating Bodies: These are usually external organizations that require compliance at some level—federal or otherwise. See also **Sarbanes-Oxley (Sarbox) Compliance Act of 2002** and **Health Insurance Portability and Accountability Act (HIPAA)**.

Release: A stable, executable (although perhaps not final) version of a system.

Requirements Discipline: A collection of activities whose goal is to elicit, document, and agree on the scope of what is and what is not to be built.

Restore Procedure: Allows the system to be revived from backed-up assets if a problem should occur.

Retirement Phase: The focus of this phase is the removal of a system from production.

Return on Investment (ROI): This metric indicates how effectively funds have been put to use. Defined as (Value–Cost) / Cost.

Reusable Asset: A robust asset that has been used at least three times on three separate projects by three separate teams. Reusability is in the eye of the beholder, not in the eye of the creator.

Risk Management: A method of assessing what can go wrong within an organization and then developing mitigation strategies to avoid these issues.

Robust Asset: A well-documented asset that is generalized beyond the needs of a single project, is thoroughly tested, and has several examples to show how to work with it.

Rolling Wave Planning: Detailed planning is performed for things closer to you (such as the relative height of the crest of a wave), and less-detailed planning is performed for things further away (the relative depth of the wave trough). As your project progresses and tasks get closer, detailed planning for them is done.

Sanitization: The process of wiping clean all data stored on computer storage media.

Sarbanes-Oxley (Sarbox) Compliance Act of 2002: U.S. government legislation that requires public companies to document their financial processes and show how the data was calculated—including traceability back to the source.

Schedule Deviation: Anything that alters the original project schedule within a portfolio. This is used to measure the ability to deliver projects according to the original baseline schedule.

Senior Management: The "C level" of management within an organization. This can include the CIO, CEO, CFO, and others who are responsible for setting the strategy within the organization.

Service-Level Agreement (SLA): Addresses both the support and operational constraints for a system running within a production environment.

Service Mark: Intellectual property such as a word, name, symbol, or device that indicates the source of the services and distinguishes them from the services of others; this is the same as a trademark except that it identifies and distinguishes the source of a service rather than a product. The terms "service mark" and "mark" are often used to refer to service marks.

Service Pack: This is a fix to a defect inserted directly into a production environment by a support developer using different types of media.

Shrink-Wrap Software: Software created for a mass-market audience with little customization.

Software Craftsperson: See **generalizing specialist**.

Software Portfolio: A collection of IT projects, both proposed and in progress, as well as deployed systems within your organization.

Software Process Engineering Metamodel (SPEM): An industry standard defined by the OMG for describing software process information.

Software Process Improvement Discipline: This discipline addresses the need to manage, improve, and support the various processes in use across your organization.

Staged Retirement: With this approach, you select portions of the system and remove them one at a time. At each stage, you convert the relevant data and migrate the subset of the interactions, leaving the rest of the system intact.

Stakeholder: Anyone directly involved with, or affected by, an activity. See also **business stakeholder** and **end user**.

Standards: A form of guidance that must be followed.

Stovepipe Application: A system that stands on its own and does not interact with or build on other systems.

Strategic Reuse Discipline: This discipline promotes development and reuse of assets across projects, the goal of which is to enable you to develop higher-quality applications more quickly by reusing assets instead of developing them anew each time. It also helps improve quality, because it allows you to use artifacts that have already been tested and proven to work.

Succession Planning: A planning process within an organization to ensure that you are ready for future generations of your IT staff to take over when your current IT staff is no longer with your organization.

Sunsetting: See **Retirement phase**.

Support: The focus of this effort is to assist end users by answering their questions, analyzing the problems that they are encountering with production systems, recording requests for new functionality, and making and applying fixes, all within the production environment.

Support Strategy: See **escalation support strategy** and **touch-and-hold support strategy**.

System Development Lifecycle: A process lifecycle that encompasses the activities required to develop a system and put it into production.

System Inventory: A current inventory of system assets within your organization.

System Lifecycle: A process lifecycle that extends the system development lifecycle to include the activities required to operate and support a system after it is in production and to eventually retire that system after it is no longer needed. The scope of a system lifecycle includes starting to develop the first version; the development, operation, and support of all subsequent versions; and the retirement of the final version.

System Uptime: The amount of time a system is continually running within a production environment. This is usually a component of service-level agreements. See also **five nines uptime**.

Technical Career Track: A term used in organizations to define a path for individuals interested in building their careers with respect to technical work.

Test Discipline: A collection of activities whose goal is to perform an objective evaluation to ensure quality. This includes finding defects, validating that systems work as designed, and verifying that the requirements are met.

Test-Driven Development (TDD): A development approach based on the idea that developers should write a test before they write new business code to ensure that they always have a 100% regression unit test suite for their system.

Time Tracking: The practice of collecting information on time spent during specific tasks throughout a project in order to compare them against a forecasted budget.

Total Cost of Ownership (TCO): Defines the cost of developing, operating, supporting, and retiring a system throughout its lifetime.

Touch-and-Hold Support Strategy: A support strategy where the initial person who took the support request follows it through to the end, although this person may have to work with other people to fulfill the request.

Trademark: Protection for intellectual property such as words, names, symbols, sounds, or colors that distinguish goods and services from those manufactured or sold by others and to indicate the source of the goods. Trademarks, unlike patents, can be renewed forever as long as they are being used in commerce.

Trade Secret: Intellectual property that contains information that companies keep secret to give them an advantage over their competitors.

Training: Focuses on teaching people specific, narrowly focused skills that are often immediately applicable to their current position.

Transition Phase: A stage in the lifecycle of a system where the primary goal is to deliver the system into production successfully. There will be testing by both system testers and end users, and corresponding rework and fine-tuning. Training of end users, support, and operations staff is also done during this phase.

Trouble Ticket: An issue from an end user about the system that can become either an enhancement request or a defect report.

Unified Method (UM): See **Unified Process (UP)**.

Unified Modeling Language (UML): An industry-standard modeling notation and semantics that maintained by the OMG.

Unified Process (UP): A framework from which system processes, such as the EUP and RUP, are instantiated.

Unified Software Development Process (USDP): See **Unified Process (UP)**.

Waterfall Development: A term indicating that development proceeds in a mostly serial manner—you identify all the requirements, then analyze them, then design the system, then build the system, then test it, and then deploy it.

Zachman Framework: Created in the 1980s by John Zachman, this framework describes a collection of perspectives pertinent to enterprise modeling. The rows of the framework represent the views of different types of stakeholders, and the columns represent different aspects or views of your architecture.

Appendix D

Acronyms and Abbreviations

AA: Agile Alliance

AD: Agile Data

AM: Agile Modeling

AMDD: Agile Model-Driven Development

API: Application Programming Interface

ASD: Agile Software Development

BI: Business Intelligence

BPMI: Business Process Management Initiative

BPMN: Business Process Modeling Notation

BSA: Business Software Alliance

CEO: Chief Executive Officer

CIO: Chief Information Officer

CMM: Capability Maturity Model

CMMI: Capability Maturity Model Integrated

COTS: Commercial Off-The-Shelf

CRM: Customer Relationship Management

CSR: Customer Support Representative

CYA: Cover Your Assets

DRP: Disaster Recovery Plan

EA: Enterprise Architecture

ECCB: Enterprise Change Control Board

EJB: Enterprise Java Bean

ERP: Enterprise Resource Planning

ETL: Extract-Transform-Load

EUP: Enterprise Unified Process

EVM: Earned Value Management

GEM: Good-Enough Metric

HIPAA: Health Insurance Portability and Accountability Act

HRMS: Human Resources Management System

IDE: Integrated Development Environment

IP: Intellectual Property

ISO: International Standards Organization

IT: Information Technology

ITIL: Information Technology Infrastructure Library

J2EE: Java 2 Platform Enterprise Edition

MDA: Model-Driven Architecture

NOC: Network Operations Center

OGC: Office of Government Commerce

OLTP: Online Transaction Processing.

OMG: Object Management Group

OS: Operating System

OSS: Open-Source Software

P-CMM: People Capability Maturity Model

PMBOK: Project Management Book of Knowledge

PMI: Project Management Institute

RFI: Request for Information

RFP: Request for Proposal

RFQ: Request for Quote

ROI: Return on Investment

RUP: Rational Unified Process

Sarbox: Sarbanes-Oxley

SLA: Service-Level Agreement

SPEM: Software Process Engineering Metamodel

SPI: Software Process Improvement

SSR: System Support Representative

TCO: Total Cost of Ownership

TDD: Test-Driven Development

UM: Unified Method

UML: Unified Modeling Language

UP: Unified Process

USDP: Unified Software Development Process

XP: Extreme Programming

Y2K: Year 2000

ZF: Zachman Framework

References and Recommended Reading

Agarwal, R. and Ferratt, T. (2002). *Enduring Practices for Managing IT Professionals.* Communications of the ACM., pp. 73–79, 45(9).

Agile Alliance (2001a). *Manifesto for Agile Software Development.* www.agilealliance.org

Agile Alliance (2001b). *Principles: The Agile Alliance.* www.agilealliance.org/principles.html

Alur, D., Crupi, J., and Malks, D. (2003). *Core J2EE Patterns: Best Practices and Design Strategies, 2nd Edition.* Upper Saddle River, NJ: Prentice Hall PTR.

Ambler, S.W. (1998a). *Building Object Applications That Work: Your Step-By-Step Handbook for Developing Robust Systems with Object Technology.* New York: Cambridge University Press.

Ambler, S.W. (1998b). *Process Patterns—Building Large-Scale Systems Using Object Technology.* New York: Cambridge University Press.

Ambler, S.W. (1998c). *A Realistic Look at Object-Oriented Reuse.* Software Development, January 1998. www.sdmagazine.com/documents/s=775/sdm 9801a/9801a.htm

Ambler, S.W. (1999a). *More Process Patterns—Delivering Large-Scale Systems Using Object Technology.* New York: Cambridge University Press.

Ambler, S.W. (1999b). *Enhancing the Unified Process.* Software Development, October 1999. www.sdmagazine.com/documents/s=753/sdm9910b/9910b.htm

Ambler, S.W. (2000). *Reuse Patterns & Anti-Patterns.* Software Development, February 2000. www.sdmagazine.com/documents/s=747/sdm0002k/0002k.htm

Ambler, S.W. (2001). *Retraining Your Staff for Modern-Age Development.* May, 2001. www.ronin-intl.com/training/ooTrainingAndEducation.PDF

Ambler, S.W. (2002). *Agile Modeling: Best Practices for the Unified Process and Extreme Programming.* New York: John Wiley & Sons. www.ambysoft.com/agileModeling.html

Ambler, S.W. (2003a). *The Elements of UML Style*. New York: Cambridge University Press. www.ambysoft.com/elementsUMLStyle.html

Ambler, S.W. (2003b). *Agile Database Techniques: Effective Strategies for the Agile Software Developer*. New York: John Wiley & Sons. www.ambysoft.com/agileDatabaseTechniques.html

Ambler, S.W. (2003c). *Model Reviews: Best Practice or Process Smell?* www.agilemodeling.com/essays/modelReviews.htm

Ambler, S.W. (2004). *The Object Primer, 3rd Edition: Agile Model Driven Development with UML 2*. New York: Cambridge University Press. www.ambysoft.com/theObjectPrimer.html

Ambler, S.W. and Constantine, L.L. (2000a). *The Unified Process Inception Phase*. Gilroy, CA: CMP Books.

Ambler, S.W. and Constantine, L.L. (2000b). *The Unified Process Elaboration Phase*. Gilroy, CA: CMP Books.

Ambler, S.W. and Constantine, L.L. (2000c). *The Unified Process Construction Phase*. Gilroy, CA: CMP Books.

Ambler, S.W. and Constantine, L.L. (2002). *The Unified Process Transition and Production Phases*. Gilroy, CA: CMP Books. www.ambysoft.com/transition ProductionPhase.html

Astels, D. (2003). *Test Driven Development: A Practical Guide*. Upper Saddle River, NJ: Prentice Hall.

Atkinson, C., Bayer, J., Bunse, C., Kamsties, E., Laitenberger, O., Laqua, R., Muthig, D., Paech, B., Wust, J., and Zettel, J. (2002). *Component-Based Product Line Engineering With UML*. London: Pearson Education.

Barnes, J. C. (2001). *A Guide to Business Continuity Planning*. John Wiley & Sons.

BARQA (2002). *Compliant Use of Computer Systems*. www.barqa.com/cms/view.php?id=21626

Bass, L., Clements, P., and Kazman, R. (1998). *Software Architecture in Practice*. Reading, MA: Addison-Wesley Longman, Inc.

Bassett, P.G. (1997). *Framing Software Reuse: Lessons From the Real World*. Upper Saddle River, NJ: Prentice Hall, Inc.

Beck, K. (2000). *Extreme Programming Explained—Embrace Change*. Reading, MA: Addison-Wesley Longman, Inc.

Beck, K. (2003). *Test Driven Development: By Example*. Boston, MA: Addison-Wesley.

Beck, K., and Cunningham, W. (1989). *A laboratory for teaching object-oriented thinking*. In Proceedings of OOPSLA '89, pp. 1–6.

Beedle, M. and Schwaber, K. (2001). *Agile Software Development With SCRUM*. Upper Saddle River, New Jersey: Prentice Hall, Inc.

Bennett, D. (1997). *Designing Hard Software: The Essential Tasks*. Greenwich, CT: Manning Publications Co.

Binder, R. (1999). *Testing Object-Oriented Systems: Models, Patterns, and Tools*. Reading, MA: Addison-Wesley Longman, Inc.

Boehm, B.W. (1988). *A Spiral Model of Software Development and Enhancement*. IEEE Computer, pp. 61–72, 21(5).

Boehm, B.W. and Turner, R. (2003). *Balancing Agility With Discipline: A Guide for the Perplexed*. Reading, MA: Addison-Wesley Longman, Inc.

Booch, G. (1994). *Object-Oriented Analysis and Design with Applications, 2nd Edition*. Redwood City, CA: The Benjamin/Cummings Publishing Company, Inc.

Borenstein, Joram (2004). *Meta-data repositories meet semantics*. The Data Administration Newsletter (TDAN.com). July 2004.

Brooks, F.P. (1995). *The Mythical Man Month: Essays on Software Engineering, 20th Anniversary Edition*. Reading, MA: Addison-Wesley Publishing Company.

Bunker, K,, Kram, K., and Ting, S. (2002). *The Young and the Clueless*. Harvard Business Review, pp. 81–87, 80 (12).

Burry, C., and Mancusi, D. (2004). *How to Plan for Data Migration*. Computerworld www.computerworld.com/databasetopics/data/story/0,10801,93284,00.html

Buschmann, F., Meunier, R., Rohnert, H., Sommerlad, P., and Stal, M. (1996). *A System of Patterns: Pattern-Oriented Software Architecture*. New York: John Wiley & Sons.

Caputo, K. (1998). *CMM Implementation Guide: Choreographing Software Process Improvement*. Reading, MA: Addison-Wesley.

Carr, N.G. (2004). *Does IT Matter? Information Technology and the Corrosion of Competitive Advantage*. Boston: Harvard Business School Press.

Clements, P. and Northrop, L. (2002). *Software Product Lines: Practices and Patterns*. Upper Saddle River, NJ: Prentice Hall, Inc.

Clements, P., Kazman, R. and Klein, M. (2002). *Evaluating Software Architecture: Methods and Case Studies*. Upper Saddle River, NJ: Prentice Hall, Inc.

Cockburn, A. (2001). *Writing Effective Use Cases*. Boston: Addison-Wesley.

Cockburn, A. (2002). *Agile Software Development*. Reading, MA: Addison-Wesley Longman, Inc.

Conger, J. and Fulmer, R. (2003). *Developing Your Leadership Pipeline*. Harvard Business Review, pp.77–84, 81 (12).

Constantine, L.L. (1995). *Constantine on Peopleware*. Englewood Cliffs, NJ: Yourdon Press.

Constantine, L.L., and Lockwood, L.A.D. (1999). *Software for Use: A Practical Guide to the Models and Methods of Usage-Centered Design*. New York: ACM Press.

Coplien, J.O. (1995). *A Generative Development-Process Pattern Language.* Pattern Languages of Program Design, Addison-Wesley Longman, Inc., pp. 183–237.

DeMarco, T. and Lister, T. (1999). *Peopleware: Productive Projects and Teams, 2nd Edition.* Dorset House Publishing Co., Inc.

DeMarco, T. and Lister, T. (2003). *Waltzing with Bears: Managing Risk on Software Projects.* Dorset House Publishing Co., Inc.

Douglass, B.P. (1999). *Doing Hard Time: Developing Real-Time Systems With UML, Objects, Frameworks, and Patterns.* Reading, MA: Addison-Wesley Longman, Inc.

D'Souza, D.F., and Wills, A.C. (1999). *Objects, Components, and Frameworks with UML: The Catalysis Approach.* Reading, MA: Addison-Wesley Longman, Inc.

Emam, K.E. and Madhavji, N.H. (1999). *Elements of Software Process Assessment and Improvement.* Los Alamos, CA: IEEE Computer Society.

Eriksson, H.K. and Penker, M. (2000). *Business Modeling with UML: Business Patterns at Work.* New York: Wiley Publishing, Inc.

Evans, G. (2001). *Palm-Sized Process.* Software Development, September 2001.

Fay, S. (2004a). *Calculating the Value of Your Asset Portfolio.* Flashline Whitepaper. www.flashline.com

Fay, S. (2004b). *Reuse Roles and Staffing Considerations.* Flashline Whitepaper. www.flashline.com

Fowler, M. (1999). *Refactoring: Improving the Design of Existing Code.* Menlo Park, CA: Addison-Wesley Longman.

Fowler, M., Rice D., Foemmel, M., Hieatt, E., Mee, R., and Stafford, R. (2003). *Patterns of Enterprise Application Architecture.* Boston, MA: Addison-Wesley Longman, Inc.

Gane, C. and Sarson, T. (1979). *Structured Systems Analysis: Tools and Techniques.* Englewood Cliffs, NJ: Prentice Hall.

Gartner Group (2000). *IT Spending: Its History and Future.* www3.gartner.com/ 4_decision_tools/measurement/measure_it_articles/july01/ mit_spending_history1.html

Githens, G.D. (1998). *Rolling Wave Project Planning.* www.catalystpm.com/NP02.pdf

Graham, I., Henderson-Sellers, B., and Younessi, H. (1997). *The OPEN Process Specification.* New York: ACM Press Books.

Graham, I., Henderson-Sellers, B., Simons, A., and Younessi, H. (1997). *The OPEN Toolbox of Techniques.* New York: ACM Press Books.

Grady, R.B. (1992). *Practical Software Metrics for Project Management and Process Improvement.* Englewood Cliffs, NJ: Prentice Hall, Inc.

Hay, D.C. (2003). *Requirements Analysis: From Business Views to Architecture.* Upper Saddle River, NJ: Prentice Hall, Inc.

Hefley, W., Curtis, B., and Miller, S. (2001). *Leading Through Today's Turmoil: Strategic IT Human Capital Management.* Cutter IT Journal, pp. 11–18, 14(6).

Highsmith, J. (2004). *Agile Project Management.* Pearson Education, Inc.

Hock, D.W. (2000). *Birth of the Chaordic Age.* San Francisco: Berrett-Koehler Publishers, Inc.

Hohmann, L. (2003). *Beyond Software Architecture: Creating and Sustaining Winning Solutions.* Upper Saddle River, NJ: Prentice Hall, Inc.

Hohpe, G., Woolf, B., Brown, K., D'Cruz, C.F., Fowler, M., Neville, S., Rettig, M.J., and Simon, J. (2004). *Enterprise Integration Patterns: Designing, Building, and Deploying Messaging Systems.* Boston, MA: Pearson Education.

Hollington, P. (2003). *Taking Emotions out of Project Decisions. Cutter IT E-mail Advisor.* May 7, 2003.

IBM (2004). *Rational Unified Process Home Page.* www.rational.com/products/rup/index.jsp

IFMA (2004). *International Facility Management Association.* www.ifma.org

ISO (1998). *Guide for ISO/IEC 12207 (Software Life Cycle Processes).* www.iso.org

ISO (2004). *International Organization for Standardization 9000 family standards.* www.iso.org/iso/en/iso9000-14000/index.html

ITIL (2003) *The ITIL and ITSM Directory.* www.itil-itsm-world.com

Jacobson, I., Booch, G., and Rumbaugh, J. (1999). *The Unified Software Development Process.* Reading, MA: Addison-Wesley Longman, Inc.

Jacobson, I., Christerson, M., and Jonsson, P., and Overgaard, G. (1992). *Object-Oriented Software Engineering—A Use Case Driven Approach.* Wokingham, UK: ACM Press.

Jacobson, I., Ericsson, M., and Jacobson, A. (1994). *The Object Advantage: Business Process Reengineering with Object Technology.* Reading, MA: Addison-Wesley Longman, Inc.

Jacobson, I., Griss, M., and Jonsson, P. (1997). *Software Reuse: Architecture, Process, and Organization for Business Success.* Reading, MA: Addison-Wesley Longman, Inc.

Jones, C. (1996). *Patterns of Software Systems Failure and Success.* Boston: International Thomson Computer Press.

Kaplan, R.S. and Norton, D.P. (2004). *Strategy Maps: Converting Intangible Assets into Tangible Outcomes.* Boston: Harvard Business School Press.

Karten, N. (2003). *Establishing Service Level Agreements.* www.nkarten.com/sla.html

Kerth, N. (2001). Project Retrospectives: *A Handbook for Team Reviews.* New York: Dorset House Publishing.

Kimball, R., Caserta, J. (2004). *The Data Warehouse ETL Toolkit: Practical Techniques for Extracting, Cleansing, Conforming, and Delivering Data*. New York: John Wiley & Sons.

Kruchten, P. (1995). *The 4+1 View Model of Architecture*. IEEE Software 12(6).

Kruchten, P. (2004). *The Rational Unified Process, 3rd Edition: An Introduction*. Reading, MA: Addison-Wesley Longman, Inc.

Krueger, C. (1992). *Software Reuse*. ACM Computing Surveys June 1992, 24(2). pp. 131–183. New York: ACM Press.

Laguna, M. and Marklund, J. (2004). *Business Process Modeling, Simulation, and Design*. Upper Saddle River, NJ: Prentice Hall, Inc.

Lim, W.C. (1998). *Managing Software Reuse: A Comprehensive Guide to Strategically Reengineering the Organization for Reusable Components*. Upper Saddle River, NJ: Prentice Hall, Inc.

Liu, K., Alderson, A., and Qureshi, Z. (1999). *Requirements Recovery of Legacy Systems by Analysing and Modelling Behaviour*. www.personal.rdg.ac.uk/~sis01kl/papers/ambols-icsm99.pdf

Loshin, D. (2004a). *Issues and Opportunities in Data Quality Management Coordination*. DM Review Magazine, April 2004.

Loshin, D. (2004b). *More on Information Quality ROI*. The Data Administration Newsletter (TDAN.com). July 2004. www.tdan.com/nwt_issue29.htm

Lunsford, D.L., Robbins W.A., and Bizarro, P.A. (2004). *Protecting Information Privacy When Retiring Old Computers*. www.nysscpa.org/cpajournal/2004/704/essentials/p60.htm

Marco, D. (2000). *Building and Managing the Meta Data Repository: A Full Lifecycle Guide*. New York: John Wiley & Sons.

Marco, D. (2003). *A meta-data repository is the key to knowledge management*. Enterprise Warehousing Solutions. www.tdan.com/i024fe02.htm

Marshall, C. (2000). *Enterprise Modeling with UML: Designing Successful Software Through Business Analysis*. Upper Saddle River, NJ: Addison-Wesley.

McBreen, P. (2001). *Software Craftsmanship: The New Imperative*. Reading, MA: Addison-Wesley Longman, Inc.

McClure, C. (1997). *Software Reuse Techniques: Adding Reuse to the Systems Development Process*. Upper Saddle River, NJ: Prentice Hall, Inc.

McGovern, J., Ambler, S.W., Stevens, M.E., Linn, J., Sharan, V., and Jo, E.K. (2004). *The Practical Guide to Enterprise Architecture*. Upper Saddle River, NJ: Prentice Hall PTR.

McGovern, J., Tyagi, S., Stevens, M.E., and Mathew, S. (2003). *Java Web Services Architecture*. San Francisco: Morgan Kaufman Publishers.

Meyer, B. (1997). *Object-Oriented Software Construction, 2nd Edition.* Upper Saddle River, NJ: Prentice Hall PTR.

Morabito, J., Sack, I., and Bhate, A. (1999). *Organization Modeling: Innovative Architectures for the 21st Century.* Upper Saddle River, NJ: Prentice Hall PTR.

Moriarty, T. (2001). *To Unify Architecture With Methodology: The Rational Unified Process Meets the Zachman Information Systems Architecture.* Intelligent Enterprise. April 16, 2001. www.intelligententerprise.com/010416/metaprise1_2.shtml

Nalbone, J., Vizdos, M., and Ambler, S. (2003a). *The EUP Enterprise Management Disciplines.* www.enterpriseunifiedprocess.com/essays/enterpriseManagement.html

Nalbone, J., Vizdos, M., and Ambler, S. (2003b). *Adopting the Enterprise Unified Process.* www.enterpriseunifiedprocess.com/essays/adoption.html

NSI (2004). *Improving security from the inside out.* National Security Institute. www.nsi.org

Object Management Group (2002). *Software Process Engineering Metamodel Specification.* OMG document formal/02-11-14.

Object Management Group (2003). *Unified Modeling Language: Superstructure version 2.0.* OMG document ad/2003-04-01.

Orr, Ken (2003a). *Five Big Questions. Cutter Agile Project Management E-Mail Advisor.* December 4, 2003.

Orr, Ken (2003b). *Answering Big Questions 1–3. Cutter Agile Project Management E-Mail Advisor.* December 30, 2003.

Palmer, S.R. and Felsing, J.M. (2002). *A Practical Guide to Feature-Driven Development.* Upper Saddle River, NJ: Prentice Hall PTR.

Pascal, F. (2000). *Practical Issues in Database Management: A Reference for the Thinking Practitioner.* Upper Saddle River, NJ: Addison-Wesley Professional.

Peter, L. (1993). *The Peter Principle.* Cutchoque, NY: Buccaneer Books, Inc.

Pigoski, T. M. (1997). *Practical Software Maintenance: Best Practices for Managing Your Software Investment.* NY: John Wiley & Sons, Inc.

Pollice, G., Curtis, E., Barnard, M., and Kruchten, P. (2002). *RUP implementation guide Part I: Recommended strategy and typical issues and risks.* www-106.ibm.com/developerworks/rational/library/1719.html

Poppendieck, M. and Poppendieck T. (2003). *Lean Software Development: An Agile Toolkit.* Upper Saddle River, NJ: Addison-Wesley.

Project Management Institute (2004). *Project Management Book of Knowledge (PMBOK).* www.pmi.org

Rittman, M. (2004). *Oracle Weblog.* June 5, 2004. www.rittman.net

Roberts, P. (2004). *The Shaky State of Security.* InfoWorld, July 26, 2004. pp. 32–41.

Roman, E., Ambler, S.W., and Jewell, T. (2002). *Mastering Enterprise Java Beans, 2nd Edition*. New York: John Wiley & Sons.

Rosenberg, D. and Scott, K. (1999). *Use Case Driven Object Modeling With UML: A Practical Approach*. Reading, MA: Addison-Wesley Longman, Inc.

Ross, J.W. and Weill, P. (2002). *Six IT Decisions Your IT People Shouldn't Make*. Harvard Business Review, November 2002.

Rothman, J. (2004). *Hiring The Best Knowledge Workers, Techies & Nerds: The Secrets & Science of Hiring Technical People*. New York: Dorset House.

Royce, W. (1970). *Managing the Development of Large Software Systems*. Proceedings of IEEE Westcon.

Royce, W. (1998). *Software Project Management: A Unified Framework*. Reading, MA: Addison-Wesley Longman, Inc.

Rueping, A. (2004). *Agile Documentation: A Pattern Guide to Producing Lightweight Documents for Software Projects*. New York: John Wiley & Sons.

Rumbaugh, J., Blaha, M., Premerlani, W., Eddy, F., and Lorensen, W. (1991). *Object-Oriented Modeling and Design*. Englewood Cliffs, NJ: Prentice Hall, Inc.

Schwaber, K. (2004). *Agile Project Management with Scrum*. Redmond, Washington: Microsoft Press.

Schwarzkopf, A., Mejias, R., Jasperson, J., Saunders, C., and Gruenwald, H. (2004). *Effective Practices for IT Skills Staffings*. Communications of the ACM. pp. 83–88, 47(1).

SCO (2004). *SCO Files Suit Against IBM*. www.sco.com/ibmlawsuit

Seiner, R. (2004). *Data Stewardship Performance Measures*. The Data Administration Newsletter, July 2004. www.tdan.com/i029fe01.htm

Sharp, A. and McDermott, P. (2001). *Workflow Modeling: Tools for Process Improvement and Application Development*. Norwood, MA: Artech House, Inc.

Shaw, M. and Garlan, D. (1996). *Software Architecture: Perspectives on an Emerging Discipline*. Upper Saddle River, NJ: Prentice Hall.

Smith, H. and Fingar, P. (2003). *IT Doesn't Matter–Business Processes Do: A Critical Analysis of Nicholas Carr's I.T.* Article in the Harvard Business Review. Tampa, FL: Meghan-Kiffer Press.

Software Engineering Institute (1995). *The Capability Maturity Model: Guidelines for Improving the Software Process*. Reading, MA: Addison-Wesley Publishing Company, Inc.

Software Engineering Institute (2004a). *Capability Maturity Model Integration*. www.sei.cmu.edu/cmmi

Software Engineering Institute (2004b). *The IDEAL Model*. www.sei.cmu.edu/ideal

Software Engineering Institute (2004c). *The People Capability Maturity Model Version 2*. www.sei.cmu.edu/cmm-p/version2/

Stack, C.M. (2004). *Asset-Based Software Engineering*. Flashline Whitepaper. www.flashline.com

Stapleton, J. (2003). *DSDM: Business Focused Development, 2nd Edition*. Harlow, England: Addison-Wesley.

Tourniaire, F. and Farrell, R. (1997). *The Art of Software Support: Design & Operation of Support Centers and Help Desks*. Upper Saddle River, NJ: Prentice Hall PTR.

Tracz, W. (1995). *Confessions of a Used Program Salesman: Institutionalizing Software Reuse*. Reading, MA: Addison-Wesley Publishing Company, Inc.

Ulrich, W.M. (2002). *Legacy Systems: Transformation Strategies*. Upper Saddle River, NJ: Prentice Hall PTR.

U.S. Department of Energy (2002). *DOE System Engineering Methodology (SEM): Computer System Retirement Guidelines, Version 3*. http://cio.doe.gov/ITReform/sqse/download/SR-V3-G1-0902.pdf

U.S .Government (2002). *Sarbanes-Oxley Act of 2002*. www.sarbanes-oxley.com

U.S. Government (2004). *Health Insurance Portability and Accountability Act (HIPAA)*. www.hhs.gov

Vermeulen, A., Ambler, S.W., Bumgardner, G., Metz, E., Misfeldt, T., Shur, J., and Thompson, P. (2000). *The Elements of Java Style*. New York: Cambridge University Press. www.ambysoft.com/elementsJavaStyle.html

Weber, S. (2004). *The Success of Open Source*. Boston: Harvard University Press.

Weill, P. and Broadbent, M. (1998). *Leveraging the new Infrastructure*. Boston: Harvard Business School Press.

Weill, P. and Ross, J.W. (2004). *IT Governance: How Top Performers Manage IT Decision Rights for Superior Results*. Boston: Harvard Business School Press.

Weiss, D.M. and Lai, C.T.R. (1999). *Software Product-Line Engineering: A Family-Based Software Development Process*. Reading, MA: Addison-Wesley Publishing Company, Inc.

Williams, L. and Kessler, R. (2002). *Pair Programming Illuminated*. Boston, MA: Addison-Wesley.

Wood, J. and Silver, D. (1995). *Joint Application Development, 2nd Edition*. New York: Wiley Publishing.

Yourdon, E. (1997). *Death March: The Complete Software Developer's Guide to Surviving "Mission Impossible" Projects*. Upper Saddle River, NJ: Prentice Hall, Inc.

ZIFA (2002). *The Zachman Institute for Framework Advancement*. www.zifa.com

Index

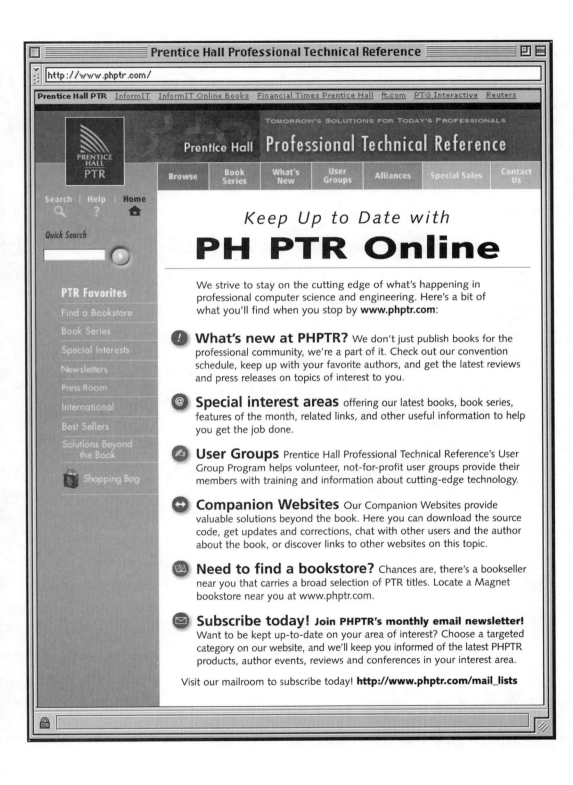

Prentice Hall Professional Technical Reference

http://www.phptr.com/

Prentice Hall PTR   InformIT   InformIT Online Books   Financial Times Prentice Hall   ft.com   PTG Interactive   Reuters

TOMORROW'S SOLUTIONS FOR TODAY'S PROFESSIONALS

Prentice Hall **Professional Technical Reference**

Browse | Book Series | What's New | User Groups | Alliances | Special Sales | Contact Us

Search | Help | **Home**

Quick Search

PTR Favorites

Find a Bookstore
Book Series
Special Interests
Newsletters
Press Room
International
Best Sellers
Solutions Beyond the Book
Shopping Bag

Keep Up to Date with
PH PTR Online

We strive to stay on the cutting edge of what's happening in professional computer science and engineering. Here's a bit of what you'll find when you stop by **www.phptr.com**:

What's new at PHPTR? We don't just publish books for the professional community, we're a part of it. Check out our convention schedule, keep up with your favorite authors, and get the latest reviews and press releases on topics of interest to you.

Special interest areas offering our latest books, book series, features of the month, related links, and other useful information to help you get the job done.

User Groups Prentice Hall Professional Technical Reference's User Group Program helps volunteer, not-for-profit user groups provide their members with training and information about cutting-edge technology.

Companion Websites Our Companion Websites provide valuable solutions beyond the book. Here you can download the source code, get updates and corrections, chat with other users and the author about the book, or discover links to other websites on this topic.

Need to find a bookstore? Chances are, there's a bookseller near you that carries a broad selection of PTR titles. Locate a Magnet bookstore near you at www.phptr.com.

Subscribe today! Join PHPTR's monthly email newsletter! Want to be kept up-to-date on your area of interest? Choose a targeted category on our website, and we'll keep you informed of the latest PHPTR products, author events, reviews and conferences in your interest area.

Visit our mailroom to subscribe today! **http://www.phptr.com/mail_lists**

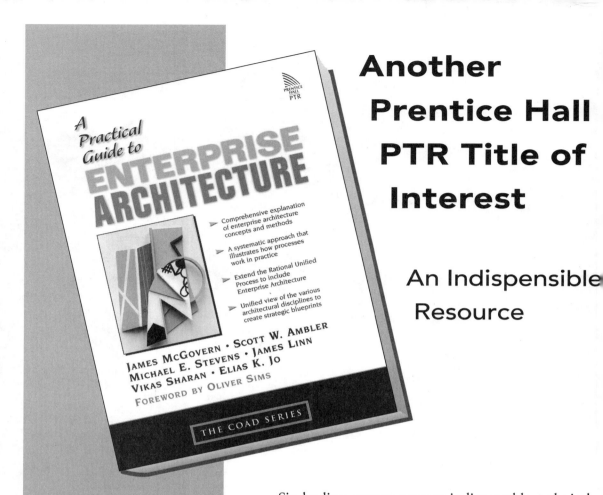

Another Prentice Hall PTR Title of Interest

An Indispensible Resource

A Practical Guide to Enterprise Architecture

by James McGovern, Scott W. Ambler, Michael E. Stevens, James Linn, Vikas Sharan, and Elias K. Jo

ISBN 0131412752

Six leading experts present indispensable technical, process, and business insight into every aspect of enterprise architecture. You'll find start-to-finish guidance for architecting effective system, software, and service-oriented architectures; using product lines to streamline enterprise software design; leveraging powerful agile modeling techniques; extending the Unified Process to the full software lifecycle; architecting presentation tiers and user experience; and driving the technical direction of the entire enterprise. For every working architect and every IT professional who wants to become one.

To find out more and read a sample chapter now, please see: www.phptr.com/title/0131412752